Still Searching for Our Mothers' Gardens

Experiences of New, Tenure-Track Women of Color at 'Majority' Institutions

Edited by
Marnel N. Niles
Nickesia S. Gordon

University Press of America,® Inc.
Lanham · Boulder · New York · Toronto · Plymouth, UK

4501 Forbes Boulevard
Suite 200
Lanham, Maryland 20706
UPA Acquisitions Department (301) 459-3366

Estover Road
Plymouth PL6 7PY
United Kingdom

Printed in the United States of America
British Library Cataloging in Publication Information Available

Library of Congress Control Number: 2011924264
ISBN: 978-0-7618-5514-9 (paperback : alk. paper)
eISBN: 978-0-7618-5515-6

Cover image by Marnel N. Niles.

™ The paper used in this publication meets the minimum requirements of American National Standard for Information Sciences—Permanence of Paper for Printed Library Materials, ANSI Z39.48-1992

Till I Rise

A strong woman knows how to bend
She unfolds herself
To heave the weight of
Broken promises
Uncertain tomorrows
Upon her soul.

Back upright
Shoulders firm
Knees descending
Hands reaching
To rescue
The lost and fallen
From the hard ground
And drowning dust.

A strong woman knows how to bend
She has had a lifetime of practice
Has learnt the balancing act
Sacrifice her staple diet. . . .

But she is woman
She is strong
She endures
With that secret smile
Knowing
That to bend is never to bow
But to crouch in waiting
To rise again.

By Nickesia S. Gordon

CONTENTS

WORKING WITH SCIENCE, TECHNOLOGY, ENGINEERING, AND MATHEMATICS (STEM)

ACKNOWLEDGEMENTS

Marnel N. Niles is especially grateful to her family and friends for their support during the writing of this book, including her parents, Dr. William Niles and Dr. Marcia Nelson Niles, and her siblings, Dwan and Norman. Thanks to Dr. Lyndrey Niles, Dr. Kesha Morant Williams, Dr. Shauneé Wallace, Dr. Cindy Griffin, and the Department of Communication faculty at California State University, Fresno for their encouragement during this process. Also, I would like to give a very special thank you to my partner, Matthew, for his constant support and love. And of course, thank you Lord for this space and place.

Nickesia S. Gordon would like to thank her family, particularly her mother, Marlene Holt, an Amazon if there ever was one, and daughter, Nakai Chinogwenya, who is always her muse. Thanks also to my partner, Farai, and all my friends and colleagues for their moral support.

The authors wish to express their profound gratitude to Dr. Alice Walker and her body of work, which serves as the inspiration for this book. They also extend their appreciation to University Press of America and the Howard University Department of Communication and Culture for their support on this project. The authors are also deeply appreciative of the keen insight and invaluable intellectual contributions leant to this book by Dr. Carolyn Cooper, Dr. Beverly Guy-Sheftall, Dr. Melbourne S. Cummings, Dr. Robin Kelley, Dr. Brenda J. Allen, Dr. Heather Harris, and Dr. Stephanie Evans. Finally, the authors would like to thank all of the contributors to this text for their very hard work and brilliant ideas—you made this book exceptional.

Foreword

CULTIVATING OUR OWN FIELDS

> "*Guided by my heritage of a love of beauty and a respect for strength—in search of my mother's garden, I found my own.*" – Alice Walker

In 1975 when I joined the faculty of a small private college in New England, I became one of only three black professors. In those days, the terms 'African-American' and 'of color' were not yet in vogue. People of African origin, whether immediately from the continent or in the Diaspora, were homogenously 'black.'

I vividly remember how surprised my 'not of color' teaching assistant was to discover that I had an M.A. and was close to completing my Ph.D. She was a senior, not much younger than I, and it simply had not occurred to her that I had earned the right to be a college professor. My appointment must have been a mistake, or a sign of 'affirmative action.'

As I absorbed the provocative essays in this penetrating collection, I kept on being reminded of my own unsettling experience three and a half decades ago. Faced with the pressing needs of black students, I was constrained to assume multiple roles beyond the ambit of my formal appointment as an Assistant Professor.

I became an amateur guidance counselor and was frequently consulted not only on academic matters but also social and financial affairs. I often functioned as matchmaker, heart-mender, financial analyst, and banker. Furthermore, the college was located in a town without public transportation. So I often provided taxi service for students. I was very young and foolish, then. But really, it was compassion. Most of the black students lived in New York City and were traumatized by the isolation the rural landscape engendered.

Coming to New England from the Caribbean, via the University of Toronto, I frequently engaged in illuminating exchanges with 'not of color' students from the hinterlands of Maine, Vermont, Rhode Island, and New Hampshire who had never experienced the pleasure of being taught by a black woman, let alone a foreigner. A male student once complained to the head of department that I couldn't even pronounce properly the word 'schedule' properly. A very wise woman, the head of the Department, confided that she had just laughed and patiently enlightened him about regional accents.

Thirty plus years after this seemingly jovial exchange, I am appalled that in the 21st century, young black women are still searching to find their proper place in academia. With literary sophistication and trenchant analytical precision, all of the scholars who document their own experiences and those of their subjects of research authoritatively tell an archetypal tale of both despair and hope.

These affirmative survival stories articulate and indubitably contest systemic alienation. Michele Foss-Snowden's compelling trope of servitude lucidly emblematizes the paradoxical placement of all of the 'outsiders within' who recount their narratives of resistance in this collection: "I earned my place at the academic table and I was free to eat (I was within the social circle), but when it was time to clear the plates, my standpoint told me that everyone else at the table was waiting for me to put on my apron and retreat to the kitchen while they enjoyed their after-dinner drinks, a clear indicator of my outsider status 'within' the group" (p. 83).

Foss-Snowden evokes the traditional spiritual, "I'm Gonna Sit at the Welcome Table," with its ironic resonances in this context. There are several variants of this poignant song but the recurring theme in all of them is the interrogation of systems of protracted social injustice. In one version of the song, explicit reference is made to racist discourses that encode discrimination against black people: "I'm gonna move those Jim Crow labels."

It is not at all easy to surmount ideologically rooted obstacles and escape restricting stereotypes of servitude. As Ahlam Muhtaseb puts it so pointedly, "One of the major challenges that I face is discussing stereotyping; many students insist that stereotypes have 'elements of truth' in them or that they must have started from a certain point in history. As I explain to students, some stereotypes have nothing to do with truth or statistics and are ideologically motivated, socially constructed, and related to the hegemonic narrative of the dominant group in society" (p. 99).

With the publication of this book, the right of women of all shades of color to sit at the welcome table is unequivocally asserted. To deploy Alice Walker's horticultural trope, these female scholars, having found the carefully tended gardens and fruit trees of their collective mother, can now cultivate with renewed passion their own fields of intellectual endeavor.

Dr. Carolyn Cooper
Professor of Literary and Cultural Studies
University of the West Indies, Mona
Jamaica

INTRODUCTION

> *This is how they seemed . . . [like] exquisite butterflies trapped in evil honey, toiling away their lives in an era, a century, that did not acknowledge them, except as "the mule of the world." They dreamed dreams that no one knew—not even themselves, in any coherent fashion—and saw visions no one could understand. . . . They forced their minds to desert their bodies and their striving sprits sought to rise, like frail whirlwinds from the hard red clay. And when those frail whirlwinds fell, in scattered particles, upon the ground, no one mourned. (Walker, 1983, p. 232)*

In 2008 in San Diego, California, a panel was presented at the annual National Communication Association Convention about the experiences of Black women assistant professors in the academy. The room was filled to capacity and the hour and fifteen minutes allotted to the session was not nearly enough time to discuss the frank narratives told by the panelists or respond to the eager questions and emotional commentaries from audience members. Afterward, the panelists and many of the panel attendees congregated in the room, excited to continue the dialogue. Even after being ushered from the room, we continued conversing in the hallway, sharing our experiences and nodding enthusiastically because finally, we were among those who understood our stories.

It seemed as if the panel and discussions opened a floodgate and our collectively fragile gardens suddenly seemed powerful and full of possibilities, despite the rocky soils and hard red clay. We once again affirmed to each other that our labor was never fruitless and that somehow, because we were all seeds buried in this unforgiving soil, we knew what the other dreamt. A vision appeared to us, not in any "coherent fashion," as we acknowledged the struggle to unbury ourselves and recommit to tending our mothers' gardens. This collection represents that vision and the heartbreak and inspiration that simultaneously emerged from the panel discussion, informing many of the narratives found in this volume.

We expanded the reach of the original panel to include women of various races, ethnicities, and religions, providing an embodiment of the variegated colors that make up our mothers' gardens. Each contributor to this text is a woman of color who has earned a Ph.D. and taught as a junior faculty member in a college or university setting. As a result, the diverse racial and ethnic backgrounds as well as similar levels of education of the chapter contributors lead to a very nuanced approach to the current examination of the experiences of women of color in academia.

Building on the groundbreaking scholarship of Dr. Alice Walker in her seminal work *In Search of Our Mothers' Gardens*, the current collection of essays looks at the issues facing women of color in academia from a communicative viewpoint, using various communication frameworks to provide realistic strategies for our survival in academic environments. Communication scholars posit that communication is the foundation from which organizations, systems, groups, and relationships are formed. Examining women of color from a communication perspective places emphasis on the meaning-construction, narratives, auto-ethnographies, symbol creation, written communication, tensions, and non-verbal communication that simultaneously inform and are formed by the experiences of the women faculty included in this volume, providing tremendous insight into the organization of academia and its treatment of tenure-track women of color. *Still Searching for Our Mothers' Gardens: Experiences of New, Tenure-Track Women of Color at 'Majority' Institutions,* while using Dr. Walker's text as its muse, thus offers a perspective that is unique in its departure from the previous literary critique of the practice of discrimination against women of color in the academy.

As intimated in the above paragraph, the first part of the title of this volume is taken from Alice Walker's text, *In Search of Our Mothers' Gardens*, a book about Black women and their creative means of surviving hardship. The play on Dr. Walker's book is appropriate because in the referenced volume, she communicates the nature of disenfranchisement from a genealogical perspective, citing that the fight for equal treatment and recognition is constant. This is similar to the lived experiences of junior, tenure-track women faculty of color who work in majority universities and colleges in North America: we watch as decades pass and note the lack of inclusion of women faculty of color. For example, Evans (2007) stated that positions for faculty of color became increasingly available in the 1970s and as time progressed, women faculty of color were provided disproportionately fewer academic positions than any other gender or racial group. Further, faculty of color are "unevenly distributed across institutional types, disciplines, and academic ranks" (Turner, 2000, ¶ 4), and this occurs even moreso regarding women faculty of color. We have consistently been overrepresented at 2-year institutions and underrepresented at 4-year institutions. We are significantly more visible in the liberal arts (inclusive of disciplines such as Communication, Sociology, English, Education, and Modern Languages) than in the Science, Technology, Engineering, and Mathematics disciplines. A 2009 publication by *The Chronicle of Higher Education* found that women faculty of color (inclusive of American Indian, Asian, Black, Hispanic, and non-resident/foreign) *combined* represent 12% of all assistant professors in the United States. This percentage decreases as these women fight to climb the tenure ladder: women of color represent just 7% of associate professors and 3.5% of full professors in the United States, suggesting that tenure-track faculty who are women of color leave academia because they have "been toiling away their lives" with no acknowledgement. As such, history and our lived experiences have taught us that the fight for equality never wanes, even as these colleges and universities increasingly advertise and proclaim their recruitment and support of diverse faculty. Instead, the same women have to constantly prove—to our universities, colleagues, administrators, students, and even ourselves—that we deserve to be in our academic places and spaces.

The first part of the text's title is also a recognition of the need for a space, a garden, where women of color may find some solace and work towards the actualization of our ambitions, not just for ourselves, but also for those who come after us. Not unlike our mothers who came before us, the strain of working as the mules of the academic world has left our butterfly wings tattered. Evil honey sits moat-like around the ivory tower, shutting us out and trapping many who attempt to cross over. It seems that women of color who teach in institutions of higher learning are still searching for this garden space, still fighting for recognition, and still devising ways to navigate this minefield called academia. However, thanks to the enduring spirits of our foremothers, we know the search will be a little less arduous because they have broken up the soil and trimmed some of the thorns.

The second part of the volume's title describes the contributors to, and participants included in, the various chapters in this text. We use the term *women of color* to encompass women who come from an array of minority racial and ethnic backgrounds, including African American, Indian, Bangladeshi, Palestinian, biracial Black, Jamaican, Bahamian, Argentinean, and Russian backgrounds. Further, we use the term *majority institution* to refer to a college or university that has a different majority student and faculty demographic than the woman of color professor. This definition extends to include colleges and universities beyond traditionally White institutions, such as historically Black colleges and universities, Christian universities, Hispanic-serving institutions, and Science, Technology, Engineering, and Mathematics institutions. Though each of these types of institutions is unique, overall, their treatment of faculty who are racially or ethnically different than their majority student and faculty body is very similar and leaves much to be desired.

Young, women, assistant professors of color endure different types of hardships teaching at institutions in which we are not part of the majority. These hardships are not a result of our junior status, gender, race, *or* ethnicity singularly; instead, these hardships are the result of the nonsummative combination of our junior status, gender, race, *and* ethnicity. Thus, this edited volume seeks to share, from a communication perspective, the multifaceted and dynamic experiences of these women in the academy and suggests ways we can keep our creative spark from being extinguished by the racism and sexism we face while going about our mothers' business.

The text also sheds light on the intersectionality of race, gender, ethnicity, and identity by offering a multiperspective approach to the interrogation of the power dynamics at play in institutions of higher learning. The contributors examine how these same forces result in the systemic marginalization of women of color working in academia. The various experiences captured in this volume engage multiple theories, methodologies, frameworks, and narratives, which bridge the chasm that often exists between theory and praxis.

The objectives of the book are two-fold. First, it shares the experiences of our contributors and their participants with others, particularly other women of color, who are in the academy or seeking to enter the academy with the intention of promoting an understanding of the struggles experienced by those in similar positions, i.e. junior, women assistant professors working in majority institutions. Second, the book seeks to empower muted groups by providing suggestions for how members from such groups may negotiate a position of strength in the academy as a minority. For far too long, women of color have individually created strategies of survival, sometimes re-inventing the proverbial wheel. It is now time to collectively share our tools for conquering our similar and unique obstacles so that we can build and expand on them, instead of continuously recreating them.

There are fifteen chapters in this collection, which are divided among five main themes: (1) Managing Tensions and Contradictions: Diversity in Question; (2) Confronting Prejudice and Discrimination: Strategies of Survival; (3) Responding to 'Otherness': Navigating Identity; (4) Experiencing Difference in the Classroom: Teaching 'Majority' Students; and (5) Working with Science, Technology, Engineering, and Mathematics (STEM). Within these themes, the contributors broach topics such as the road to tenure, student perceptions and stereotypes, unsupportive colleagues, otherness, denial of discrimination, teaching strategies, and muted voice, among others. In general, these chapters offer a tightly focused read on timely issues such as the rhetoric versus practice of diversity on college campuses, the complexities of identity negotiations, and globalization and its influences on faculty composition in institutions of higher learning. For example, several of the chapters (i.e. Gentles-Peart; Jaya & Ahmed; Muhtaseb; Wilson) offer important global perspectives on the experiences of women of color in academia. Though the chapters in this text cannot fully describe all of the experiences of junior women faculty of color in the academy, they do add significantly to the small body of knowledge that currently exists about this subject.

Several books that have been published about women of color in the college or university setting must be acknowledged, for they also helped provide the foundation for this text. The publication of these texts indicates a growing interest in the intersectionality of gender and race at academic institutions. For example, *Black Women in the Ivory Tower, 1850-1954: An Intellectual History* (Evans, 2007) provides a detailed account of Black women professors working in traditionally White institutions. Similarly, *Telling Histories: Black Women Historians in the Ivory Tower* (White, 2008) and *Outsiders Within: Black Women in the Legal Academy After Brown v. Board* (Watson, 2008) both discuss the experiences of Black women in specific disciplines of the academy. Other notable texts include *The Pursuit of Race and Gender Equity in American Academe* (Witt, 1990), *Black Women in the Academy: Promises and Perils* (Benjamin, 1997), and *A Broken Silence: Voices of African American Women in the Academy* (Myers, 2002).

In spite of the aforementioned texts, the documentation and analytical discussion of the experiences of newly minted women faculty of color who wish to advance along the tenure-track largely remain underresearched. Based on the significant interest that the editors' call for abstracts generated among women and other members of academia, there is a need for this type of research due to its present paucity. In addition, *Still Searching for Our Mothers' Gardens: Experiences of New, Tenure Track Women of Color at 'Majority' Institutions* is a unique text for several reasons: (1) it focuses on the communication that takes place between women of color in the academy and their colleagues, superiors, and students; (2) it specifically examines women of color who are *new* to the academy; and (3) it focuses on the experiences of women from diverse races, ethnicities, and nationalities, as well as those who occupy an immigrant status, thus allowing for a greater breadth and depth of material.

This text represents an academic response to the underrepresented experiences of new, tenure-track women of color and provides a theoretical volume that maps out the problematic relationships between this community of faculty members and academic institutions. As such, it is geared toward several different audiences. It is aimed at researchers, activists, and academic professionals who seek frames of reference for related epistemological discussions for which very little documentation exists in a collective format. The book is also very appealing to junior faculty, given its address of the challenges associated with the tenure process from the perspective of those who have successfully navigated that course or who are currently along that path. It offers survival strategies and coping mechanisms that women of color in majority institutions have used or are using to attain success. As such, the collection can be used as a handbook on how to steer through the tenure process.

Based on its critical examination of the gendered and racialized relationships of power in academia, this volume also appeals to feminist scholars, particularly those engaging in "minority" studies (which may intersect with African American, Asian, and Hispanic scholarship) and those pursuing research in critical race issues or discourses of power in institutions. Additionally, because of its interconnections with the discipline of teaching and pedagogy, this book is aimed toward scholars, researchers, and students in the field of education, especially those interested in the dynamics of the teacher/student relationship in the ever increasing multi-cultural classroom. Similarly, scholars from cultural studies may use this text for the aforementioned reasons. The volume will be most useful for a graduate student audience given its strong theoretical bend and focus on meaning construction. It is best suited for the research community; this is better represented at the graduate level. Notwithstanding, the book may also be used as a text for senior undergraduate classes that substantively engage in applied research, feminisms, race, or other related theoretical discourses.

Regardless of who you are as a reader or peruser of this text, it is the editors' hope that it will inspire you to take action to better the experiences of tenure-track women of color in the academy. We desire that the reading of this edited book will be therapeutic for women of color who are struggling in the academy and enlightening for all others. Ultimately, we hope that with this book, women of color in the academy will no longer continue to, in the words of Alice Walker (1983), "[perish] in the wilderness" (p. 235).

Dr. Marnel N. Niles
Dr. Nickesia S. Gordon

REFERENCES

Benjamin, L. (Ed). (1997). *Black women in the academy: Promises and perils* Gainesville, FL: University Press of Florida.

Chronicle of Higher Education (2009). Number of full-time faculty members by sex, rank, and racial and ethnic group, fall 2007. Retrieved from http://chronicle.com/article/ Number-of-Full-Time-Faculty/47992/

Evans, S. Y. (2007). *Black women in the ivory tower, 1850-1954: An Intellectual history.* Gainesville, FL: University Press of Florida.

Myers, L. W. (2002). *A broken silence: Voices of African American women in the academy.* Westport, CT: Bergin and Garvey.

Turner, C. S. V. (2000, September/October). New faces, new knowledge. *Academe Online.* Retrieved from http://aaup.org/AAUP/CMS_Templates/AcademeTemplates/ AcademeArticle.aspx?NRMODE=Published&NRNODEGUID={CB90DAAC2F91-480E-9B18C9E6AD67AA61}&NRORIGINALURL=%2FAAUP% 2Fpubsres%2Facademe%2F2000%2FSO%2FFeat%2Fturn.htm&NRCACHEHINT=NoModifyGuest

Walker, A. (1983). *In search of our mothers' gardens: Womanist prose.* Orlando, FL: Harvest.

Watson, E. D. (2008). *Outsiders within: Black women in the legal academy after Brown v. Board.* Lanham, MD: Rowman and Littlefield.

White, D. G. (2008). *Telling histories: Black women historians in the ivory tower.* Durham, NC: University of North Carolina Press.

Witt, S. L. (1990). *The Pursuit of Race and Gender Equity in American Academe.* New York, NY: Praeger.

MANAGING TENSIONS AND CONTRADICTIONS

DIVERSITY IN QUESTION

Chapter 1

Disclose and Demystify

The Discrepancy between the Concept of Diversity and the Action of Diversity in the Face of "Stubborn Faculty, Wary Students, and Unsupportive Administrators"

Angela Prater
Yuping Mao
Marnel N. Niles
Yuxia Qian

The call for diverse individuals to apply for tenure-track positions is clear on almost every job announcement: "Women and minorities are encouraged to apply." What happens after minorities apply and achieve these positions? We would like to call attention to what appears to be a gap between the *concept* of diversity and diversity in *action* when double minorities, i.e. women of color, occupy these positions. The discrepancy between diversity in concept and diversity in action is well captured by Allen, Orbe, and Olivas's (1999) statement: "Whereas most institutional mission statements centralize diversity within their public identities, 'doing difference' in the academy reveals that such ideologies are not necessarily part of the everyday culture of these institutions" (p. 402).

While diversity in the U.S. typically considers ethnicity, race, gender, and other material characteristics of the body, the significant role that culture plays is easily overlooked. Diverse persons comprise more than the material bodies that physically and superficially define them as "diverse." More importantly, women of color also bring with them the culture from which they emerge—and which inform those diverse experiences and perspectives that propel them into the academy. Indeed, minority women's individual or personal characteristics that are deeply rooted in their unique culture sometimes may not smoothly "fit" into the mainstream and institutional cultures. Female assistant professors of color, the subjects of this chapter, sometimes struggle with the slippage between the "perfect" concept of diversity and the subtle/manifested resistance to diversity from students and colleagues in their daily interactions. Thus, this chapter aims to increase the understanding of the challenges that women assistant professors of color face with diversity issues and provide suggestions for how these challenges can be overcome.

In this chapter, we interviewed six women of color who work as assistant professors at majority institutions to better understand their experiences with diversity at their respective institutions. Higher education institutions are important sites for educating citizens and initiating positive cultural shifts and behavioral change. We hope the experiences the female assistant professors of color have shared with us in this chapter can be transformative, leading to a higher level of cultural sensitivity in both the academy and society and ultimately creating a more diverse reality that can benefit both the individual and her institutional community.

For the purposes of this discussion, we use the term *diversity* to refer to university outreach to and socialization and retention of faculty of color in majority institutions. This concept includes the fact that diverse ideas, teaching styles, and communication patterns among colleagues are respected and appreciated along with the material characteristics of the body. Diversity in *action* then indicates an appreciation of the everyday communication patterns of minority female tenure-track professors as they begin their careers at majority institutions.

THEORETICAL FOUNDATIONS

Critical theorists believe that it is necessary to understand the lived experiences of people in the context in which particular phenomena occur (Littlejohn, 1999). These contexts can be specific social contexts in society such as families, religions, or educational systems. Traditionally, critical theorists invested their time in various social contexts to uncover oppressive power structures with the intention of freeing oppressed individuals (Littlejohn, 1999). These individuals are freed through the knowledge of such oppressive structures and are then able to overcome them. The typical method used to uncover oppressive structures is discourse analysis. Discourse analysis is a way of purposely investigating the hidden, or "situated," meaning behind a text, which, in the case of this chapter, is in the form of participant narratives (Gee, 1999).

Feminist theory is one theoretical and methodological foundation in which critical theorists can employ discourse analysis. Feminist theory is unique in that it focuses on the oppressive nature that gender imposes in society (Littlejohn, 1999). Feminist theories have also provided critiques from the perspectives of race, class, and gender, citing that the struggle against oppression is one that affects all humankind. Foss, Foss, and Trapp (2002) expand on this notion, stating:

> Any efforts made to free oppressed people must be on behalf of all who are oppressed and not just a particular group. . . . The system of white-supremacist capitalist patriarchy is not maintained solely by white folks. It is also maintained by all the rest of us who internalize and enforce the values of this regime and who act unconsciously, in complicity with a culture of domination. (p. 271)

A feminist critique examines the interconnectedness of race, class, and gender, allowing for the understanding of the lived experiences of women in everyday contexts. By using a feminist critique, we seek to uncover social oppressive structures in order to enlighten all participants in the higher education system, including women of color who are junior faculty, so that collectively, they can overcome them. For the purposes of this chapter, we employ feminist critique as a lens in which we analyze the diversity discourse of females of color in the academy. As such, we view the discourse on diversity as predominantly masculine, majority raced, and oppressive toward women of color. However, the uncovering of these oppressive discourses begins with the stories told by women of color in academe. These women hold but a small minority, but as feminist theory teaches us, every story matters (Foss & Foss, 1994).

In this chapter, the female assistant professors' experiences were analyzed within organizational contexts from a feminist critique. Taking a critical approach, we hope the voices of female assistant professors of color in this study can help to "create a society and work places that are free from domination and where all members can contribute equally to produce systems and meet human needs and lead to the progressive development of all" (Deetz, 2000, p. 26), resulting in a true appreciation of and action toward diversity.

LITERATURE REVIEW

Over the past 20 years, the demographics of the student body of higher education institutions have become more diverse, while "the challenges with the curriculum, institutional practice, climate, and hiring remain unresolved" (Wolf-Wendel, 2005, p. iii). Decision makers in universities reached the agreement that diversity of faculty and staff is essential for higher education institutions. Ayers, Wheeler, Fracasso, Galupo, Rabin, and Slater (1999) argue that "the university will become a community of international scholars whose members will be represented by people historically isolated from the academy" (p. 165). In spite of this call for diversity, women of color make up approximately 2% of all full-time professors in the United States (Evans, 2007). Recruiting and retaining women of color faculty members also poses a challenge. Compared with males and White women, fewer women of color have completed doctoral degrees, resulting in few female candidates of color in higher education institutions (Gregory, 2001). In addition, ignorance and insensitivity existing among faculty, administrators, and students in majority higher education institutions create pedagogical and professional challenges for women of color professors, which become a great barrier to minorities fully immersing themselves in their institutions. Therefore, the rhetoric of diversity has become one of the mainstream ideologies in today's society and universities, while the practice diversity remains challenging.

The challenges faced by women of color in academia are not new. Evans (2007) traced the history of Black women in predominantly White institutions and found that in the 1920s, Black women professors' pay was lower than their White and male counterparts. These women were also "relegated to lower ranks, doing much 'invisible work,' such as counseling, coordinating meetings, stretching meager resources, and organizing grassroots civil rights campaigns that improved their campuses and communities" (Evans 2007, p. 132). Evans finds that this treatment, or "extraordinary scrutiny" (p. 134), is due to the magnification of gender and racial stereotyping. It is unfortunate that the treatment of women of color in the academy is very much the same today.

Many higher education institutions have tried different ways to change their treatment of women of color and achieve diversity within the institutions. Wolf-Wendel (2005) suggests that organizations that succeed in meeting the challenge of diversity can provide a good model for other institutions in functioning in a diverse manner. Bentley University is one institution that has made significant diversity changes in the past decade. Spelman, Addison-Reid, Avery, and Crary (2006) argue that one key successful characteristics of the initiative that Bentley University took to achieve diversity was to hire "managers that make the university more demographically diverse, faculty members that enrich the diversity-related offerings in the curriculum, and student affairs professionals that prepare the resident assistants to manage diversity-related conflicts in the residence halls" (p. 23). The lessons that Bentley University share in diversity initiatives confirm that having a diversified faculty and staff body is key for higher education institutions to achieve diversity. Therefore, it is very important to understand minority faculty members' experiences in higher education institutions and find ways to improve their experiences in order to create an environment with visible actions toward diversity.

Smith and Wolf-Wendel (2005) further explain the reasons for the emphasis on a diverse faculty and staff in higher education institutions. A diverse group of faculty and staff can provide support for students from particular groups, be important role models and symbols to minority students about their future and the institution's commitment to them, and create a more comfortable environment for minority students as well as for faculty and staff. Research shows that minority students' lack of support is negatively correlated with their overall satisfaction levels with their university (Helm, Sedlacek, & Prieto, 1998); therefore, having minority faculty members provide support for minority students is crucial for the success of higher education institutions. In addition, White students who are not used to having members of minority groups in positions of authority and power can also benefit by having this new experience. The diversification of faculty members and staff can contribute to the curriculum, the content of teaching, and the style of teaching. Minority faculty members can bring new and alternative perspectives and approaches, which in the past have often been ignored or devalued by "mainstream" culture.

Smith and Wolf-Wendel (2005) discuss the significance of practicing diversity at a deep level by stating that, "as long as the leadership of our institutions contains only token representation of persons from diverse backgrounds, institutions will not be able to claim that the goals for society or our educational institutions have been achieved" (p. 51). This token representation is evident by the fact that minority faculty members historically comprise disproportionately low percentages in universities and colleges in the U.S. For example, as reviewed by Hendrix (1998), prior to 1900, there were only two Black professors teaching in predominantly White colleges/universities in the U.S. In 1985, 90% of the full-time faculty in higher education institutions in the U.S. was White, while only 4.1% was Black (Guess, 1989). In 1996, Black faculty represented 4.4% of senior faculty members and 5.4% of new faculty hires in higher education institutions in the U.S. (Magner, 1996). Black faculty also had the lowest faculty progression, retention, and tenure rates in academe (Moses, 1997).

Black professors are also challenged by research and publications. Gregory (2001) argues that most Black faculty members are expected to publish their research in mainstream journals that are widely accepted by White scholars, while in many cases, Black faculty members' research topics on people of color and their qualitative methodological approaches are not embraced by White editors with different research interests. Furthermore, Branch (2001) points out that some Black scholars' research is rejected because the personal experience, reflection, and emotion they put in their writing make their research more likely to be viewed as sloppy and non-academic.

Due to different challenges that Black faculty members have in teaching, research, and service, Black faculty members are promoted at slower rates than White faculty members. In the diverse spectrum of faculty members, female Black professors are at the lowest position of the hierarchy of promotion. Black female professors are paid less and promoted more slowly than their Black male and White female counterparts (Gregory, 1995). Some scholars argue that universities should adjust their tenure promotion policies to acknowledge and reward Black faculty members' special contributions to working with Black students on campus, bringing in new research topics, and diversifying different committees (Astin, 1982; Graves, 1990; Turner & Meyers, 2000).

Diversity issues do not just affect Black faculty; rather, these issues involve all members in higher education institutions. Appel, Cartwright, Smith, and Wolf (1996) argue that while faculty issues are some of the most difficult to address, they are simultaneously some of the most important to which to attend. In spite of this, Sedlacek (1995) explains that most faculty members do not see themselves playing a role in diversity issues and are not willing to be seen as social change agents (Helm et al., 1998), leaving minority faculty to bear the burden of addressing diversity alone. For example, Butner, Burley, and Marbley (2000) suggest that minority faculty members initiate more research collaborations with colleagues to make connections with other faculty members and reduce feelings of isolation. This could also help such faculty become more productive as scholars.

Based on the discussion above, it would appear that although diversity has been widely discussed in higher education institutions, such talks are based more on rhetoric than praxis. That is, many higher education institutions are interested in the concept of diversity, which results in a steady increase of minority faculty at institutions of higher learning. However, this increase also leaves minority faculty members isolated to represent and "act out" diversity once they begin their positions at majority institutions. Further, much of the existing research focuses on Black professors, while the experiences of other faculty of color, and specifically, female faculty of color, remain underexplored. This study extends the literature by exploring African American, Native American, and Asian female professors' experiences with diversity at their majority institutions. This chapter focuses on both positive and negative feelings and experiences that such female faculty of color face in higher education institutions. Specifically, the following question is explored: How do female faculty of color understand their institution's ideology of diversity and how do their understandings compare with their everyday experiences?

DATA COLLECTION AND ANALYSIS

To understand how the everyday experiences of diversity compare to the institutional conceptualization of diversity, we interviewed six female assistant professors at majority institutions. Through personal networks, professional networks, and e-mail lists, we extended our invitation to participate in this study to as many female assistant professors of color as possible. Two African American men expressed great interest in participating in the study but the authors decided that it would be beyond the scope of this chapter to include them and declined their inquiry. However, this is certainly a fruitful area of research that should be explored.

With IRB approval from both Canadian and U.S. universities, we initiated the dialogue of participants' living experiences of diversity through e-mail exchanges after the women responded to our research invitation. We began our study with eight confirmed participants but two, one Asian female and one African American female, withdrew. The Asian female committed to participate but after several attempts by the authors to collect information, never responded. The African American female said that she did not want talk about issues that were too emotional and still at the surface.

As such, the six remaining participants represented are all tenure-track women of color professors from four-year colleges and Ph.D.-granting institutions. To protect their identities, the participants were given pseudonyms by the authors. They were: Caroline, an African American female teaching at a midsize public university in the southeast United States; Lee, an Asian American female teaching at a midsize university on the East Coast of the United States; Angel, a Chinese female working at a private Christian university in the Western United States; Flower, a Chinese female teaching at a historically Black institution on the East Coast of the United States; Lauren, an Asian female working at a Catholic university in a major metropolitan area in the East Coast; and Margaret, an American Indian (Cherokee/Choctaw) female working at a New England state college. Margaret and Caroline are the only United States-born participants; the other four women are not originally from the United States.

Our dialogue with the participants focused on how their stories and perspectives related to diversity issues at their institutions. All participants were sent the aforementioned question in addition to follow-up questions based on those answers. By facilitating the discussions and initiating dialogue with these female assistant professors of color, we were able to listen to and try to understand their experiences regarding diversity, allowing us to provide our readers with more awareness of diversity in action in the academy.

The analysis of the dialogue was completed by the authors. Specifically, we created primary themes by constant reading and comparing of the data transcripts (Riessman, 1993), using the research question to guide the coding process (Lindlof & Taylor, 2002). Lindlof and Taylor recommend interrogating the text in a "sensitive, reflexive fashion" (p. 217) and making initial linkages between incidents in the data. After reading and rereading the transcripts, the researchers began looking for the overarching themes across the narratives and categorizing them. Categorization basically means "[identifying] a chunk of or unit of data (e.g., a passage of text of any length) as belonging to, representing, or being an example of some more general group phenomenon" (Spiggle, 1994, p. 493). The themes included in the study were shared and agreed upon by the authors.

RESULTS

Three themes emerged from the experiences of the six women; these themes provided us with insight into the everyday communication strategies used by women of color in majority institutions. These themes are: 1) tension between the universities' definitions and the participants' personal understandings of diversity, 2) tokenism/lack of cultural sensitivity, and 3) greater understanding from students than colleagues.

TENSION BETWEEN THE UNIVERSITIES' DEFINITIONS AND PERSONAL UNDERSTANDINGS OF DIVERSITY

The tension in the first theme is that of the discrepancy between the institutional and personal definitions of diversity. Among our participants we found that some institutions do not even have a clear definition of the term. Thus, the tension is due to the fact that most of the respondents did not know or could not find an official definition of diversity. Instead, they understand the definition based on their everyday communication with students, faculty, and administration. For example, the following are how some of the participants replied to the initial research question about their universities' definitions of diversity compared to their personal definitions. First, Caroline stated:

> Diversity regards difference and having participants from different backgrounds and walks of life to add a more eclectic mix of experiences to a social situation. I believe, however, that [my university's definition] is probably different than my own. The difference is important because people should know I add more to the university than having more of a racial mix. A unique set of experiences comes with that that helps enrich the community and the students' lives. I think the leadership and my department understand that, but I'm not sure about how that's interpreted by others at my university. I wouldn't say there is a discrepancy, but my definition goes beyond racial diversity. I'd say that the university's definition is part of my definition, but does not address the totality of experiences of difference.

Margaret also spoke of a difference between her and her university's interpretations of diversity:

> I try to think of [diversity] in terms of inclusivity; actually, I'm gonna plug in a committee definition that I helped craft: the objective is to remove the barriers that block faculty and students from using the full range of their competencies

> and skills . . . in the classroom and world. I think the definition is good, but such ideals can crumble in the face of stubborn faculty, wary students, and unsupportive administrators. We might understand diversity as an inclusive pedagogy, for instance, and then be faced with provincial students in the classroom who inadvertently believe in stereotypes that readily offend other students. There is a slippery slope between realization and idealization and I think issues of self-discovery and "trumping" each other with specific categories of diversity are stumbling blocks in moving beyond good-hearted dialogue. There are discrepancies because of the aforementioned difference between idealized mission statements and putting the rubber to the road, so to speak.

Lee also expanded on the issue, explaining that her university does not have a clear definition of diversity:

> My institution does not have a definition on diversity; along with civic manner, integration, [and] leadership, diversity is among them. . . . It's the browning of the America; it's the tolerance and understanding of differences in beliefs, cultures, and customs. [There is a] huge difference [that] exists between my institution's definition and my definition. Currently I am experiencing racial discrimination regarding my English speaking. It's an institutional racism; some of the colleagues of different races also had the same experience. We are seeking justice externally. In teaching and research, diversity has been idealized. In reality, it's so hard to make the administrators appreciate the virtue of diversity. [It's] totally two different things in teaching/research and in existence.

Based on the responses and the typical job call that encourage minorities to apply, one can project that institutions may refer to "diversity" as either difference in race/ethnicity or as part of their discrimination policies. For instance, according to Angel, her university does not have an official definition, though diversity is identified as one of its core values for 2010-2015. Lauren was the only respondent that sent a university definition; however, she did state that her university's policy relating to diversity was based on a discrimination policy:

> [Name of University omitted] is committed to the policies, principles and practices of equal opportunity, affirmative action and nondiscrimination in all of its activities, including, but not limited, to employment. [Name of University omitted] commits itself to maintaining a welcoming environment for all people and extends its welcome in particular to those who may be vulnerable to discrimination, on the basis of their race, ethnic or national origin, religion, color, age, gender, marital or parental status, sexual orientation, veteran status or disabilities.

While participants reported ethnicity as the basic understanding of diversity, their concept "diversity" coincides with the authors' definition of diversity mentioned at the beginning of the chapter. Respondents shared similar views towards diversity and Angel's definition seemed to capture the totality of their understanding:

> [Diversity] basically boils down to respect and acceptance of difference. Difference can be racial, political, religious, physical, or other things, both visible and invisible. Diversity is not simply about having faces of color in a university or a workplace. It should be about acknowledging and respecting the intrinsic value of a human being.

With this understanding of diversity from our participants, we asked them to share how they reconciled any discrepancies between their definitions and their universities'. Lee responded,

> I am frustrated. To me, [it] is so obvious, even my students could better understand the problems, but it's hard to get the opinions up to the community level. There is no way to reconcile. In the past year, I have tried to reach each level of administration, but failed to get an answer. Have to look for outside help.

In Flower's case, the discrepancy between her personal definition of diversity and that of her institution made her feel a deep sense of frustration and resignation:

> There shouldn't be any hierarchy among the differences in my understanding. . . . I don't like [discrepancies]. I constantly feel my status of being a minority. I didn't know I had to reconcile. But now I have to accept it and deal with it, and perform my foreignness to an acceptable degree and in a positive light.

It is evident that these junior faculty members know that they have very different understandings of what diversity means compared to the official definitions of their universities (or lack thereof). It seems that they are frustrated with this tension and are trying to find ways to make sense of and deal with their frustrations.

TOKENISM/LACK OF CULTURAL SENSITIVITY

Tokenism/lack of cultural sensitivity is a second theme that emerged from the interviews with the participants. Tokenism is defined as making an obligatory effort toward including minorities. According to Yoder (1991), tokens represent a subgroup that is less than 15% of the larger group. In terms of their ethnic, racial, and gender backgrounds, the participants find themselves underrepresented in their institutions. Several have even come to the conclusion that they are mere tokens in their institutions as a result of their races/ethnicities and their institutions' diversity initiatives. Interestingly, the women simultaneously accept and reject their tokenism. For example, Caroline's comment shows her acceptance of the fact that she is a token, but also shows her attempt to reject her tokenism:

> I feel like I have extra service demands for mentoring students of color since I'm the only African-American tenure-track professor in the department. Because I research women of color, I feel obligated to work with Women's Studies and African-American Studies. I am happy to network with people in these areas, so I hope this doesn't come across the wrong way. I just feel like I need time to get myself situated and find my place with the department first. Sometimes I wonder about these obligations because I have no written or specific guidelines, but there seems to be an understanding that I will be actively involved with these programs when I speak to people.

While Caroline is at predominantly White institution, Flower, a Chinese faculty member, finds herself at a historically Black institution dealing with a similar phenomenon. Though the authors posit that the experiences of faculty at historically Black institutions and predominantly White institutions are not the same, a lack of cultural sensitivity toward the minority faculty can still exist at both institutions. For example, Flower explains:

> I came to this institution from a predominantly White institution. . . . I thought I would feel less foreign here, but it turned out to be the opposite—I feel more foreign here than anywhere else. It was very frustrating when I found that everything was outside my cultural repertoire when I first started teaching here. I couldn't pronounce most of my students' non-Anglo names, could barely recognize the differences of their faces (as they also confuse me with other very few young Asian females on campus), and I knew so little about their academic and cultural experiences. They are close to a different body of academic "canon" than the "America" that I was familiar with. For example, they often quote Malcolm X, whom at first I have never heard of. They mention their experiences at Black churches in class discussion that made me feel that I truly AM from a different world.

Flower admitted that she thought her experiences at the historically Black institution at which she works would lead her to fit in more than at her previous predominantly White institution. Unfortunately, it seems that both she and her students had difficulties embracing the other's difference and individuality.

Overall, the participants are very aware of their minority statuses on campus as female faculty of color. They accept that they are different from the other faculty and students, but do not want to be recognized only for their race, ethnicity, and/or gender.

Greater Understanding From Students Than Colleagues

The final theme relates to participants' relationships with their students and colleagues. Even though the respondents have concerns about teaching majority students, their experiences with the students are positive most of the time. Angel stated that although her authority was sometimes challenged by the students, she used media tools to help them understand and respect people from different backgrounds, as the following statement demonstrates:

> I guess it is not too overstretched when I say that most of the students still expect a white male professor taking the center stage in class. When a female and colored body assumes the authority figure, sometimes it is challenged. However, instead of getting frustrated, I engage in more proactive pedagogical practices. I often use news outlets as a source to discuss diversity issues. Last April when an 11-old Hispanic boy by the name of Jaheem Herrera committed suicide as a result of being bullied at school, we, as a class, discussed the impact of racism and homophobic language. When Attorney General Eric Holder's "A Nation of Cowards" speech caused a lot of debate in the media, it created a moment for my students to reflect on their own take on whether this is a country of equal opportunities for everyone. Many students think that racism is a story in the past and that in this post-racial society everyone is equal. Activities like these provide moments for everyone to face their own hidden biases.

Similarly, Lee stated that she had positive experiences with students. She said that it was easier to build common ground with students than with colleagues. The problem with this is that, unlike Angel and others who are able to transform their experience with difference in the classroom, it is very difficult to confront the issue as a non-tenured female faculty member of color, especially when it comes to faculty and administration. In fact, most of the respondents demonstrated professional ethics in face of students' resistance to minority professors and took proactive strategies to address the problems. Their frustrations as minority faculty members came more from the administration than from the students. Caroline's comment illustrated this point:

> I'm careful how I phrase my comments so I don't come off like I'm complaining. I also want to emphasize the positive aspects of my identity. My chair and two of my colleagues are especially responsive and make sure to protect my time and check with me to see how I'm doing. I primarily talk to them about it when it relates to my job duties.

Angel supported this as well in her statement:

> I am here in the U.S. on a H1-B visa. When I told a colleague about my need to apply for green card, her response was: 'We would love to have you here. You are also Chinese. Now our government has borrowed so much money from China. We'd better treat the Chinese well.' I cannot recall the exact conversation between us. However, this outsider-who-wants-to-stay undertone is what remains in my memory. I do understand, against the background of recession, when people are struggling to put food on their table, it is difficult for them to focus on larger issues. But is it the reason for us to brush the issue of diversity aside? No. I personally think that individual effort is important. But if it is not supported by the large institutional culture, individual impact will be limited.

Many of the participants have more positive experiences with their students than with faculty, staff, or administrators. Students seem to be more willing to implement diversity in action, whereas the participants' colleagues are far less accepting. Lee reminded us that, "Without a downward effort in promoting diversity from institutional level, it's hard to work upward."

SUMMARY

The shared experiences of the female assistant professors of color revealed the difficulties and challenges in negotiating their double minority identities with students, colleagues, and administrators. While their respective university or college tries to project a public image of being a "diverse" institution, in reality, there is a long way to go to truly embrace the idea of "diversity" and integrate female assistant professors of color on the interpersonal and structural levels. The results indicated that the participants are cautious to talk about diversity issues with their colleagues because structurally, institutions did not fully integrate the female assistant professors of color across functions, levels, and workgroups. They became tokens when they were only invited to speak concerning topics of their own races/ethnicities/gender.

Noticeably, our research findings confirm the existing literature that states minority faculty members must make more efforts to establish their credibility, but will be favored by students once the credibility is established (e.g. Hendrix, 1997, 1998). In general, they had no extremely negative experiences with students, as the teaching credibility and student-professor relationship are things they can improve through constant effort. For example, in the case of her authority being challenged by students, one female faculty of color demonstrated professionalism and took proactive strategies, such using media outlets, to help the students understand and respect people from different backgrounds.

In contrast, when it came to the administration and the colleagues, the female faculty of color could not find an easy way to transform their experiences into positive institutional and societal change in action. Some indicated their frustrations with the hierarchy of their institutions and their colleagues' attitudes toward minority faculty members. Having sensed their limited individual impact, most of the participants chose to be silent about their everyday frustrations and struggles.

In summary, the findings of the study indicate that there is indeed a discrepancy between the concept of diversity and diversity in action. The problems experienced by the participants cannot be easily resolved due to the lack of informal and structural support. While the participants are able to negotiate their identities successfully with their students, they do not feel comfortable communicating about diversity issues with their colleagues and the administration. It requires the efforts from the minority faculty, the majority faculty, and the administration to bridge the gap between the idea of diversity and diversity actualized.

DISCUSSION

This section provides a discussion of the initial question posed in this chapter, "How do women faculty of color understand their institution's ideology of diversity and how do their understandings compare with their everyday experiences?" This question seeks to understand the discrepancy between the ideology of diversity in higher education institutions and the participants' everyday experiences of diversity. The results reveal that the institutions tend to define diversity as difference in race/ethnicity and/or as part of their discrimination policies. Instead, the participants recommend that the action of diversity must begin with having the definition of diversity be more inclusive of culture within institutional discourse. A feminist critique provides further insight into the participants' discussions.

Institutions of higher learning represent socially oppressive structures that privilege the majority-race male voice, resulting in the suppression of the voices of racial and gender minorities. From the narratives of the participants, it is evident that the treatment they receive at their universities suppresses their identities in favor of dominant-culture led institutional initiatives toward diversity. For example, Affirmative Action has helped increase the number of diverse "faces" in academe, but the treatment of these same diverse individuals as cultural beings free to express their individuality within and outside of the classroom has not occurred. Though racial and gender integration was initially about giving minorities access to the same educational opportunities as White men, women of color in higher education still struggle with truly being accepted. Unfortunately, the daily experiences of the female faculty of color interviewed for this chapter tell us that their perception of diversity as difference in cultures, values, and perspectives is a constant struggle in daily communicative patterns. This struggle is a result of the women competing with their institutions' definitions of diversity in isolation, resulting in further marginalization. Angel's statement summarized the primary issue: "Diversity is not simply about having faces of color in a university or a workplace. It should be about acknowledging and respecting the intrinsic value of a human being." Thus, the concept of diversity is the result of a majority-race, male dominant discourse, which seems to have no true intention of implementing diversity that genuinely includes minority voices. Instead, the intent of these male-dominated institutions is to satisfy the diversity "talk" by fulfilling minority quotas. As a result, female junior faculty of color feel that their colleagues and administrators lack cultural sensitivity.

It is also clear from the dialogue with the participants that they feel that they need more support from colleagues and administrators. Compared to their students, colleagues seem the least accepting when it comes to interacting with others from different cultural backgrounds. Although they may have some difficulties with students, they are able to confront these issues in the classroom. Difficulties with senior faculty, however, are much harder to overcome. In this sense, issues of power are most likely the reason for this discrepancy. In the classroom setting, students are viewed as less powerful than our participants, so it is easier for minority female faculty members to address diversity issues with students (Golish & Olson, 2000). As such, students are more likely to be willing to negotiate their stereotypes and dominant-culture beliefs.

On the other hand, among faculty, female assistant professors of color are at the bottom of the hierarchy because of their racial, gender, and junior statuses and there might be some unintended consequences that could affect their careers if they were to broach diversity issues with their colleagues and administrators who may be in more senior positions than they. This confirms the findings of 1997 University of California, Los Angeles (UCLA) study that found that "higher education in the United States falls short in its faculty diversification efforts" (par. 1). A feminist view of the social institution of academia shows that the power is in the hands of senior, majority-race male faculty, who also control the diversity discourse. The consequence of this is the silencing of the junior minority faculty. As Caroline stated, "I primarily talk to [my colleagues] about [diversity] when it relates to my job duties" and not about how diversity in action can take place at her institution.

For these junior, female faculty of color, hoping that academe is a place that understands racial politics does not always have positive results. Many felt they were blindsided after realizing that not all universities have faculty and administrators in higher positions who are even willing to entertain the conversation about truly advancing diversity. Instead, it should be that minority and majority faculty, staff, and administrators alike are willing to engage in the same practices of inclusion and cultivate those affective dimensions inside and outside of the classroom. This will allow them to build relationships with each other, leading to the freeing from the aforementioned domination that is evident in the oppressive power structures of higher education.

Implications and Conclusion

Changes in workforce demographics have inspired a new surge of interest in diversity in the workplace. Although colleges and universities often claim promoting diversity as their goal, there is often a discrepancy between diversity as described in the institutions' mission statements and the everyday experiences of female junior faculty of color with diversity. The purpose of the chapter was to disclose and demystify the discrepancies between the concept of diversity and diversity in action through exploring the experiences of female assistant professors of color in the academy.

Though this study included a small number of participants, the stories they tell are no less significant, for there is much power in the story of even one marginalized woman faculty member of color. This study, which highlights the experiences of six women of color, has several research and practical implications in the increasingly diverse workplace. First, the daily experiences of female faculty of color tell us that diversity is not simply about having faces of color in an organization, but about respect and acceptance of difference. However, there is no easy way to reconcile the discrepancies between the concept of diversity and diversity in practice. Female faculty of color have learned to live with this gap by not talking about it with colleagues, yet they should not have to, particularly because these silenced struggles could increase minority faculty's feelings of isolation and marginalization in the workplace. As a result, it will become harder to recruit and retain female faculty of color in academia.

Second, the current chapter contributes to the diversity literature by calling special attention to the experiences of junior faculty of color in majority institutions. The common experiences among different minority groups in the academy carry a strong message regarding diversity issues that reinforce current trends. For example, recent trends inform us that faculty of color in the United States are dissatisfied with most parts of their jobs (UCLA, 1997) compared to White colleagues. Similarly, faculty of color feel higher levels of stress due to retention, tenure, and subtle discrimination (UCLA, 1997), indicating that the issues experienced by the women faculty of color in this study are not experienced in isolation; they are felt by countless numbers minority faculty at majority institutions. Future studies should be devoted to exploring the work experiences of a much broader and diverse population in the academy.

Finally, the research has important practical implications. As acknowledged by one of the participants, individual efforts to increase the action of diversity are necessary, but their impact on diversity will be limited without institutional support. While minorities must speak up for themselves in certain situations dealing with diversity, mainstream American faculty members and administrators have to acknowledge their part in the struggles minority faculty face as well. In the words of Warren (2003), "Just because one does not intend to oppress others with an utterance or nonverbal expression does not mean that s/he is not responsible for the effects such communicative messages might have on others" (p. 55). Therefore, it is imperative that we bring to light the unconscious operation of oppression among some faculty and administrators. Dialogue, as uncomfortable as it may be, is the only way that we will be able to transform and go beyond the concept of diversity.

Higher education institutions should reach out more to female faculty of color. The goal is not simply to achieve diversity demographically, but to create a positive diversity environment in which differences are valued and appreciated. The current research will help institutions realize the gap between the concept of diversity and diversity in action as reflected in the daily experiences of the female faculty of color. By raising awareness, we hope institutions will be more proactive in the socialization and retention of minority faculty and provide more structural and informal network support to reduce their challenges and struggles. In this sense, the experiences shared by the female assistant professors of color have the potential to transform the academy into one with a heightened level of cultural sensitivity and openness to differences.

REFERENCES

Allen, B. J., Orbe, M. P., & Olivas, M. R. (1999). The complexity of our tears: Dis/enchantment and (in)difference in the academy. *Communication Theory, 9*(4), 402-429.

Appel, M., Cartwright, D., Smith, D. G., & Wolf, L. E. (1996). *The impact of diversity on students: A preliminary review of the research literature.* Washington, DC: Association of American Colleges and Universities.

Astin, A. W. (1982). *Minorities in American higher education: Recent trends, current prospects, and recommendations.* San Francisco, CA: Jossey-Bass.

Ayers, J. F., Wheeler, E. A., Fracasso, M. P., Galupo, M. P., Rabin, J. S., & Slater, B. R. (1999). Reinventing the university through the teaching of diversity. *Journal of Adult Development, 6*(3), 163-173.

Branch, A. J. (2001). How to retain African American faculty during times of challenge for higher education. In L. Jones (Ed.), *Retaining African Americans in higher education: Challenging paradigms for retaining students, faculty and administrators* (pp. 175-192). Sterling, VA: Styles.

Butner, B. K., Burley, H., & Marbley, A. F. (2000, January). Coping with the unexpected Black faculty at predominately White institutions. *Journal of Black Studies, 30*, 453-462.

Deetz, S. (2000). Conceptual foundations. In F. M. Jablin & L. L. Putnam (Eds.), *The new handbook of organizational communication: Advances in theory, research, and methods* (pp. 3-46). Thousand Oaks, CA: Sage.

Evans, S. Y. (Fall 2007). Women of color in American higher education. *The NEA Higher Education Journal*, 131-137.

Foss, K. A., & Foss, S. K. (1994). Personal experience as evidence in feminist scholarship. *Western Journal of Communication, 58*, 39-43.

Foss, S. K., Foss, K. A., & Trapp, R. (2002). *Contemporary Perspectives on Rhetoric* (3rd ed.). Prospect Heights, IL: Waveland Press, Inc.

Gee, J. P. (1999). *An introduction to discourse analysis: Theory and method.* New York, NY: Routledge.

Golish, T. D., & Olson, L. N. (2000). Students' use of power in the classroom: An investigation of student power, teacher power, and teacher immediacy. *Communication Quarterly, 48*, 293-310. doi: 10.1080/01463370009385598

Graves, S. B. (1990). A case of double jeopardy? Black women in higher education. *Initiatives, 53*, 3-8.

Gregory, S. T. (1995). *Black women in the academy: The secrets to success and achievement.* New York, NY: University Press of America.

Gregory, S. T. (2001). Black faculty women in the academy. *The Journal of Negro Education, 70*(3), 124-138.

Guess, J. M. (1989). Race: The challenge of the 90s. *Crisis, 96*, 28-30, 32-33.

Helm, E. G., Sedlacek, W. E., & Prieto, D. O. (1998, Fall). The relationship between attitudes toward diversity and overall satisfaction of university students by race. *Journal of College Counseling, 1*, 111-120.

Hendrix, K. G. (1997). Student perceptions of verbal and nonverbal cues leading to images of Black and White professor credibility. *The Howard Journal of Communications, 8*, 251-273.

Hendrix, K. G. (1998). Student perceptions of the influence of race on professor credibility. *Journal of Black Studies, 28*, 738-763.

Lindlof, T. R., & Taylor, B. C. (2002). *Qualitative research methods*. London, England: Sage.

Littlejohn, S.W. (1999). Critical Theories. *Theories of Human Communication* (6th ed.). Belmont, CA: Wadsworth Publishing Company.

Magner, D. K. (1996, February 2). The new generation: Study shows proportions of female and minority professors are growing. *The Chronicle of Higher Education*, pp. A17-18.

Moses, Y. T. (1997). Black women in academe. In L. Benjamin (Ed.), *Black women in the academy: Promises and perils* (pp. 23-38). Gainesville, FL: University Press of Florida.

Riessman, C. K. (1993). *Narrative analysis: Qualitative research methods volume 30*. Newbury Park, CA: Sage Publications.

Sedlacek, W. E. (1995). *Improving racial and ethnic diversity and campus climate at four-year independent Midwest colleges* (An evaluation report of the Lilly Endowment Grant Program). Indianapolis, IN: Lilly Endowment.

Smith, D., & Wolf-Wendel, L. (2005). *The challenge of diversity*. Washington, DC: ASHE-ERIC.

Spelman, D., Addison-Reid, B., Avery, E., & Crary, M. (2006). Sustaining a long-term diversity change initiative: Lessons from a business university. *Diversity in Higher Education, 14*(4), 19-25.

Spiggle, S. (1994). Analysis and interpretation of qualitative data in consumer research. *Journal of Consumer Research: An Interdisciplinary Quarterly, 21*(3), 491-503.

Turner, C. S. V., & Myers, S. L. (2000). *Faculty of color in academe: Bittersweet success*. Boston, MA: Allyn and Bacon.

University of California, Los Angeles (1997). UCLA study show nation's college faculty of color still low in number, still occupy lower tiers. Retrieved from http://www.gseis.ucla.edu/heri/race_pr_95.html

Warren, J. T. (2003). *Performing purity: Whiteness, pedagogy, and the reconstruction of power*. New York, NY: Peter Lang Publishing.

Wolf-Wendel, L. E. (2005). New forward. In A. J. Kezar, K. Ward, & L. E. Wolf-Wendel (Eds.), *The challenge of diversity: Involvement or alienation in the academy?* (p. iii). ASHE Higher Education Report, *31*(1).

Yoder, J. D. (1991). Rethinking tokenism: Looking beyond numbers. *Gender and Soci ety, 5*(2), 178-192.

Chapter 2

A Muted Voice on Holy Ground
Reflections on the Dialectics Experienced as an African American Female Professor in a Christian University

Jeanetta D. Sims

> *I am always answerable for the response that is generated from the unique place I occupy in existence. My responses begin to have a pattern; the dialogue I have with existence begins to assume the form of a text, a kind of book. (Holquist, 1990, p. 28)*

Given the increased significance of racial and gender diversity in higher education (Hale, 2004), Christian colleges and universities have implemented key initiatives in order to advance their diversity efforts. The nature of these initiatives typically involves faculty training, student multicultural days, increased efforts at attracting faculty and students of color, and symposia designed for reflection and planning about the leadership required to sustain diversity in the Christian university environment—all activities in which I have participated, advocated for, facilitated, championed, and sponsored. As an African American female communication "teacher scholar" whose program of research includes social influence, public relations, marketing communications, and strategic communication in organizations, this "diversity" discussion represents a unique place of personal intersection across, between, and among my teaching, scholarship, race, gender, and Christianity.

The process of negotiating the tensions associated with these multiple roles is a challenge that I continue to welcome and the result of my experience with one Christian institution is this brief essay which, although not exhaustive of my experiences in a Christian university, examines the dialectics observed while working as a minority faculty member. The essay first considers Baxter and Montgomery's (1996; Baxter, 2004a, 2004b) relational dialectics and Bakhtin's (1975/1981) dialogism influences as well as the utility of such a framework. Next, the dialectics inherent to the nature of a Christian institution are examined. Then, the dialectics that best illuminate my experiences in a tenure-track position at this majority institution are shared. Additionally, suggestions from my experiences as an active participant are offered to women of color who are seeking to cope and thrive in majority institutions, whether religiously affiliated or not.

DIALECTICS AS AN EXPLANATORY FRAMEWORK

AN OVERVIEW OF RELATIONAL DIALECTICS

Baxter and Montgomery's (1996) dialogical perspective is heavily influenced by M. M. Bakhtin, an early 20th century Russian cultural theorist, whose 50-year body of work became known as a theory called dialogism (Holquist, 1990). Bakhtin's dialogism argues that all meaning "comes about only as a result of the relation between two bodies occupying simultaneous but different space" (Holquist, 1990, p. 19), which makes the position of the observer (one who Bakhtin also regarded as an active participant) fundamental. Bakhtin (1975/1981) argues that any utterance of social life is "a contradiction-ridden, tension-filled unity of two embattling tendencies" (p. 272), and his focus on the contradictions present in the discourse of social life served as the initial catalyst for Baxter and Montgomery's work. His writings prompted Baxter and Montgomery's reconsideration of how the self both influences and is influenced by the other (the "other" is regarded as ideas, people, or institutions) through dialogue, which is conceptualized as more like a medieval carnival of contrasts than a flippant conversation (Baxter, 2004b).

Perhaps an additional catalyst for relational dialectics were Baxter and Montgomery's (1996) frustrations with the "theoretical one-sidedness and neglect of the 'both/and'-ness of relating" (p. 6) in communication theories and research. The scholars began re-conceptualizing relational development theory and research by focusing on the contradictions and inconsistencies (e.g., closedness/openness, independence/interdependence, etc.) present in relational communication (Baxter, 1990).

Four key assumptions associated with all dialectical approaches and with Baxter and Montgomery's (1996) early dialogical orientation are worth referencing. First, *contradiction* is regarded as opposing forces that drive social change and that are inherent in relationships; they are not indications of failure, but are a part of the realities of routine social life. Second, *change* is punctuated by stability, which enables the interplay and flux of social life to be detected. Third, *praxis* regards people as social actors and reactors to their own actions as it relates to their communication decisions. Fourth, *totality* is regarded as the interdependent nature of phenomena as they are only understood in relation to one another.

Dialectics may be internal (between the self and the other in the relationship) or external (between the relationship and the broader community). From a relational dialectics perspective, relational development is not viewed as navigating the relationship through various relational stages (e.g., beginning, middle, end, etc.) toward some ultimate end state or position of balance (Baxter, 2004a, 2004b; Baxter & Montgomery, 1996). Instead, relationships are thought to be a process or a change that consists of negotiating the internal and external tensions that are present. To have relational balance is to be void of the presence of opposing forces or contradiction and is conceived "as a state of nondialogue" (Baxter, 2004b, p. 19). Dialogue is steeped not in conversational exchanges, but in the contrasts associated with perceiving.

The academic journey of relational dialectics began as a unique metatheoretical perspective (Baxter & Montgomery, 1996) with a dominant focus on contradictions and continues today with Baxter's (2004b) second-generation refinements and clarifications that re-focus the theory on five Bakhtinian conceptions of dialogue. The full array of Baxter's enhancements go beyond the scope of this brief essay[1]; however, the framework of relational dialectics has provided great utility among communication scholars in examining intercultural couples' communication (Cools, 2006), social networking site communication (Kim & Yun, 2008), the discourse of bereaved parents (Toller & Braithwaite, 2009), and social influence (Baxter & Bylund, 2004), just to share a few of the recent contextual areas of inquiry from this perspective.

Relational Dialectics as a Framework

In his perspective on dialogism, Bakhtin (1975/1981) was insistent on the essential relevance of one's position in time and space for deriving meaning. To be dialogical "means that reality is always experienced, not just perceived, and further, that it is experienced from a particular position" (Holquist, 1990, p. 20). This role of self as a being is not a central position of superiority but is co-constituted and reflective of its place relative to other people, other ideas, and other institutions. Later, four dialectics (present but absent, fighting but flighting, connected but disconnected, and thriving but struggling) associated with my experiences are offered. Deriving meaning in this way is different than conducting an experiment, collecting survey data, or analyzing conversational talk; however, this approach of being reflective of the self in a particular place in time lends itself nicely to discussing my experiences in a majority Christian institution for this edited volume.

A key tenant of relational dialectics is its focus on the complexities of a phenomenon rather than attempting to bring all of its intricacies to a nice, satisfying resolution. A dialogic approach positions this chapter as reflecting on the disorder and disarrays of my experience, "not with a goal of 'smoothing out' its rough edges, but with a goal of understanding its fundamental ongoing messiness" (Baxter & Montgomery, 1996, p. 3). Additionally, a dialectical approach is well positioned to acknowledge the "both/and" nature of human relating and relationships rather than juxtaposing them in a bipolar fashion. This is a useful framework when attempting to explain the likes and dislikes of my work and speaks to the potential of having work that is both loved and dreaded simultaneously. Without this nature of "simultaneous demand," much of the double-sided interplay in the tensions between and among my roles as a minority, teacher, Christian, and scholar would go unaccounted for in an effort to resolve these mixed elements of my experiences. Thus, using a dialectical framework to share and reflect on my experiences of having shared time and space with faculty, students, administration, and the majority institution itself provides the opportunity to collectively appreciate and regret aspects of the tenure-track journey. Perhaps, best put, the use of relational dialectics as a framework for this essay is simply my effort to have an appreciation for the disorder that is often criticized, yet that continually permeates the dialogue present between minority faculty and majority Christian institutions.

DIALECTICS AND THE IDEALS OF A CHRISTIAN COLLEGE

THE MESSINESS OF CHRISTIAN EDUCATIONAL INSTITUTIONS

In a multitude of areas, religiously affiliated educational institutions are unique and complicated (given their quote offered above, Baxter & Montgomery, 1996, would likely use the term "messy"[2]) places to pursue tenure. The academic missions are steeped in religious heritage and traditions with rhetoric that are connected to heavenly outcomes directed at carrying out God's purpose. A hallmark of this type of educational institution is the desire to remain intentionally Christ-centered and to allow "a lively and rigorous interpenetration of liberal learning with the content and commitment of Christian faith" (Holmes, 1987, p. 7). Failure to put Christian values at the forefront results in an institution void of its vision and its ethos, leading, most likely, to the irrelevance of its Christian heritage (Benne, 2001). Not only are Christian values at their core, but numerous calls of reconciliation as well as scriptural justifications (see Breems, 2001, 2002) have been offered by Christian universities for their diversity efforts.

Thus, intentional Christian values are not surrendered in this setting but serve as the foundation of the Christian university mission. The success of tenure-track faculty is inextricably linked to their ability to integrate faith and learning for students as well as to enrich the dialogue about faith and learning in their scholarly pursuits. As Davis (2002) argues, "faith has much to say about the conversion of information into knowledge" (p. 135). He contends that for scholars in a Christian university, faith provides a window of understanding and is a legitimate factor that both contributes to methodological processes and "directs the collection and interpretation of observations" (p. 133).

The mission-minded focus of the Christian college or university, with its centrality of Christian values and its focus on the integration of faith and learning, would almost have the appearance of "holy ground." The Christian university would appear to be a type of spiritual utopia for tenure-track women of color who desire to make a meaningful impact with an opportunity to influence young minds not just for the four- to five-year academic window of time, but also for eternity. Certainly Menjares' (2003) research confirms that faculty of color choose Christian universities because of the institutions' spiritual missions. From his research, the top three reasons faculty of color make the choice to teach at a Christian university are a sense of God's call, the opportunity to engage in Christian ministry, and the prospect of challenging students spiritually, socially, and racially.

However, in accounting for the experience of my tenure-track journey, one would have to consider that the same centripetal forces that propel a sense of cohesion and unity are also centrifugal catalysts that highlight the numerous ways in which differences are neither tolerated nor celebrated. So, let us consider some of the opposing forces that permeate the Christian university context, bearing in mind that from a relational dialectics perspective, contradictions are not negatively valenced nor should they be regarded as pessimistic points of contention with Christian colleges and universities. Instead, the aim is to attain an understanding of the "messiness" without seeking a shift towards resolution.

Opposing Forces and Institutional Diversity

By their very nature, Christian institutions (at least those seeking to preserve their distinctiveness) have cultural environments marked by contradictions or opposing forces that drive change, which sustains a complicated or "messy" state of flux. Certainly, the following three dialectics (changing/changeless, inclusive/exclusive, and unity/disunity) are an incomplete account of all dialectics that could be offered. Other minorities and non-minorities, who occupy different spaces simultaneously in Christian educational institutions, could very well extend, adjust, or clarify this list. However, based on my experiences of having conducted diversity training with faculty and diversity steering committees, and having shadowed coordinators and participated in national diversity symposia all with and for Christian educational institutions, these three dialectics best account for my observations of the most noteworthy tensions inherent in institutional diversity discourse and the Christian educational institution.

The changing/changeless dialectic. Arguably, any educational institution must adapt to or change with the environmental and/or social demands of its time if it is to stay current and relevant in the 21st century academy. Yet, Christian universities are plagued with a genuine need to hold fast to key values and doctrines lest they become unprincipled. This means that Christian colleges and universities are constantly challenged to retain that which makes them uniquely Christian while at the same time attempting to thrive and adapt to modern day demands. For example, the Christian university must weigh retaining the principle of a university-wide commitment to worship against the scheduling demands of having classes or meetings at the same time. Or, the university might have to protect against decreasing required religious courses in an effort to increase the curriculum hours associated with enhancing a particular major. "Simply put, the status of many Christian colleges and universities as distinctly evangelical is only tenuous at best unless certain safeguards keep them accountable to their own theological convictions" (Thornbury, 2002, p. 48). The desire to safeguard or protect these convictions often runs in opposition to pursuing institutional diversity change. This is an interesting tension given the fact that research (Haralu, 2005; Kratt, 2004) documents that many religiously affiliated educational institutions lag behind their secular counterparts in matters of diversity, suggesting less change rather than more change has taken place.

For women of color, this is a foremost tension to be negotiated. Advancing diversity, which I define as "managing the full contributions of people with *different identities*[3] into the social, structural, and power relationships of an organization or institution" (Sims, 2008, p. 7), to include the contributions of more women of color will, in most cases, place the initiative in opposition to a Caucasian male-dominated faculty, administration, and board of trustee leadership that has remained relatively changeless. Given the previous definition for diversity, this lack of structural change within the institution makes advancing diversity problematic. Certainly, some change occurred as institutional efforts were made to hire more women and people of color in faculty and staff positions; however, the perceived visual display of these efforts was in the cafeteria and janitorial services rather than in faculty or administrative offices (based on focus group research associated with Sims, 2007). Whether the reasoning for the lack of change is to stay aligned with doctrinal concerns or to preserve control and power, women of color face the challenge of contradicting the status quo associated with a conservative evangelical culture (Menjares, 2003).

Not only would the structural presence of women of color across all organizational levels provide a visual change, their presence would also permit a change in leadership style and communication. For example, Parker's (2005) work suggests the leadership themes associated with African American females are markedly different than their counterparts. The use of interactive leadership, empowerment of employees, openness in communication, participative decision making with argument and refutation, and boundary spanning communication are unique to African American female leadership. The structural presence of women of color would exert tension on the status quo.

To advance racial and gender diversity, women of color will face the need to change the Whiteness and maleness of the institution and its corresponding leadership styles. This will have to be done in an environment where institutional budgets are managed and decision-making occurs (something that may lie outside the scope of their duties in their tenure-track positions), even as women of color seek to assist the university in having a distinctiveness that is unchanged (something that can be impacted in a tenure-track position).

The inclusion/exclusion dialectic. Related to, but different from, the previous dialectic is the notion that while all individuals are welcome in the Christian college and while God's truth is capable of being infused into any topic (Guthrie, 2002), only certain types of individuals are truly granted acceptance and certain topics of conversation truly given utterance. Holmes (1987) argues that the lack of inclusion and engagement with various, even differing, perspectives and viewpoints among Christian colleges is a pitfall that must be avoided. He argues that if students are to "act creatively and to speak with cogency and clarity to the minds of [their] fellows, the educated Christian must be at home in the world of ideas and people" (p. 5). Though this effort may be a teleological aim of Christian educational institutions, women of color in tenure-track faculty positions will be challenged by the simultaneous demands of inclusion and exclusion present "in the process" of the institution achieving the end state that Holmes describes.

Perhaps, the best metaphor is inviting guests into the home, but only allowing them to stand in the living room for the length of their visit rather than to sit comfortably on the sofa. For a friend and even an acquaintance, this would be an unacceptable occurrence. So, when the metaphor is considered against the backdrop of a Christian worldview, it becomes interesting, annoying, perplexing, and detestable all at the same time. Menjares (2003) labels this challenge for people of color as being placed in a box. My metaphor extends more broadly but also encompasses Menjares' finding. When a "minority expert" is needed, the faculty member of color is "let out of the box" and offered inclusion for the purposes of engaging in and often leading diversity discussions. Once discussions have expired, the faculty member is put back in the box. Thus, routine inquiry about the ways in which the campus climate excludes diversity in the occurrences of everyday institutional life goes unexamined, remaining intact in the box. This is similar to having an invitation to someone's home without the added courtesy of being granted a place of prominence or comfort. In essence, the contradictory and metaphorical message is, "You're welcome to be here, but don't get too comfortable."

Another aspect of this dialectic is seeking to understand the types of individuals who are granted comfort and inclusion. Rather than attempt to offer the defining traits and characteristics of the "type" of persons who are welcome in a Christian university, allow me to share some brief descriptors used by Caucasian faculty, administrators, and students to describe African Americans in meetings in which I participated: "a Whitey/Blacky," "more White than Black," and "not really Black." The use of these terms as descriptors for individuals suggests a need to label African Americans against the backdrop of a White persona, a rhetorical practice that is steeped in race-based comparisons. When "White" is used as the standard for comparison to establish normalcy and privilege, non-White individuals are automatically reduced to a place of inferiority and "otherness." Though indirectly implied, the meaning derived from the use of these descriptors is that the closer one's behavior, manner, and carriage are to being "White" and not "Black," the greater the inclusion. The interplay of these utterances suggests a greater level of acceptance and comfort for people of color who culturally "behave" in ways that are like their Caucasian counterparts. The nature of this inclusion is predicated on the exclusion of (in this case) their African American identities.

The candor, openness, lack of a hidden agenda, and explicit refutation that characterize African American female leadership communication (Parker, 2005) may very well be the evidence cited to justify why a woman of color is just not "White" enough for a new position or for advancement. Given that most Christian colleges and universities are dominated by Caucasian males in leadership positions, the normative leadership behavior in these organizations will be distinctly different than the leadership displayed by African American females. In interpersonal interactions and meetings where indirect communication styles and more covert aims are the norm, the directness and openness associated with African American female leadership may not be celebrated or appreciated and instead, may be viewed negatively. African American females will need to negotiate two types of tensions: the tensions associated with "behaving" by displaying the normative leadership style in an effort to be included; and the tensions associated with "misbehaving" in an effort to retain one's racial identity by displaying a uniquely different leadership style. The persistent conciliation associated with this dialectic will need to be negotiated on the tenure-track journey and beyond.

The unity/disunity dialectic. Given the importance of retaining its religious traditions, distinctiveness, and ideals, the Christian university has a unified worldview, unified educational goals (Holmes, 1987), and typically a time designated for a campus-wide unified worship (Benne, 2001). The benefits of working and worshipping alongside faculty, staff, and students who share the same religious affiliation, Christian doctrine, and worldview are rewarding.

The commonalities and unity infuse a much easier path to relating; however, they also contribute to the friction that occurs when one seeks to travel off the beaten path. And travelling off the beaten path is exactly where diversity dialogue must be designed to go. Acknowledging the commonalities while simultaneously advocating for the contributions of *different identities* can often become a fragile enterprise. In order for the institution to advance its espoused value of diversity, multiple voices and perspectives must be engaged in the dialogue. These utterances will manifest the disunity and contradictions in the commonalities, even as individuals seek to uphold the unification. Negotiating the contradictions of this dialectic is central when considering faculty-required worship times where the Caucasian-led majority culture often leaves little room for the emotional connections, rhythms, speaker cadence, and upbeat musicality that are typically a part of the African American style of worship, and other non-majority styles of worship face the same tensions.

Also, negotiating this dialectic is central to discussions about institutional policies (ideally more past than present), which have often isolated, misled, or mistreated people of color. When stakeholders (both internal and external) who are diversity advocates consider the university's historical record, their expectations are for the institution to give an account or reconcile the previous acts of intolerance in institutional memory with the university's current diversity efforts. However, resurrecting, addressing, and reconciling these grievances threaten the unity by publicly acknowledging the times of disunity and institutional intolerance. By virtue of the focus on *different identities,* diversity dialogue then is riddled with the tensions of unity and disunity as the opposing forces of commonality and difference are negotiated.

These three dialectics are not "necessary evils" associated with working in the Christian university cultural environment. Instead, they are "necessary acknowledgements," which can enable the dialogue to be better understood and which can enhance the relating with and among women of color in tenure-track positions. Perhaps elements of these three dialectics are certainly present in other educational institutions. However, the centrifugal and centripetal forces play out in a slightly different state of messiness and flux given the Christ-centered values and worldview associated with the Christian university.

DIALECTICAL TENSIONS IN THE MAJORITY INSTITUTION

The previous dialectics have centered on the tensions germane and inherent to the very nature of the Christian college or university. They were offered first because "the meaning of whatever is observed is shaped by the place from which it is perceived" (Holquist, 1990, p. 20). This created the foremost necessity of exploring the characteristics of the Christian institution as a place of higher learning. Now, I turn to the tensions experienced as a female, African American in a tenure-track position at this majority institution. In this section I will intentionally reflect on aspects of my own personal accounts with hopefully the candor and honesty of "scholarly girl talk" over a nice cup of hot tea or coffee.

THE ONGOING FLUX OF MY EXPERIENCE

Speaking from a relational dialectics and dialogic perspective, balance in my minority experience was continually displaced by an ongoing "dialogic flux" (Baxter, 2004b, p. 18). The nature of my experience formed, re-constituted, disintegrated, and recomposed itself in a dynamic swirl of tensions, tensions that "are a fundamental feature, and are not to be considered as equal to conflict or problem" (Cools, 2006, p. 264). These opposing forces or tensions are what constituted my experiences in the majority institution. Indeed, as I reflect, the tensions were what made the experience simultaneously vibrant, challenging, frustrating, and rewarding.

In the process of negotiating the aforementioned tensions, my "voice" was often muted. Similar to the playing of a favorite soundtrack which, when muted, continues on but is inaudible, often my muted voice became a silent soundtrack in the midst of conversation and resulted in a failed attempt at dialogue. When a voice is muted, dialogue is not only damaged, but it is also dangerously manipulated. Dialogue is damaged because while the utterance occurs, meaningful exchanges are incapable of taking place without participants "tuning in" to the soundtrack. Dialogue is also dangerously manipulated because, since the utterance occurs, conversational participants are capable of claiming that "voice" was given, despite the fact that the voice was muted. This process is an interesting dynamic of my speaking, but being silenced and of my being heard, but not being listened to. Elements of the "speaking, but inaudible" nature or "muted voice" of my experience were present in the process of managing the tensions and contradictions associated with the Christian majority institution. Four dialectics (present but absent, fighting but flighting, connected but disconnected, and thriving but struggling) will be discussed in sharing the tensions associated with this experience.

It should be noted that only brief examples associated with each tension are shared; however, several more examples could be provided if reader time, hot tea/coffee, and space were allowed. Also, it should be noted that the tensions may appear to be similar to those experienced by minorities in all majority educational institutions, regardless of whether they are religiously affiliated or not. However, the previously mentioned dialectics inherent in the Christian institution itself permeated the perceptions associated with the author's ongoing flux of opposing forces. Since the place associated with this experience was a Christian institution of higher learning, the author has a strong belief in the importance and preeminence of an unchanging spiritual focus (aligned with the changeless aspect of the changing/changeless dialectic), in the inclusion of an African American self despite racial dissimilarities (aligned with the inclusion aspect of inclusion/exclusion dialectic), and in the unifying effects of a common faith (aligned with the unity aspect of the unity/disunity dialectic). These beliefs would not have held such a central position for the author had the experience been in an educational institution that had no religious affiliation. This is because these types of institutions typically have no espoused Christian ethos infused into their institutional missions that presuppose an atmosphere of inclusion and unity. Subsequently, being in a Christian institutional space permeated my set of beliefs, expectations, and experiences.

I contend that the bolstering of these religious-based beliefs alone (without discussions similar to those offered in this chapter) results in one being unprepared and defenseless when seeking to understand the complexities of the ongoing oppositions in the Christian institution of higher learning. Thus, what makes the following tensions unique and indeed germane to the Christian majority institutional setting is the notion that the tensions occur in an environment where they are often not expected to occur, where defenses are weakened from bolstered religious beliefs, and where cognitions have not been properly prepared to face opposition. The aim in offering the opposing forces below, based on my own personal accounts, is to ready the defenses of minorities for managing the tensions rather than merely bolstering the benefits associated with a Christian majority institution.

Present but absent. This tension best explains how I, as an African American assistant professor, was physically in existence. I taught a four-course teaching load in the Spring and Fall semesters, engaged in a program of research, contributed to departmental work, and provided service to the university; however, as the "only" African American female tenure-track faculty member and one of three (which eventually dropped to two) tenure-track African American faculty, my ability to see others who looked like me (and for my students to do so as well) was absent.

Being absent in the "monocultural" majority institution enhances at least two misperceptions. First, it perpetuates the notion that all African Americans both know one another well and are good friends. And second, it misguidedly suggests that all African Americans are in agreement about the "Black experience," which inaccurately assumes that any one of them is capable of sharing the unified feelings of the whole, particularly as it relates to advancing diversity. For example, many colleagues and administrators were surprised to hear contradictory philosophical approaches from minority faculty and staff for advancing diversity. The assumption was that each of us would and should "be on the same page." This stipulation of unanimity of thought is not placed on our majority counterparts during discussions where their opinions are being sought. They are thus granted the luxury of having their own individualized thoughts and concerns despite their racial similarity. African Americans, on the other hand, are denied this "privilege."

Though one is actively present and engaged in a tenure-track position, the full impact of the absence of other women of color creates the continuous need to remind students, faculty, and administrators that one's individual voice is meaningful and important, but the utterance of that single voice is insufficient in accounting for the multitude of other minority voices on campus. Additionally, and perhaps more dangerously, that single voice can be used to mute other voices when other minorities are not asked to share their own modes of thinking.

Fighting but flighting. This tension addresses the fighting and clashing of routinely combating stereotypes and flawed thinking, and at the same time, acknowledges the anxiety and weariness that often propel one toward flighting instead. The fighting aspect underscores the importance placed on infusing discussions of different identities into the Media and Society, Advertising, Public Relations, Business Communication, and Oral Communication courses taught while simultaneously lamenting "having to go there" again once the difficulties of dialoguing about race and cultural issues were realized. From a pedagogical perspective, the pendulum would swing more to the flighting side of the tension when student-teacher evaluations were considered; some students' ratings reflected an appreciation for being challenged while others blamed the dissonance of their own confrontations or irresolute state on my teaching abilities rather than it being just the dynamic process of individual growth. In striving to teach and combat the narrow-mindedness of students, it was often a challenge to force more engagement with and appreciation for racially different others. A personal struggle in the classroom was having the courage to continually press play on my own soundtrack rather than assuming or "playing the role" of least resistance in the Christian environment.

The fighting element of this dialectic for me has involved serving on the university's diversity initiative steering committee, creating and facilitating a half-day diversity seminar for the university president with key internal and external stakeholder groups, conducting diversity committee training, contributing to and leading all-faculty discussion sessions, and co-founding and spearheading the inception of a six-month minority mentoring project, along with ongoing advisement for the Minority Student Association. In the classroom, guest lectures in the senior-level philosophy course and the Race, Gender, and Class course housed in the Honors Program were also a part of my efforts to assist in diversity advancement.

Each of these activities was completed in addition to the typical duties of a tenure-track faculty member with no release time or additional compensation. Often these activities were additional reasons for my tendency toward flight. There were numerous inappropriate remarks, heated emotional discussions, moments of celebration, and cause for pause or tears throughout these efforts. Yet these were all ways in which I carried out the intersections of my own personal identity and negotiated the flux of contradictions in the majority institution.

Connected but disconnected. This tension represents enjoying the connections of collegiality with faculty and from mentoring students, while simultaneously experiencing the disconnections. The commonalities and Christian values referenced earlier made the everyday chatter of relating to colleagues and students incredibly fun and rewarding, even as the same relationships faced instability.

Relationships on campus with a core group of faculty provided the opportunity to connect. Through exchanging classroom ideas, discussing student conduct, debating metatheoretical underpinnings, and sharing research projects, my colleagues and I developed a unique bond. With students in my classrooms (the majority of whom were Caucasian with the same religious affiliation), questioning, complaining, and learning were all common threads running through our joint discourse in the process of connecting during class meetings. Outside of the classroom, additional connections occurred during student advisement sessions and random drop-ins to my office (sometimes during office hours, but usually not) during which students would want to discuss course assignments, their latest love interest(s), résumé and internship opportunities, appropriate attire for an upcoming interview or professional gathering, future plans after graduation, my parenting and marital relationships, conflict and how to resolve it, and a host of other matters. Certainly, these students and I were connected as I enjoyed being their advocate and witnessing their growth.

The true nature of these connections was also manifest when my four-year old son was diagnosed with a very rare type of brain cancer. The colleagues that I had connected with covered my classes without compensation for three months as his health declined, and the students that I had connected with put their social influence, public relations, and communication skills to exceptional use by leading a movement of support with heartfelt activities—including a 24-hour prayer-a-thon, a benefit concert, flowers, cards, quilts, gifts, and numerous other acts of kindness. They also served my family at the gathering following our son's memorial services.

Even off campus, several opportunities for connecting with women who worked in Christian universities existed through attendance at two advancing intercultural competencies symposia hosted by the Bill and Melinda Gates

Foundation as well as through women's leadership development institutes hosted by the Council for Christian Colleges and Universities. Each of these opportunities refined my thinking and re-energized my spirits for the flux associated with the tenure-track journey. In addition, they provided exposure to women with similar, but different, tensions and struggles.

Simultaneous to these relationships were real disconnects that needed to be negotiated, even as genuine connections were being enjoyed. Not attending the same congregation for Sunday worship or mid-week Bible study with others in the majority institution also meant participation in a different set of social networks than the majority of my students and colleagues. The result was at times a feeling of being "out of the loop" concerning campus politics because interpersonal campus-related discussions often extended to the church parking lots and other social activities that were associated with congregational gatherings. The disconnect also became apparent when African American students would share their frustrations about campus life issues, offensive comments made by fellow faculty, and efforts made by advisors to re-direct the student of color toward a major that was less challenging and thus deemed "a better fit" for his or her abilities. Often these concerns were voiced in semesters following the faculty diversity discussions, which again demonstrated the ways in which several of my colleagues and I were not connected.

In the classroom, disconnects were present as well. Given the fact that many of my classes were void of any person of color, my classroom examples needed to relate to students whose frames of reference were very different from my own; this also contributed to this particular tension. For example in Media Writing, discussions about *how* to avoid sexism, racism, and ageism in writing first had to begin with *why* these topics should matter to the students along with a justification for why other content was not being covered instead. Even after classroom discussions and exercises, some students still saw no merit in such classroom conversations. Many touted traveling on the university's study abroad programs to Europe and Asia as well as their "good intentions" (despite the offensive slights) as sufficient evidence for their abilities at relating to minorities and writing on minority topics without offense.

An additional layer of disconnect occurred when I was navigating the tenure-track journey in a male-dominated departmental environment through pregnancies and young children. The multiple roles of mother, professor, researcher, wife, and colleague, not to mention the differences in racial identity, exacerbated the ways in which I was not connected to colleagues. For example, after having a child near the end of July, I was asked to attend an orientation session for advising new students that was scheduled in mid-August. Certainly within the department there were limited examples of how to work towards tenure while balancing the demands of motherhood with teaching, scholarly research, and service. The only other female, a tenured Caucasian, chose to work as a stay-at-home mom and assume an adjunct position with the university so connecting with her and witnessing her example was short-lived. To be fair, both departmental chairs that I worked with followed my preferences for teaching assignments as well as worked the times for assigned classes around my schedule; however, the process of relating from a gendered as well as racial perspective encompassed the inconsistencies associated with the opposing forces of disconnecting and connecting.

Thriving but struggling. To better understand this final tension, one must consider the layered totality (or interdependence) of the previously referenced dialectics about the Christian majority institution itself and the opposing forces of my own experience. Despite a 4/4 teaching load, advising more than 50 students, and maintaining service commitments, all indications from performance benchmarks were remarkable. Along with assisting the university in beginning to have institutional dialogue about diversity, a trend within the communication department during my window of time was a more than 70% growth in the number of students majoring in public relations. Public relations students won competitive internships, scholarships, and other statewide student public relations awards. In addition, the university was granted a charter for establishing a student association in public relations. I was also honored with a university-level outstanding teaching award and received overall positive student evaluations.

Though these were definite signs of my thriving, the combined dialectical forces and tensions worked to weave a web of marginalization. Despite the diversity activities and discussions, faculty of color new hires, board trustees of color, and administrators of color never materialized, and few accomplishments of substantial progress could be found. Haralu (2005) argues that this occurred because some Christian colleges "may have intentionally adopted core values which exclude diversity" (p. 13), even as they are striving to advance it.

Another aspect of the struggle lay in maintaining the pace of this expected additional workload, which left little to no time for scholarly output and academic research. In the weekly schedule of teaching, service, one-on-one advisement sessions, and sponsoring two student associations, I was indeed thriving. However, I was thriving in many areas that were in direct competition with my ability to achieve tenure, to sustain my own marketability, and to contribute to my own career growth as a young scholar. How does one carry out an active program of research with consistency when the time commitments for advisement, teaching, mentoring, service, and sponsoring are so great?

Negotiating the messiness of thriving by engaging in some activities, while simultaneously struggling to avoid other activities is an interchange that women of color will contend with in majority institutions. These opposing forces of flux swirl to create a unique dynamic because women of color are inextricably linked to the diversity dialogue, whether they care to be active diversity conversationalists or not—they are formed by it, re-constituted by it, dependent upon it, and influenced by it.

Ultimately, the flux of my negotiations created a sense that dialogue was engaged with the Christian campus community; however, the reciprocal nature of the discourse was not apparent. Indeed the best summation of my experience is a messy continuous spiral of speaking, but being inaudible and of voicing, but being muted.

SUGGESTIONS FOR ENGAGING THE FLUX

Eventually, I left the Christian institution to pursue tenure in a different state of flux where there are more minority voices to negotiate the tensions of diversity dialectics as well as more students of color in my classrooms. After thriving and struggling now in both types of institutions, what has made the tenure-track journey most compelling is being an exemplary role model for scholarly engagement through an active research program as well as sharing that scholarly focus with students through teaching and mentoring. This, rather than a more dominant focus on engaging in campus diversity dialogue, legitimately clears a path for justifying one's presence as a teacher scholar and defies the appearance of tokenism when proven teaching and publication records are consulted. Out of the messiness and flux of the dialectics experienced, the following suggestions are offered for consideration for tenure-track women of color:

Be honest about the type of teacher scholar you aspire to be. Based on the assumption that a teacher scholar is responsible for producing knowledge through an active program of research and sharing that knowledge with her students, the real question is, at what pace would you like to produce and share knowledge in your tenure-track journey? The production of knowledge (research) at a faster rate might suggest publishing four articles every two years with a lighter teaching load, while sharing knowledge (teaching) at a faster rate might suggest a 3/3 teaching load with a publishing rate of two articles every five years. Numerous colleagues are content with either option; however, all have their own preference. Know your scholarly self well enough to know if you have a preference, and if so what that preference might be.

Select an institution that best fits your aspirations but do so with an understanding of the institutional culture. As discussed earlier, by necessity an irreversible feature of a Christian college or university is a focus on retaining cultural aspects that make the institution uniquely Christian. This creates an institutional culture with an irrevocable set of challenges and tensions from the onset. Since no educational utopia exists and every educational institution has its own distinctive culture, learning as much as you can about the cultural components (e.g., institutional history, values, assumptions, heroes, etc.) can provide useful information about what behaviors are expected and whether those are the same behaviors that get rewarded. Weighing these expected and rewarded behaviors with your own set of aspirations can better inform your selection of the educational institution with the best fit.

Know what it takes to obtain tenure and focus your time on that which moves you closer to it. While this suggestion may appear obvious, a challenge for many women of color is being "needed" for advising minority students or associations, for speaking at diversity symposiums, days, or seminars, and for weighing in on diversity-related campus-wide issues. Regardless of the type of request, each of these "needs" likely falls into the single category of service, which may not be regarded by majority colleagues as equal to the service commitment of work that is not diversity-related. Agreeing to every diversity "need" can result in a lopsided tenure-track endeavor with ample time not being devoted to teaching and scholarship.

Select students who are women and people of color to work alongside you at graduate and undergraduate levels. Rather than saying "yes" to every opportunity to discuss or speak about diversity, model diversity as a teacher scholar by seeking students to work with you through independent study, research assistantships, or teaching assistantships. During the two-year window of time in my current position, I have passed up all but two diversity-related service opportunities and instead devoted my time to securing women and students of color to work with me through independent studies and grants on research projects. This work has generated four student co-authored poster presentations, two student co-authored conference presentations (one of which was awarded a Top Paper), and three funded on-campus grant proposals, which included three different paid research assistants all involving work with seven undergraduate students (two Caucasian males, two Caucasian females, two African American females, and one African American male). In alignment with suggestion two mentioned previously, the institution's espoused value of transformative learning through the involvement of undergraduate students in research is being enacted in my work, while at the same time I am making progress toward tenure. This is a "win" for the university, a "win" for the students, and a "win" for me.

Don't be afraid to both appreciate and regret aspects of your tenure-track journey. All situations demand an assessment of the "good" and the "in need of adjustment." Appreciation of "the good" suggests a distinctive type of thankful state that is called into remembrance and labeled. Surely, there are or will be elements of the tenure-track journey worth reflecting on with gratitude and celebrating either alone or with like-minded colleagues. A conference paper accepted, a journal submission published, a fantastic class discussion, a candid conversation with a colleague, outstanding teacher evaluations, or a successful committee assignment—each of these successes should be celebrated and appreciated. Regretfulness, or the "in need of adjustment" category, suggests an opportunity to re-commit to engaging in an alternative activity and is not simply an emotional state frozen in space and time. Properly channeling regret can assist you in noticing that change is necessary and can help you make sense of what needs to be changed. You will likely find it useful to share your regrets and planned adjustments with like-minded colleagues who can provide support during your tenure-track journey.

Conclusion

In sharing this essay, my hope is for this to be a single contribution in an ongoing conversation rather than a place where "discourses of closeness, certainty, and candor [are] privileged and opposing discourses [are] muted" (Baxter, 2004a, p. 188). Certainly, more is to be mocked, shared, discrowned, and celebrated about the dialectical tensions experienced by faculty women of color in majority institutions. Though I acknowledge the contradictions and inconsistencies in reflecting on my own experiences that are steeped in a particular place and time, the experience of my being is only made more meaningful by the joint activity of communication in an ongoing interplay with others who have occupied different spaces in time. Relational dialectics allows, and indeed requires, the multi-strandedness and multiple perceptions associated with all ways of being. In that spirit of relational dialectics, I hope this essay has represented an initial foray into a continued future dialogue rather than the "final word" on the experiences of women of color in majority Christian college or university settings.

Notes

1. In sharing the overview of relational dialectics, I have endeavored to stay consistent with Baxter's (2004b) terminology, which means the reader will likely notice the use of dialectic, dialogic, dialectical, and dialogical. Baxter clarifies that Bakhtin's influence on relational dialectics and his notion of dialogism provides a differentiating view of dialogue from most dialectical approaches. She concludes, "Dialogue is dialectical, but not all dialectical approaches are dialogic" (p. 19).

2. The terms "complicated" and "messy" are used interchangeably here and throughout the essay. This is not derogatory but is similar to Baxter and Montgomery's (1996) use, which suggests a complicated or complex arrangement. This section of the essay speaks to the unique disarray of the complexities associated with religiously affiliated educational institutions. This is *not* to suggest that non-religiously affiliated educational institutions are somehow less complicated, in better order, or are not "messy" and in disarray. Instead from this perspective, all educational institutions are beset with different types of disarray, flux, and messiness.

3. While the *different identities* associated with this working definition of diversity include race, gender, sexual orientation, ethnicity, disability, class, and job tenure, as well as other dimensions, this essay intentionally focuses on racial and gender diversity given the nature of this edited volume.

References

Bakhtin, M. M. (1981). *The dialogic imagination: Four essays by M. M. Bakhtin* (C. Emerson & M. Holquist, Trans.). Austin, TX: University of Texas Press. Original work published 1975.

Baxter, L. A. (1990). Dialectical contradictions in relationship development. *Journal of Social and Personal Relationships*, *7*, 69-88.

Baxter, L. A. (2004a). A tale of two voices: Relational dialectics theory. *The Journal of Family Communication*, *4*(3/4), 181-192.

Baxter, L. A. (2004b). Distinguished scholar article: Relationships as dialogues. *Personal Relationships*, *11*, 1-22.

Baxter, L. A., & Bylund, C. (2004). Social influence in close relationships. In J. S. Seiter & H. Gass (Eds.), *Perspectives on persuasion, social influence, and compliance-gaining* (pp. 317-336). New York, NY: Allyn & Bacon.

Baxter, L.A., & Montgomery, B. M. (1996). *Relating: Dialogues and dialectics.* New York, NY: Guilford.

Benne, R. (2001). *Quality with soul: How six premier colleges and universities keep faith with their religious traditions.* Grand Rapids, MI: Erdman's.

Breems, B. (Fall, 2001). A biblical rationale for diversity at Trinity Christian College. Retrieved from http://www.cccu.org/resourcecenter/resID.2324,parentCatID.192/rc_detail.asp

Breems, B. (Spring, 2002). A biblical rationale for diversity at Trinity Christian College. Retrieved from http://www.cccu.org/resourcecenter/resID.2324,parentCatID.192/rc_detail.asp

Cools, C. A. (2006). Relational communication in intercultural couples. *Language and Intercultural Communication*, *6*, 262-274.

Davis, J. H. (2002). Faith and learning. In D. S. Dockery & G. A. Thornbury (Eds.), *Shaping a Christian worldview: The foundations of Christian higher education* (pp. 129-148). Nashville, TN: Broadman & Holman Publishers.

Guthrie, G. H. (2002). The authority of scripture. In D. S. Dockery & G. A. Thornbury (Eds.), *Shaping a Christian worldview: The foundations of Christian higher education* (pp. 19-39). Nashville, TN: Broadman & Holman Publishers.

Hale, F. W. (Ed.). (2004). *What makes racial diversity work in higher education: Academic leaders present successful policies and strategies.* Sterling, VA: Stylus.

Haralu, M. (2005). *Minority student perceptions of diversity initiatives in a Christian liberal arts college.* Unpublished doctoral dissertation, Trinity International University.

Holmes, A. F. (1987). *The idea of a Christian college.* Grand Rapids, MI: Erdman.

Holquist, M. (1990). *Dialogism: Bakhtin and his world.* New York, NY: Routledge.

Kim, K. H., & Yun, H. (2008). *Cying* for me, *Cying* for us: Relational dialectics in a Korean social network site. *Journal of Computer-Mediated Communication*, *13*, 298-318.

Kratt, W. E. (2004). Diversity in Evangelical Christian higher education. Unpublished doctoral dissertation, Claremont Graduate University.

Menjares, P. (2003, March 29). *Campus climate.* Paper presented at the 2003 Presidential Symposium on Advancing Intercultural Competencies. Retrieved from http://www.cccu.org/resourcecenter/resID.2099,parent CatID.192/rc_detail.asp

Parker, P. S. (2005). *Race, gender, and leadership: Re-envisioning organizational leadership from the perspectives of African American women executives*. Mahwah, NJ: Lawrence Erlbaum Associates, Inc.

Sims, J. D. (2007). Beneath the cloak of Christianity in handling diversity: Understanding the selves and emotional responses of racioethnic identities. Paper presented at the annual National Communication Association Convention, Religious Communication Division, Chicago, IL.

Sims, J. D. (2008). Communicating value-in-diversity campaigns: The role of reactance and inoculation in accomplishing organizational aims. Unpublished doctoral dissertation, University of Oklahoma.

Thornbury, G. A. (2002). The lessons of history. In D. S. Dockery & G. A. Thornbury (Eds.), *Shaping a Christian worldview: The foundations of Christian higher education* (pp. 40-61). Nashville, TN: Broadman & Holman Publishers.

Toller, P. W., & Braithwaite, D. O. (2009). Grieving together and apart: Bereaved parents' contradictions of marital interaction. *Journal of Applied Communication Research*, *37*(3), 257-277.

Chapter 3

WATCHING MY B/LACK

THE NOT SO COLORBLIND WORLD OF ACADEMIA

Nickesia S. Gordon

This chapter is written from the perspective of a young, female graduate student pursing academia and represents a discussion of how discourses of colorblindness and meritocracy affect black women in academia, and more specifically, black women who are international graduate students from developing countries. Black, female international students from developing countries are defined as female students of African descent who come to the U.S. on an international F-1 visa to study for a master's or doctoral degree in a given field and whose country of origin is identified by the World Bank as a developing country or as belonging to the global south. This category of students often face institutional and personal discrimination on their campuses, even while being sold the rhetoric of merit-based and colorblind treatment.

Meritocracy refers to the idea that social selection, in employment and in education, is based increasingly on individual achievement and, most importantly, on formal qualifications (Goldthorpe, 2003), while the idea of colorblindness infers that race does not matter in the way that individuals are treated nor affect their outcome in life (Knowles, Lowery, Hogan, & Chow, 2009). However, in institutions of higher learning, the application of both the ideas of meritocracy and colorblindness operate ideologically to serve opposing goals and agendas and maintain the socio-economic status quo (Knowles et al., 2009). That is to say, in practice, despite stating otherwise, these principles function to marginalize certain groups based on their racial, gender, or ethnic backgrounds. Further, research has shown that "consistent with the notion that color blindness can serve hierarchy-enhancing ends, White people induced to adopt a colorblind perspective tend to exhibit greater explicit and nonconscious racial bias" (Knowles et al., 2009, p. 859).

The present discourse of meritocracy and colorblindness, as outlined above and as practiced by academic institutions, has serious consequences for black women who are international students from lesser developed societies. Not unlike their African American counterparts, these women are rendered invisible through such discourses, making them outsiders within (Collins, 1986) the spaces of tertiary institutions in which they find themselves. Black international female students face similar disadvantages as those endured by African American women in academia because they share the same skin color and are often identified as black Americans. One explanation given by Hilaire (2006) for this conflation of identities is that "black immigrants to the United States are more often perceived as blacks than as immigrants" (p. 49). This happens because of the racial hierarchy in the U.S., which imposes the same types of stereotypes (and identities) on black immigrants as those associated with the most disadvantaged black Americans (Rong & Fitchett, 2008). Another reason behind lumping black immigrants in with African Americans in terms of how they are identified is that initially, when blacks from places such as the West Indies began arriving in the U.S., they had little choice but to settle in the spaces that black Americans traditionally occupied, such as Harlem, New York and Detroit, Michigan (Freeman, 2002). In order to survive and because of the laws of segregation, black immigrants had little choice but to assimilate an African American identity despite their obvious cultural differences. Freeman (2002) elaborates on this idea when he says:

> Prior to the Civil Rights Movement, race was unquestionably a 'master' social characteristic in the US that dictated social outcomes for all Blacks, including those who were immigrants. . . . For these earlier Black immigrants, assimilation meant assimilation into Black America, not White America. Malcolm X, Louis Farrakhan, Stokely Carmichael, and Colin Powell are examples of well-known second-generation West Indian immigrants for whom assimilation meant melting into Black America. (p. 186)

Subsequently, the proclivity to identify newly arrived black immigrants as African Americans remains very strong. As such, black international female students categorized as black Americans suffer many of the same indignities meted out to their cohorts on campus.

However, despite the similarities among the experiences of black international women and their African American colleagues, a key difference lays in the fact that the former group of women suffers other forms of discrimination not felt by other black women. Many new black immigrants, international students included, are subjected to both xenophobia (discrimination against foreigners) and racism in their social and academic lives (Rong & Fitchett, 2008). They encounter multiple forms of invisibility based on their race as well as their national origins. These students are often seen as "foreign invaders" because they are not American and so face discrimination not just from white Americans but non-whites as well. As Ying, Lee, & Tsai (2000) point out, in some cases, discrimination experienced by international students is brought on by non-white students from the host nation or other international students. In fact, both immigrant and international students experience or perceive more discrimination than do non-white U.S. students (Ying, et al., 2000). In addition, because the countries from which these students hail are often regarded as underdeveloped, they are viewed as inferior and are thus excluded as meaningful contributors to American culture and society in general. In this sense, black international female students face a type of ethnocentric monoculturalism[1] or cultural racism (Jones, 1997), wherein they are treated as inferior because their societies may be perceived as less developed, primitive, or even pathological (Sue, 2003).

As previously mentioned, the chapter focuses on the experiences of black female graduate students who are international. The rationale behind this decision is twofold. First, research supports the idea that the experiences students have during their graduate studies impact their ensuing professional development and career. For example, Pomrenke (2010) notes that "it is . . . easier to move into careers within academia, post-doctoral work or alternatively explore non-traditional employment opportunities with the 'connections' or knowledge of the 'system' that a mentor can provide" (par. 2). Further, Pomrenke found that "in order to complete a graduate degree and/or move forward into employment in academia, substantial personal and institutional social support systems need to be in place" (par. 3). What these findings suggest is that having a supportive environment during one's graduate career significantly increases the chances for success among students. This is especially true for female graduate students who, while constituting 51% of all U.S. citizens who earn a Ph.D., have the greatest difficulties acquiring and are underrepresented in academic jobs because of discriminatory practices (Dua, 2008).

In the case of international black female graduate students, having a negative experience during their graduate years has even greater implications regarding their professional success. Since their institutional experiences may be related to their national and racial background, these students may be multiply alienated from their institutions and prevented from accessing the benefits of mentoring and other inside connections to which their peers have access. This kind of discrimination clearly places them in a disadvantageous position when it comes to their professional development. On entering the professional world of academia, if they make it, as young, tenure-track assistant professors, these women will be in an even more unfavorable position than their majority colleagues. Given that the tenure process is wrought with many obstacles, the marginalization and lack of support that black international female graduate students often face during graduate school potentially raises their risk of not attaining success.

The second half of the rationale to focus on this category of students rests with the fact that discrimination experienced or perceived by international students can be harmful to their identities (Ying et al. 2000), which again, can limit their chances of professional success as young, tenure-track assistant professors in U.S. academic institutions. Having a strong sense of self is usually associated with confidence and high self-esteem, qualities that can be invaluable in helping newly minted assistant professors navigate the tenure track. Therefore, if one's identity is compromised or negated, it can have an adverse effect on her self worth. For example, it has been found that international female students who experienced discrimination in academia were likely to develop low self-esteem as a result (Ying et al., 2000). While both male and female international students face discrimination in general, research shows that women tend to have lower self-esteem than men when they experienced discrimination (Ying et al., 2000). They also experience higher levels of stress as a result. For black female international graduate students from developing countries, this situation is magnified by the added discriminatory elements of race, gender, and their "third world" national origin.

It is important to pay attention to these issues as there is very little research that focuses on the experiences of graduate female students in general, and next to none that deals with the ordeals faced by international female graduate students of African descent who are from the global south. The contribution that international students make to American academic life is well documented. As Ku, Lahman, Yeh, and Chen (2008) note:

> The benefits of recruiting and retaining high caliber international students to United States postsecondary institutions are numerous. . . . International students who stay in the U.S. to work in faculty positions bring much needed international perspectives to the academic culture, which may foster the ability of domestic graduates to operate more successfully in an increasingly global community. (p. 366)

It stands to reason that the more positive their graduate experience, the more effective and successful these students will be, yet there are very little academic support mechanisms in place to assist them. In fact, international female graduate students of African descent are almost routinely discriminated against during their years of study.

It is from this perspective that this chapter seeks to explore how the discourses of meritocracy and colorblindness create negative experiences for black female international graduate students from developing countries, or the global south, the geopolitical term often used to describe these countries, who are studying on U.S. campuses. The discussion aims to illuminate the pitfalls but also provide suggestions that can help this category of students better prepare themselves for life during, and more significantly, after graduate school, where they may find themselves struggling in their new roles as young assistant professors on the tenure track.

The motivation to write this chapter stems from two sources: the author's personal experience, which provides an autoethnographic account of marginalization, and the experiences of classmates and colleagues who faced similar situations as international students. Together, these narratives provide theory-driven accounts of our formative years in academia and how those experiences shaped our graduate studies and subsequent careers in academia. These experiences will be "sampled" through anecdotes presented to illustrate how the concepts of colorblindness and meritocracy operate to render us invisible. They also inform the author's understanding of the position of this category of women in academia. In order to demonstrate how this invisibility is created, it is necessary to establish the theoretical framework that aided the conceptualization of how the experiences of black international female graduate students are linked to colorblindness and meritocracy. Black feminist thought, critical race theory, and ethnocentric monoculturalism were particularly useful in unveiling how an institutional culture of race neutrality is de facto a policing of "third world-ness." However, a note first about the relevance of auto-ethnography to this discussion.

AUTO-ETHNOGRAPHY

According to Crawford (1996), the practice of auto-ethnography presents an opportunity to probe the human experience by using personal life experience as a source of data. It allows for the accounting of the experiences of marginalized groups whose positions are often negated by a mainstream positivist framework that discredits the notion of the subject standpoint. It is now accepted that knowledge can be created through lived experiences (Nicotera, 1999) and that such knowledge can be intellectually generative. Auto-ethnography describes one's life to illustrate a way of life, connecting personal and cultural worlds (Ellis & Bochner, 2000). It is the interplay of this connection between the personal and cultural, which is epistemological. Using auto-ethnography permitted the author's experiences, as well as those of other colleagues expressed in the anecdotes, to play a valid role in the study. This is because the genre includes the researcher as a participant. As Gergen and Gergen (2002) stated, "in using oneself as an ethnographic exemplar, the researcher is freed from the traditional conventions of writing. One's unique voicings—complete with colloquialisms, reverberations from multiple relationships, and emotional expressiveness—are honored" (p. 14). The accounts contained in this essay therefore represent a legitimate perspective from which to extract a standpoint for understanding the experiences of black international female graduate students pursuing academic careers in American colleges and universities. The narratives have the potential to advance knowledge about this group of students through a theory-driven processing of their experiences on college campuses.

THEORETICAL FRAMEWORKS

ETHNOCENTRIC MONOCULTURALISM AND THE VEIL OF INVISIBILITY

Finding and applying theoretical constructs that are appropriate to describe the experiences of the women described above can be challenging. Traditional theories used in cultural studies, women's studies, or even black studies, for example, are general and sometimes do not account for key issues, such as educational imperialism and being treated as subjugated others, that are encountered by this group. It is important to understand why the experiences of black international female graduate students from developing countries may be different from others with a similar ethnic background because efficacy of strategies developed to address their needs can only be achieved if such measures are tailored to meet the specific problems that this group of students faces.

In general, the perceptions of peoples from developing countries, particularly those of African descent, have been molded by a Euro-American worldview, which constructs them as being less qualified, less capable, unintelligent, inarticulate, unmotivated, and lazy. These perceptions are steeped in the dichotomy of developed/underdeveloped created by global intuitions such as the World Bank which, through their economic policies, promote the assumption that people from "underdeveloped" or "third world" societies are inferior because they are unsophisticated and often in need of Western modernization (Biccum, 2002). The World Bank first posited the notion of development after World War II (Biccum, 2002). In doing so, it established a dichotomous relationship between developed and underdeveloped; that is, it construed development as inevitable for everyone, yet only necessarily undertaken in Third World contexts (Biccum, 2002). Consequently, development "would only naturally spring from Europe and the West, whereas the 'third world,' characterized within most development theories as backward, static, traditional, and lacking in the capacity to produce wealth, would 'naturally' require the assistance of the West" (Biccum, 2002, p. 39). These assumptions are rife on American college campuses and inform the relationships between international graduate students from the global south and their American counterparts. The former are viewed through an ethnocentric lens wherein the latter strongly believe in the superiority of their national culture and the inferiority of others. This forms the basis for inequities and the creation of roadblocks for black international female graduate students in pursuit of a career in academia. The selection of an appropriate theory to illuminate their experiences is therefore important in developing insight into the issue.

One theoretical framework that offers promise of understanding and explaining the unique experiences of this category of women in academia is ethnocentric monoculturalism. This concept comes from the discipline of psychology and states that there is a basic paradoxical denial of difference within mainstream American society through the imposition of a monolithic worldview on diverse cultures. While this construct generally addresses the "invisible veil of a worldview that keeps White, Euro Americans from recognizing the ethnocentric basis of their beliefs" (Sue, 2004, p. 764), it is also applicable to the issues faced by the above mentioned female students studying on American university campuses as it highlights the type of discrimination they face from Americans in general and not just white Americans. Ethnocentric monoculturalism creates a "strong belief in the superiority of one group's cultural heritage" (Sue, 2004, p. 264). Subsequently, because of the developing world's construction as an underdeveloped space, students on campus from these countries are viewed as less intelligent and less capable. They often speak with an "accent," which immediately announces their "otherness" and so puts their intellect in question.

SPACE INVADERS: THE OUTSIDER-WITHIN STATUS

Another theory that helps illuminate the experiences of discrimination black international female graduate students face based on the intersection of their race and gender is Black Feminist Thought. Black Feminist Thought suggests that African American female scholars (and students alike) occupy marginal positions on college campuses, both institutionally, meaning as faculty or staff, as well as psycho-socially, referring to their lack of inclusion in the campus community. This marginality is generally viewed as the "outsider within" status where black women have been invited into spaces occupied by the dominant group but remain outsiders as they are still invisible and have no voice when dialogue commences (Howard-Hamilton, 2003). As such, these women do not achieve a sense of belonging because there is no personal or cultural fit between them and the dominant group.

This perspective of the marginalization of black women through their insider-outsider status offers a valuable lens through which to evaluate the experiences of black international female graduate students on college campuses because the latter often assume the identity of their African American counterparts as a result of their skin color, as previously discussed. As a result, they tend to receive similar treatment. However, an important addendum to this perspective must be noted in that, because of the "third world" status of these international students, they bear an additional burden or layer of exclusion that is not necessarily within the realm of the African American female experience. As Collins (2002) points out, women from different racial groupings may have similar gendered interpretations of an experience, yet their diverse racial standpoints and pasts create distinctly different experiences. I would like to add national origins to the points of differentiated gendered experiences as a context from which to view and understand these experiences. This represents a cultural dimension, which may offer a nuanced look at the evidence of marginalization encountered by these particular women of color in college institutions.

MERITOCRACY AND THE MYTH OF COLORBLINDNESS

It is often believed that universities and colleges are institutions that embrace diversity in terms of ideas, ethnicities, and lifestyles (Patton, 2004). This rhetoric promotes the idea of equality, race neutrality, and meritocracy. The ideas that the best will rise to the top, that all perspectives will contend in the market place of ideas, and that everyone has an equal chance to succeed and will be treated fairly are the hallmarks of academia. However, in reality, these discourses are constructs that operate to perpetuate inequality and oppression. Rather than universities being places to explore and embrace diversity, they often become complicitous in domination and oppression (Patton, 2004). Critical race theory deconstructs the myths and exposes the falsity of neutrality, objectivity, meritocracy, and colorblindness (Howard-Hamilton, 2003). While critical race theory is often used to delineate the racialized content of policies and policy-making regarding black/white relations in America, it is also very useful in examining the experiences of black female international graduate students on U.S. college campuses, especially given that the identities of African Americans are often projected unto them because of their skin color. These international students encounter similar attitudes when it comes to meritocracy and neutrality. Their third world identities however, compound the issues and present an additional layer of disenfranchisement where the rhetoric of inclusion and equality are concerned. The discussion now turns to an exploration of the accounts of marginalization given by members of this group of women who have studied as graduate students at U.S. academic institutions.

NARRATIVE ACCOUNTS OF EXCLUSION: ETHNOCENTRIC MONOCULTURALISM

As previously mentioned, ethnocentric monoculturalism refers to a kind of cultural racism in which whiteness is privileged. This privilege is made "invisible" and represents a worldview that "keeps White Euro Americans from recognizing the ethnocentric basis of their beliefs, values, and assumptions" (Sue, 2004, p.

764). Despite the fact that Sue uses the term to describe the psychological state of white Euro Americans regarding their cultural assumptions about non-whites, I argue that in principle, the term can be applied more broadly to include the cultural relations between American nationals in general and those from developing countries. This is because the latter is often constructed through a discourse of imperialism by the former and subsequently, in academia, international students are many times viewed through an imperialist lens (Rhee & Sagaria, 2004). In addition, because the eventual outcome of ethnocentric monoculturalism is cultural oppression of the other according to Sue, the term can indeed be applied to describe the cultural relations between international students and their American cohorts on college campuses since subjugation of their culture is precisely what occurs as a result of being viewed through an imperialist lens. Based on my experience as an international graduate student from the Caribbean, as well as the narratives of colleagues from other developing countries, it was evident that a strong sense of cultural superiority/inferiority informed our interactions with professors and classmates, the latter two assuming the mantle of the culturally superior.

In the classroom, this belief in the inferiority of international graduate female students is often translated into the domination of class discussions by American students who sometimes possess an inflexible assumption about the absoluteness of their knowledge. It is assumed that international graduate students hailing from lesser developed sections of the globe have an inferior intellect and so have little knowledge of issues that may fall outside of their "narrow" third world sphere. As a result of this kind of mindset, these international female graduate students are treated as having no right to participate in certain class discussions, especially if these discussions pertain to issues facing American society or that have to do with the theoretical positions of major scholars who happen to come from European or American societies. Our American cohorts often thought such arguments too complex or too sophisticated for someone formerly educated in the third world and assumed the position that their international classmates needed to be "told" about such issues as opposed to participating in any discussions about them.

As a result of this kind of attitude, comments from international students are often ignored or invalidated by questions such as, "Do they even speak English in your country?" or, "How do you know about that?" These perceptions set in motion a whole set of interlocking systems grounded in a false reality that has negative consequences for international female graduate students. For instance, they may be unfairly graded by professors who find it necessary to re-inform their intellect. Two particular anecdotes illustrate this aspect of ethnocentric monoculturalism at play.

First, after querying a failing grade given for a paper (an analysis of a poem written by British-turned-American author T. S. Elliot), I was told the reason for not doing well on the paper was because my writing was "too pompous," which, when translated, means that it was too British, or more precisely, not American enough. I was being critiqued not based on the content or intellectual contribution of the paper, but on something more superficial and integrally related to my origins, i.e. Jamaica, which is an ex-British colony. Similar comments were made by the same professor to another colleague from the Caribbean about her writing, thereby evaluating her cultural standpoint instead of the content of her paper.

In the other extreme of this emphasis on writing style, professors would return my papers with comments relating their surprise at how well I wrote English. Comments would range from "nicely written" to "great writing" or "you have a way with words" and "excellent writing." These represent comments from different professors on papers that I have written both during my master's and doctoral programmes. While these comments might appear flattering and might have reflected professors' admiration for my writing skills, what stood out most for me was the inherent surprise expressed in their commentary. The various graduate programmes of which I have been part were replete with great writers, none of whose skills were ever really in question. This therefore made me question whether or not the issue of writing had more to do with where I was from than a general problem with writing among graduate colleagues. Based on these examples, it would be fair to say that neither I, nor my colleague, were being evaluated based on the intellectual merit of our work but moreso on where we were from and the assumptions held by our professors about those cultural spaces.

Under these circumstances, the academic careers of black international female graduate students are jeopardized. Failing grades compromise their academic record, making them appear as underachievers while the puerile comments about their writing hinders their intellectual growth as substantive feedback on the content of their work is not offered. In both situations, what is apparent is that a strong belief in the intellectual inferiority of international students informs professors' reactions to their work. This worldview represents a dimension of ethnocentric monoculturalism "which creates a strong belief in the superiority of one group's cultural heritage, history, values, language, beliefs, religion, traditions, and arts and crafts" (Sue, 2004, p. 764). As such, this belief in one's superior status in society makes them prone to believing that their definitions of problems and solutions are the correct ones (Sue, 2004). The natural outcome that these mindsets have for international female graduate students on American college campuses is cultural oppression since, "in many respects, the belief in individual or group superiority often results in an inability to empathize or understand the viewpoints or experiences of other individuals who are different" (Sue, 2004, p. 765). As previously mentioned, female international students are especially vulnerable to perceived discrimination on college campuses and are more likely to suffer from depression as a result; therefore, marginalization faced by female students regarding their intellect affects them more insidiously.

Outside of academic performance, the economic well-being of black international female graduate students is also compromised as a result of the effects of ethnocentric monoculturalism. For example, their ability to secure jobs on campus may be severely hindered by the superior/inferior dichotomy that informs cultural relations between American nationals and international students on campus. One graduate student, who was also a colleague of mine, related the story of applying for a job at the writing centre on the campus of a majority institution in the Northeast United States. The job entailed helping undergraduates with their writing and academic papers. However, after sending in her resume and not getting a response, the student called to determine the status of her application. It was then that she was informed that she did not qualify for the position based on the Centre's evaluation of her competence. They determined she was not competent enough given that English was not her native language. To the contrary, not only was the student's national language English, as she was Anglo-Caribbean, she was also an 'A' student in her major, English Literature, with a stellar GPA of 3.98. It may be assumed that stereotypes about the student's Caribbean origins or third world-ness functioned to limit her access to economic resources on campus. These types of experiences serve to marginalize and invalidate these international female graduate students.

Embedded in the practice of ethnocentric monoculturalism is the ability of the dominant cultural group to define reality. According to Sue (2004), the cultural group that is dominant in any given society has the power to impose its ideas about reality, as well as its belief systems, on others. On U.S. college campuses, American culture is dominant and its members, if they so desire, can use that power to impose a certain set of cultural beliefs on their international cohorts. Usually, when such power is exercised, it is done through communicative discourses such as inclusiveness and equality. These discourses have ideological functions that disadvantage international female graduate students from developing countries in that they reify and naturalize American cultural hegemony on campus. One of the consequences of maintaining cultural hegemony is that the above mentioned student group gets arbitrarily excluded from visibly occupying campus spaces. For international female students, this invisibility is quadrupled in the sense that they are black, female, and most significantly, are from the so called Third World. The latter is what quadruples their marginalization on college campuses, thus making them outsiders within in multiple ways.

NARRATIVE ACCOUNTS OF EXCLUSION: OUTSIDERS WITHIN

The term *outsiders within* is invariably used to describe "the positions inhabited by groups who are included in dominant cultural practices but are nevertheless, and for various reasons, unable to fully participate in them" (Lenz, 2004, p. 99). Consequently, these groups are rendered invisible and disempowered. Within this context, black international female graduate scholars often find themselves as outsiders within on American college campuses. They are often invited into these academic spaces through scholarships, grants, or fellowships. As such, these academic awards become gateways through which these women are invited to become insiders in a "First World" college space. However, this insider status is marked by boundaries which delineate "the limits of place, space, and territory" (Patton, 2004, p. 191). According to Patton (2004), boundaries serve to maintain hegemony because of their inherent design to include or exclude. They also have the ability to shape social relations through establishing the dichotomy of "us" or "them," insider or outsider, and in the case of black Caribbean female students, American or foreign, but more precisely, developed or underdeveloped. These boundaries further translate into intellectual hierarchies of superior and valued knowledge versus inferior and less valued knowledge and are manifested in the classroom through the curriculum design. For example, materials selected for general courses that are supposed to span the gamut of any particular subject, often inflexibly focus of a singular aspect of a canon, usually the European or American contributions to that canon. Black international female graduate students from developing countries often find themselves literally and figuratively left out of the classroom as their cultural contexts are devalued. Two examples illustrate this point.

The first example relates the experiences of a colleague while attempting to select a thesis topic for her master's degree. This colleague was studying Literature and wished to pursue a topic relating to a writer from the Caribbean. On making her desires known to her advisor (this professor became her advisor de facto, being the only black faculty member), she was promptly dismissed and told that if she wanted to study Caribbean literature she should have remained in the Caribbean. Her only alternative was to pursue a topic on an African American author that was deemed more suitable. This exchange emphasizes the binary created by the boundaries of the insider-outsider status, namely, inferior knowledge versus superior knowledge. Although Caribbean literature is a part of the literary canon, the work produced by such writers is considered intellectually inferior because it is created by people from supposedly underdeveloped societies. It is therefore excluded from academic consideration, its exclusion marking the marginalization of the student's cultural experiences. It represents a colonization of the mind as well as an ontological erasure that is in keeping with the developed-underdeveloped dichotomy.

The second example comes from my own personal experience in a course that examined political writings in literature. Despite the fact that the course's title suggested an inclusion of works from across the canon globally, the material selected was narrowly confined to writers from Euro-America. When I attempted to introduce a few pieces from the Caribbean that resonated with the overall theme of the course, I was told that these writings did not qualify, despite the fact that were chronicling or responding to political turmoil in a Caribbean country, Guyana, during the 1960s. No specific explanation was given regarding their unsuitability for the course, just that, from the perspective of the professor, the poems were not considered to be political in nature. The dismissal of the poems on such a nebulous premise was made even more questionable when it was revealed during a conversation with the same professor afterwards, that the latter had no clue where the country of Guyana was. Therefore, his decision to dismiss the poems as non-political was not grounded in any informed view or knowledge of the country's political history, or apparently, on any knowledge of Guyana at all. This raises questions about the professor's motivation for excluding literary works from outside Europe and America and also illustrates that despite being invited to study on these campuses, international graduate students are expected to remain "unseen" as a cultural force and therefore, outside the academic mainstream.

These particular examples reinforce the idea that although international female graduate students of African descent are invited into American academic spaces as insiders, they occupy a marginal status given that the institutional practice only welcomes "diversity" as long as it is prepared to assimilate to mainstream norms (Williams, 2001). International female students from developing countries quickly learn that that despite this invitation, they are in fact outsiders, space invaders at best. Their presence is only barely tolerated intuitionally so that the diversity discourse of academia can be legitimated and international demographic quotas for which colleges and universities get funding satisfied. For the most part, these students are viewed by colleagues as viral at best.[2] Academia's claims of being a marketplace for the exchange of diverse ideas are therefore challenged by these practices of marginalization and exclusion.

NARRATIVE ACCOUNTS OF EXCLUSION: MERITOCRACY AND COLORBLINDNESS

In their book, *The Meritocracy Myth*, McNamee and Miller (2004), describe meritocracy as an ideology in which individuals can go as far as their own merit takes them. Accordingly, getting ahead is "ostensibly based on individual merit, which is generally viewed as a combination of factors including innate abilities, working hard, having the right attitude, and having high moral character and integrity" (McNamee & Miller, 2004, par. 1). The concepts of meritocracy and colorblindness are closely related in that they both suggest that individuals will achieve success based on nothing else but their own efforts. Therefore, neither race, social class, gender, nor any other social or cultural category will play a role in how one's life progresses, and those who end up at the bottom of society "'rightfully' belong there" (Saunders, 2006, p. 184). This discourse is very prevalent among academic institutions, which try to present academia as a space that promotes openness, fairness, equality, and fraternity for all. However, as research has shown, this is far from the case when it comes to certain cultural groups such as women, people of color, and gays and lesbians. Black international female graduate students from developing countries can also be added to the list based on their experiences of being treated unfairly by the academic system. Their narratives indicate that they are not treated equally and their levels of academic and professional success have plenty to do with their race, gender, and where they come from.

As previously mentioned, these students are often invited into the spaces of tertiary institutions through scholarships, fellowships, and grants. By virtue of the selective nature of these awards, it is well established that these students are invited based on academic merit. The assumption is thus made that they will be treated as intellectual equals as a result of having met and even surpassed the scholarly requirements that are the standards of the recruiting institution and country. However, as the following examples illustrate, this is not necessarily the case. It is an illusion that the academic playing field is level and that merit is all that is needed to succeed. Individual, institutional, and cultural prejudices place barriers in the way of academic attainment for the previously mentioned category of students. In the classroom, biases in teacher-student relationships often impede their full academic and professional development. They are overlooked and neglected, especially in informal classroom proceedings or activities that take place outside the classroom.

First, marginalization for these graduate students occurs at the level of gender as the following quotation indicates:

> Faculty members, usually males, provide their favored and preferred students, usually male, the research training and experience necessary for professional and intellectual development, nominate them for fellowships and awards, take stands for them in the perennial disputes surrounding qualifying exams and degree requirements, furnish professional visibility by introducing them at meetings and conferences to others in the discipline and co-author papers and articles with them. (Jones-Johnson, 1988)

Clearly, based on the proceeding quote, there is a fair amount of preferential treatment that takes place in academia. Female students are at the bottom of the food chain, not because of their abilities, but because of their gender. For black international female students in graduate school, the issue of gender is compounded by the intersection of their race and geographic origins. Not only do blacks on American college campuses perceive significantly more discrimination from administration, peers, and faculty (Poyrazli & Lopez, 2007, p. 266), non-European international students perceived or experienced the most discrimination than any other category of students on campus (Poyrazli & Lopez, 2007). Black international female graduate students therefore experience unfair treatment on multiple levels and are shoved even deeper to the bottom of the academic pool, not because they are incapable, but as a result of their race, gender, and national origins.

This professional and social neglect was experienced by a colleague and me on several occasions during our sojourn as graduate students at a majority institution in the Northeast U.S. For instance, whenever there were invited professional guests at our monthly colloquium, we would never be introduced. Instead, the chair of our department would invariably draw the guests' attention to the two international students from Europe who would be presented as representing the sum total of department's international student body. They would also be introduced as the "brightest and the best" students the department currently had. In other instances, the chair would arrange to have special lunch meetings with these students to check on their academic progress and social well-being, the rationale being they were away from home and needed academic mentorship and social support. We would only learn about these lunch/ mentorship meetings in passing, when the invited students happened to mention them. As Jones-Johnson (1988) points out, this kind of omission from the rituals of academia that often ensure the scholarly success of graduate students has negative consequences for those not included. Academia is an institution based on faculty sponsorship and support, without which students find it difficult to locate jobs and upward career mobility. When mentorship is lacking, students are often left to struggle and figure out things on their own. This unfair treatment emphasizes the hollowness of the academy's claims about meritocracy and equality in institutions of higher learning. Black international female students are at a disadvantage as they are operating on a playing field that is not level.

However, the myth of meritocracy dismisses the fact that individual, institutional, and cultural discrimination places barriers in the way of these students' achievement. Their third world identities predispose them to this disenfranchisement given the discourse constructed around their origins. Third world is equated with inferiority and given that "graduate, and to some extent professional education, is a kind of cloning process in which faculty members seek to reproduce themselves or at least those who will fill their intellect shoes" (Jones-Johnson, 1988, p. 315), faculty do not readily imagine themselves incarnate in a person deemed by the discourse as having a third-rate intellect. It is well established that discourses are ways of constituting knowledge or truth (Patton, 2004) and the group in control of a particular discourse shapes the power relations in a society or institution. In academia, the discourses of meritocracy and colorblindness favor those considered to be part of the "developed" world and exclude those are thought not to be. The category of students being discussed, who are not part of the so-called developed world, are not treated equally as they are not appraised based on their merit but their gender, race, and origins.

Recommendations and Conclusion

The information contained in this chapter attempts to illuminate the challenges faced by black international female graduate students pursuing a career in academia in American colleges. The author makes the argument that in academia, what are thought of as standard and fair operational procedures serve to deny equal access and opportunities to these students. What the expressed experiences of such students reveal is that academia does not necessarily embody a marketplace for the exchange of diverse views but instead embodies a colonizing space that reifies the superiority of the developed world. As Patton (2004) argues, "by its very nature, the university recreates the hegemonic order of, [in this instance, developed/underdeveloped,] and contributes to the reification of disenfranchised persons because it operates by constructing and has constructed an impassable boundary—the outsider within" (p. 193). The concept of the outsider within, provided by Black Feminist Thought, presents a helpful framework within which to explore and understand the experiences of black international female graduate students inhabiting university spaces. However, their "third world" origins create a unique dimension to their experiences that is not applicable to their African American counterparts, the experiences of whom Black Feminist Thought is often engaged.

Understanding that these differences between African American women and those from developing countries are steeped in the cultural construct of developed/underdeveloped is important to acknowledge because it presents a platform from which the situation of the latter may be addressed. In addition, the discourse of ethnocentric monoculturalism that construes people of non-European origins as prone to being less qualified, less capable, unintelligent, inarticulate, unmotivated, and lazy must be confronted and replaced in the classroom with an ethos of multiculturalism wherein students from varying ethnic and national backgrounds can have their experiences validated. As with national economies and markets, tertiary education has become globalized. If we are to lay credence to the rhetoric of globalization, then we must begin to retreat from our boundaries established to keep the other out and the insider perennially privileged. On that note, I offer a few suggestions that could help black international female students cope with the graduate experience, especially since their chances of success as young assistant professors on the tenure track, if they should choose that path, often depends on the quality of the experience they have while pursuing their higher education.

Seek mentorship, get connected; your life after graduate school depends on it. The benefits of mentorship for female graduate students cannot be emphasized enough. As one female graduate student puts it, "Mentoring is key! It is the business of who you know and how connected you are" (Pomrenke, 2010, par. 1). For black female graduate students from the developing world, mentoring is not only key, it is indispensible. Because such students are coming from further behind the academic tenure and promotion track, compared to other traditionally marginalized groups such as African American women and women in general, a mentor can help them get that proverbial leg up or foot in the door when their independent/individual efforts will not. As Pomrenke points out, it is easier to get into academic careers, post doctoral work, and even nontraditional jobs with the connections or knowledge of the system that a mentor can provide. Therefore, students should make it a top priority to seek a mentor as soon as they enter their graduate programmes. This enables them to build a solid relationship with their mentor over an extended period of time, i.e. the entire duration of their graduate studies, and also gives them time to find an alternative person if the person with whom they started out is not the right fit. It may not always be easy to find a mentor in the same department or even institution, so it is important that students be open to looking beyond their own departments and universities and even gender. Don't be afraid to consider having a man as mentor!

A good place to start is at professional or academic conferences where many established faculty who have been in their professions for many years converge. Black international graduate students can always search the programme to see who may be attending/presenting and if she or he working in an area of research that is similar or compatible to theirs. They should attend those sessions and introduce themselves and always follow up immediately after returning from the conference with an email reminding the scholar of who they are, where they met, and asking about their work. Individuals often enjoy talking about their research with others and are also flattered by genuine interest shown by others. Another way to seek a mentor is through good old fashion journal sleuthing, i.e. reaching out to individuals through the contact information they provide in their journal articles. International graduate students should read a little bit about these individuals and their work first before making contact so that they can establish a good connection.

In terms of making connections, black female graduate students from the developing world should also consider reaching out to other graduate students from different disciplines or universities for possible research or other forms of collaboration. In making these connections, students can keep abreast of and participate in/attend research forums or colloquia that often take place on university campuses. These events give students an added opportunity to meet students like themselves engaged in research as well as other faculty who could potentially serve as mentors. It also opens up the possibility of becoming involved in cross-disciplinary research, which raises students' visibility and helps them explore potentially valuable alternative research agendas.

Work it from the outside; the view from the fringes can be spectacular. The final suggestion that I will present is for students to create spaces of power from the margins that can help mitigate some of the more negative effects of racism, sexism, and imperialism they experience on campus. For centuries, marginalized groups from various societies have managed to find ways to establish and assert influence despite being on the fringes. The idea is not to become an insider but to exploit the view from the outside that makes one privy to many insights and even "secrets" not discernable by the dominant group. Patricia Hill Collins (1986) uses the example of how black domestic workers in America during the time of segregation managed to attain a sense of self-affirmation after seeing white power demystified. They were only able to do this by being "outsiders" within who witnessed from that position that it was not the talent, intellect, or humanity of their employers that secured the dominant group with their superior status but rather pure privilege (Collins, 1986). This revelation immediately demythifies the rhetoric of meritocracy and simultaneously places superior/inferior, developed/underdeveloped dialectics in proper perspective. Armed with this understanding, black female graduate students from developing countries can position themselves at academia's "blind spot," seeing what their institutions cannot and using the knowledge gleaned from this spot to create critical discourses that can challenge existing norms as well as aid in the creative development of their disciplines.

NOTES

1. The term *ethnocentric monoculturalism* was coined by psychologist Derald Wing Sue (2004). It describes the invisibility created by the imposition of a dominant worldview on culturally diverse groups in a society (in this case American). This imposition is tantamount to a denial of difference and the creation of monolithic values and belief systems that ultimately oppress other cultural groups that may not be American.

2. The outsider status that these boundaries create for black female graduate students from developing countries students is often manifest in barely masked resentment often felt toward them by their American counterparts, who sometimes see them as interlopers who have "stolen" an educational opportunity from a more deserving American student. As previously stated, many black international female graduate students become "insiders" on campuses as a result of scholarships and fellowships offered by colleges. These are opportunities that American students view as legitimately theirs and sometimes resent their international colleagues for having been awarded these chances. The latter often encounter a chilly climate and isolation on campuses. They may experience microaggressions wherein unconscious or conscious, verbal or non verbal, and visual forms of insults are directed towards them (Howard-Hamilton, 2003).

References

Biccum, A. (2002). Interrupting the discourse of development: On a collision course with postcolonial theory. *Culture, Theory and Critique*, *43*(1), pp. 33-50.

Collins, P. H. (1986). Learning from the outsider within: The sociological significance of Black Feminist Thought. *Social Problems*, *33*(6),14-34.

Collins, P. H. (2002). Some groups matters: Intersectionality, situated standpoints, and Black Feminist Thought. In T. Lott & J. Pittman (Eds.), *A Companion to African-American Philosophy* (pp. 205-229). Boston, MA: Blackwell.

Crawford, L. (1996). Personal ethnography. *Communication Monographs, 63,* 158-170.

Dua, P. (2008). Impact of gender characteristics on mentoring in graduate departments of sociology. *American Sociology*, *39*, 307-323.

Ellis, C., & Bochner, A. P. (2000). Auto-ethnography, personal narrative, reflexivity: Researcher as subject. In N. K. Denzin & Y. S. Lincoln (Eds.), *Handbook of Qualitative Research* (2nd ed., pp. 733-768). Thousand Oaks: CA: Sage.

Freeman, L. (2002). Does spatial assimilation work for black immigrants in the US? *Urban Studies*, *39*(11), 1983-2003.

Gergen, M., & Gergen, K. (2002). Ethnographic representation as relationship. In A. Bochner & C. Ellis (Eds.), *Ethnographically speaking: Autoethnography, literature, and aesthetics* (pp. 11-33). Walnut Creek, CA: Altamira.

Goldthorpe, J. (2003). The myth of education-based meritocracy: Why the theory isn't working. *New Economy*, pp. 234-239.

Hilaire, D. (2006). Immigrant West Indian families and their struggles with racism in America. *Journal of Emotional Abuse*, *6*(2/3), 47-60.

Howard-Hamilton, M. F. (2003). Theoretical frameworks for African American women. *New Directions for Services*, *104*, pp. 19-27.

Jones-Johnson, G. (1988). The victim-bind dilemma of black female sociologists in academe. *The American Sociologist, Winter*, pp. 312-321.

Jones, J. (1997). *Prejudice and racism.* New York, NY: McGraw Hill.

Knowles, E. D., Lowery, B. S., Hogan, C. M., & Chow, R. M. (2009). On the malleability of ideology: Motivated construals of color blindness. *Journal of Personality and Social Psychology*, *96*(4), 857-869.

Ku, H. Y., Lahman, M. K. E., Yeh, H., & Chen, Y. (2008). Into the academy: Preparing and mentoring international doctoral students. *Education Tech Research Dev*, *56*, 365-377.

Lenz, B. (2004). Postcolonial fiction and the outsider within: Toward a literary practice of feminist standpoint theory. *NWSA Journal*, *16*(*2*), 98-120.

McNamee, S. J., Miller, R. K. (2004). The meritocracy myth. *Sociation Today*, *2*, *1*. Retrieved from http://www.ncsociology.org/sociationtoday/v21/ merit.htm.

Nicotera, A. M. (1999). The woman academic as subject/object/self: Dismantling the illusion of duality. *Communication Theory*, *9*(4), 430-464.

Patton, T. O. (2004). Reflections of a Black woman professor: Racism and sexism in academia. *Howard Journal of Communications*, *15*, 185-200.

Pomrenke, M. (April 13, 2010). Mentoring is key! Success for female graduate students [Weblog comment]. Retrieved from http://blog.fedcan.ca/2010/04/13/%E2%80%9Cmentoring-is-key%E2%80%9D-success-for-female-graduate students/

Poyrazli, S., & Lopez, M. D. (2007). An exploratory study of perceived discrimination and homesickness: A comparison of international students and American students. *The Journal of Psychology, 13*(3), 263-280.

Rhee, J., & Sagaria, M. D. (2004). International students: Constructions of imperialism in the Chronicle of Higher Education [Abstract]. *Review of Higher Education, 28*(1), 77-96.

Rong, X. L., & Fitchett, P. (2008). Socialization and identity transformation of black immigrant youth in the United States. *Theory Into Practice, 47*, 35 -42.

Rowney, J., & Taras, V. (2008). Crosscultural differences in perceptions of justice: Consequences for academia. *ISEA, 36*(3), 104-123.

Saunders, P. (2006). Meritocracy and popular legitimacy. *The Political Quarterly Publishing Co. Ltd.*, pp. 183-194.

Sue, D. D. (2003). *Counselling the culturally diverse: Theory and practice* (4th ed.). New York, NY: Wiley.

Sue, D. (2004). Whiteness and ethocentric monoculturalism: Making the "invisible" visible. *American Psychologist*, pp. 761-769.

Williams, C. (2001). The angry black woman scholar. *NWSA Journal, 13(2)*, 87-97.

Ying, Y. W., Lee, P. A., & Tsai, J. L. (2000). Cultural orientation and racial discrimination: Predictors of coherence in Chinese American young adults. *Journal of Community Psychology, 28*, 427-442.

Confronting Prejudice and Discrimination

Strategies of Survival

Chapter 4

A Different Kind of Professor

Marcia Alesan Dawkins

In what the media refers to as a *post*-racial and *post*-feminist Obama America, questions of prejudice and discrimination can often be treated with ambivalence, if they are treated at all. In a recent interview with CNN's John King, President Obama himself suggests that racism exists, but more so in our imaginations than our intentions ("Race Not 'Overriding Issue,'" 2009). Others, like Faludi (1992), comment that making "a fuss about sexual injustice is . . . now uncool" (p. 95). One reason for this ambivalence is the argument that the United States has reached a *post*-racial and *post*-feminist moment in which basic rights for all have been won. Constituents who support this perspective remind mainstream society that multiracialism and gender equality are not only our destiny but our reality. They refer to our current generation as "Generation Mix" and celebrate the Obamas' success as the latest in a growing trend of multiracial-, gender-, and diversity-oriented milestones (Mavin Foundation, 2009). Because everyone can be successful and independent, not to mention an "empowered consumer," our society is now said to have transcended our culture wars (Tasker & Negra, 2007, p. 1).

Despite this peaceful ethos, culture wars are always lurking. Such has been the case since May 26, 2009, when President Obama announced Federal Appeals Court Judge Sonia Sotomayor as his nominee for filling the vacancy left by outgoing federal judge, Justice Souter, on the United States Supreme Court. Almost immediately, conservatives branded Sotomayor a racist because of remarks she made at a 2001 address to the "Raising the Bar" symposium at the University of California Berkeley School of Law. The remarks in question are the final 32 words of the following statement:

> Whether born from experience or inherent physiological or cultural differences . . . our gender and national origins may and will make a difference in our judging. Justice O'Connor has often been cited as saying that a wise old man and wise old woman will reach the same conclusion in deciding cases. . . . I am also not so sure that I agree with the statement. First, . . . there can never be a universal definition of wise. Second, I would hope that a wise Latina woman with the richness of her experiences would more often than not reach a better conclusion than a white male who hasn't lived that life. (Sotomayor, 2001, par. 21)

While many conservatives were up in arms over these "reverse racist" words and busied themselves making pointed *ad hominem* attacks via Twitter, I began to realize that what they were really objecting to was Sotomayor's standpoint, or expression of her powerful and legitimate voice as a "wise Latina judge." According to *Time Magazine*, this is a standpoint Sotomayor has articulated at least seven times between 1993 and 2003 (Rosen, 2009). Thus, the "challenge" Sotomayor poses to her opponents "is in the critical constitution of the-self-in-the-world that does not undermine or forego the societal structures that exceed the self" (Bow, 2004, p. 134). In other words, her critics were unwilling to acknowledge that members of certain groups may have special insights into particular lives and issues. More to the point, critics were unwilling to acknowledge that Sotomayor's membership in these groups comes with privileges that can be considered a form of epistemological expertise, especially in a national context in which the racial majority is changing. At the same time, critics used the articulation of her standpoint to discount her ability to appeal to the law as the ultimate authority when exercising her profession, thus pitting her ethnic or "folk" knowledge against official judiciary objectivity.

The discursive struggle over Sotomayor's identity, legitimacy, power, and voice dovetail with the ways in which I am experiencing my multiracial and gendered identity on a day-to-day basis in the academy—as a historical, rhetorical, institutional, intersectional, and personal set of communication relations that require some working through. I have been working my way through these relations since I was an undergraduate student at a majority institution. Coming from a diverse public high school in New York City, my undergraduate years at a suburban private institution on the East Coast of the United States that was over 90 percent white can best be described as an experiment in cognitive dissonance, leaving me as one of the *isolani*, known only to myself, knowing only myself. As an Assistant Professor at a public institution on the West Coast, however, I now see two major differences. I realize that the identity of the nation's racial majority is changing, bringing with it the need for newer and more realistic models of communication and identification, and that there is often an unwillingness to relinquish ideals from the past. I also realize that by mobilizing my identity and standpoint I can harness the power of change as a communication device and a creative emotional experience that inspires others to dream, struggle, and achieve.

But what does that mean exactly? First, it means recognizing that I have a standpoint. And, like Sotomayor's, my standpoint allows me to reach "better conclusions" about how to view and exercise my profession among a changing majority than those who do not share my background and experiences. Second, it means recognizing that up until now I have been part of an endangered species. As in many other fields, in a world where gender and racial inequalities still prevail, multiracial women have been given a real chance only during the last decade to check "all that apply" and show what we can do. Many have profited from those opportunities, sharing their multi-faceted and dynamic experiences in classrooms and scholarly writing. But we still face preconceptions growing out of the longstanding mystique of the professor as a mainstream authority figure. To hear many colleagues tell it, they continue to confront barriers and discrimination in forms ranging from the blatant, including lower salaries and difficulties with tenure approval, to the latent, including an expectation to address exigencies of marginalized on- and off-campus communities that hamper traditional scholarly productivity.

In the pages that follow, I will discuss my professional experiences through the lens of Standpoint Theory and articulate my vision for a different kind of professor, as an agent of change with others instead of merely for others. I will explain the development and expression of my own standpoint along with some blatant and latent forms of discrimination that have contributed to my status as part of the endangered species of young, multiracial, and female tenure-track professors. These contributing factors include predators inside and outside of the classroom, exploitation, a small network of identifiable peers, and unique vulnerability to heavy traffic at intersections of racial and gender discrimination (Crenshaw, 1989). I will then address ways in which young, multiracial, and female tenure-track professors can fight extinction by questioning our environments. I will conclude by focusing on change, the power of changing demographics, and ways in which my own creative spark thrives by transforming today's discrimination into tomorrow's opportunity. In so doing, I hope to make the most of my opportunity to educate, emancipate, and stir a "critical consciousness," as Paolo Freire (Freire & Ramos, 2002) would say. I will conclude with my vision for a different kind of professor as one who proclaims a standpoint and practices it by learning from the past and present, replacing existing dichotomies with new possibilities for teaching and researching, and connecting these new possibilities to academic and non-academic audiences in meaningful and innovative ways.

Standpoint Theory

Introduced in the 1970s and 1980s as a feminist critical theory and methodology, Standpoint Theory describes the "relations between the production of knowledge and the practice of power" as they relate to women's lives (Harding, 2004, p. 1). Theorists such as Hartsock (2003) combined and extended Hegelian and Marxian thought for feminist ends. Specifically, Hartsock linked the development of women's intellectual and political positions to their social locations in day-to-day life. These locations are called "standpoints," which lend an interpretive aspect to a person's life that would, for instance, allow "a wise Latina woman with the richness of her experiences . . . [to] . . . more often than not reach a better conclusion than a white male who hasn't lived that life" (Sotomayor, 2001, par. 21). In this respect, Standpoint Theory can be considered a philosophical statement, a research and analytical tool, a way of knowing and living, a cultural tactic, and a communication theory.

It is important to note several assumptions that underlie this approach. First, a standpoint is not a perspective. A standpoint recognizes subjectivity and partiality and is always under construction, whereas a perspective is a fully formulated "attitude towards or way of regarding something" ("Perspective," n.d.). Consequently, a standpoint emphasizes context and circumstance and may not be fully formed, asserting that all knowledge is "situated" (Haraway, 1988). Therefore, those who wish to discover their standpoints must recognize their social privileges and understand their social locations. This means a person may have some insights, but is also limited in some of his or her views.

Second, Standpoint Theory puts essentialism and dualism in conversation with vision and liminality. The theory assumes that when material life is structured in opposing ways for different groups, the understanding of each will be an inversion of the other. However, since the vision of the ruling group structures the material relations in which all groups are forced to participate, choices are removed from subordinates. Thus, the vision available to members of an oppressed/subordinate group represents both a struggle and an achievement. This leads to the assumption that understanding visions of the oppressed exposes the inhumanity of existing intergroup relations and creates a move toward a more just world. Yet, the theory maintains that the reverse does not hold true for the ruling group. Why? Because it is rare that members of the ruling group are able to shrug off their power positions to achieve an "outsider within" standpoint. According to Collins (1998), an "outsider within" standpoint reflects a plural identity formation developed through engagement with positioning among communities. Outsiders within, like Sotomayor, can access the knowledge of the ruling group but are questioned when they claim that knowledge and seek the full power given to members of that group. Insiders fear that because Sotomayor may not share all of the assumptions traditionally held by members of the Court and may find some of these assumptions inaccurate or even implausible, she may advocate on behalf of new issues that require a new type of decision-making process that they cannot master.

The third assumption is that standpoints and communication are reciprocal. In other words, those with similar standpoints adopt similar communication styles. This belies the notion that those with differing standpoints will adopt different communication styles. As Sotomayor's comments suggest, (Latina) women's experiences and perspectives differ from (white) men's, thus producing different communication and identification styles. This is why the communication of Sotomayor's standpoint can be named "reverse racism" from the perspective of Newt Gingrich, even if he would later state that his critique was "perhaps too strong and direct" (Amato, 2009, par. 2; Cillizza, 2009, par. 1). Sotomayor's and Gingrich's public miscommunications reveals that we can best understand a person's experiences by paying attention to that person's own interpretations and articulations of these experiences. It also forces us to ask ourselves the questions that guide the remainder of my discussion: For whom do I speak? As whom do I speak? From where do I speak? I will answer these questions in the next section by articulating clearly what I offer and the value of my identity, social location, privileges, praxis, and goals.

FINDING AND EXPRESSING MY STANDPOINT

As a young, multiracial, female tenure-track professor at a majority institution, I often wonder if anyone can hear the sound of my voice. Though the transition from life as a graduate student to life as a new professor has been exhilarating, I am disillusioned. Some of my disillusionments are fiscal, leading me to ask if I can really afford to work as a public educator amidst the twin realities of extensive budget cuts and increasing living and professional expenses. Rejections from academic journals make me doubt the scholarliness and importance of my research. These concerns extend to my teaching, leading me to speculate whether I assign my students enough texts about marginalized groups. Obvious resistance from male students, as they insist on addressing me by my first name and challenging my intellectual authority along with those of the theorists I present during lectures, causes me to rethink my classroom management strategies. This feeling of inferiority is reinforced as my elder colleagues, though generally supportive of my professional efforts and innovations, refer to me as a "kid." Discussions with colleagues and students behind closed doors make me wonder whether I am seen as a person of color, and if so, what color. In addition, hearing the personal sacrifices many have made to achieve academic success makes me wonder how I will get tenure while maintaining healthy relationships with my partner, family, and friends. These questions and doubts guide my attempts to adjust to, what Taliaferro Baszile (2006) called, "the realm of academic abstraction" (p. 196).

After much introspection I reached an epiphany. I realize that all of the questions I am asking center around an important concept—identity, or lack thereof. I do not use the term identity for the sake of categorization or data collection, though those are important ways in which to measure and mobilize. Rather, I realize that what I am dealing with in classrooms, in faculty meetings, and in my own head, is a lack of identity so great that it hinders human potential. I realize that the ancient Greeks were right when they inscribed "know thyself" on the forecourt of the Temple of Apollo at Delphi. They understood that when we truly know ourselves and our capabilities, we can impact and transform our communities and environments in powerful ways. Later theorists such as Habermas (1973) echoed this theme, explaining that self-reflection is the key to liberation. These questions, doubts, and realizations also connect to the first assumption of Standpoint Theory: understanding my social location and recognizing my social privileges.

I am beginning to realize that while my social location is one of an "outsider-within," I am the beneficiary of many social privileges. First, I have an education that has taught me how to think critically for myself and communicate my thoughts ethically and persuasively. Second, as a teacher and scholar with my own experiences and standpoint, I have the opportunity to engage the academy differently. I have begun initiatives to teach innovative classes incorporating multiple communication contexts, such as Communication and Culture, New Rhetoric and New Media, and Racial Rhetoric and Representations in online and on ground settings (Babb & Mirabella, 2007). I also have the opportunity to develop new paradigms by researching and writing critical accounts of social relations, human nature, and the changing nature of human communication. By modeling this behavior, thereby engaging with my institution as a place laden with possibilities for generating change instead of stifling change, I am also investing in the identity formation and mobilization of students for campus, local, national, and even global change. By finding their purposes and goals, and understanding who they are, I believe that students will be empowered to accomplish great things. The wonderful reward is that I continue to develop my own identity and standpoint in the process and get closer to my goal of becoming a different kind of professor.

As a different kind of professor I am conscious of the fact that all the things I perceived as liabilities—my multiracial identity, youth, and gender—are my greatest assets. Consequently, my insider/outsider positionality is transformed. I realize that I do not have to carry the burden of speaking for all multiracial women under 35 years of age in the United States because no one person is capable of doing so. To quote Sotomayor (2001),

> I accept that our experiences as women and people of color affect our decisions. The aspiration of impartiality is just that—it's an aspiration because it denies the fact that we are by our experiences making different choices than others. (par. 19)

I understand that my assets empower me with the ability to identify with my students in a way that few other professors at my institution are able. Because I can speak the language of my students and the languages of traditional (on ground) and changing (online) academics, I am able to link these seemingly disparate discourses. My youth gives me the time and energy to understand my own and others' experiences, as well as understand how some people's experiences limit their abilities to understand the experiences of others. My gender allows me to relate with the 60 percent majority of college students who are women. My racial identity allows me to identify with students from European, Hispanic, African American, Arab, and Asian backgrounds. This is, as U.S. Census Bureau (2000, 2001) statistics reveal, practically everyone.

As a professor, I am fortunate enough to have a self-selected audience that meets with me weekly in the communication classroom. Each day I have the privilege of learning something new with my students about how to identify and express ourselves in a world that all too often looks at us with doubt. I have learned that the results are best when I teach theory through identification—by reminding students that the tensions and ambiguities with which they are grappling also affect others concretely. For instance, many of my "millennial generation" students are struggling to communicate their vision of a post-racial society as liberating from the burdening of historical narratives. At the same time, I help them come to grips with the racial struggles and theoretical perspectives of prior generations through class discussion and readings. I endeavor, in my teaching, to express as clearly as possible my own "mental movie" of the complex phenomena that underlie human communication and affect daily life on both microscopic and macroscopic levels. I accomplish this by providing students with a variety of approaches to a given topic. For instance, we update McGee's (1980) take on social activism by using our cell phones for electronic civil disobedience. We interpret Bandura's (1989) Social Cognitive Theory through the model of behavior change presented in NBC's television series, *The Biggest Loser.* We understand Black's (1970) and Wander's (1984) rhetorical theories of the Second and Third Personae by watching President Obama's 2009 "A New Beginning" speech to Muslim audiences in Cairo on YouTube. Or, we seek our own standpoints through the example of a leader like Sotomayor.

These experiences underscore the privilege I have as a teacher and scholar of communication. Moreover, they allow my students and me to link our conversations to the second assumption of Standpoint Theory: to expose disparities in social relations that can affect access to information and power. Since my field is an inherently interdisciplinary one, I am able to utilize history, media, cultural studies, sociology, literature, psychology, political science, and law in my teaching to reflect today's social and cultural tensions and ambiguities. In addition to making connections between theory and life in my own ways, I understand that some students may identify with guest lecturers who provide new perspectives and expertise from which we all can benefit. It is my desire that through such encounters students begin to see the possibilities for their own lives—both inside and outside of the classroom. As a result, I have also begun to understand that as a different kind of professor I too have a certain degree of power both inside and outside of the classroom. It is not my goal to replicate myself or to further my own political agenda. Instead, my goal is to harness the power I do have to empower my students ethically. In so doing I encourage them to take as much responsibility for their learning as I take for their teaching. I encourage them to defend and debate their ideas and regard them as individuals with unique standpoints that are constantly under construction. Thus, I hold fast to the third assumption of Standpoint Theory: that standpoints and communication are reciprocal. As my standpoint evolves, so does my ability to communicate and teach effectively. As my students' standpoints evolve, so too will their communication skills. I remember that the classes in which I felt most comfortable contributing when I was a student were those in which I felt the safest. Unsurprisingly then, the learning environment that I strive to recreate as a different kind of professor is one that is mutually beneficial: where I learn as much as I teach and where my students and I become a learning community that sees the world differently enough to challenge assumptions and convention together. By requesting a clear and concise statement of expectations early on, I force students to think about what they hope to gain from our interactions, what they believe to be their roles in their learning, and how they might use what they hope to learn in their future endeavors. Moreover, I believe that education should be critical and dynamic. Rather than simply dole out answers that I believe to be true, I act as a facilitator with the expectation that asking provocative questions will lead to a discovery of interesting answers and new possibilities. Seeing new possibilities is a critical element in the process of identifying and expressing one's standpoint publicly.

This is why I believe that identification must be extended from theoretical models to students themselves. For instance, while pursuing my doctoral studies I noticed that the undergraduate curriculum at my institution was lacking a focus in African American rhetoric and media image. I proposed a class to fill this void and designed a course outline that gained curriculum committee approval. I successfully taught this class with a focus on exploring how African Americans have used symbols to discover, maintain, and mobilize their identities. Using a mixture of public address, music, and visual images, we studied the impact of racialized communication on individual, collective, and intercultural identity formation and its ability to catalyze social change in national and transnational contexts.

I am proud to report that 50 students enrolled in that first section of African American Rhetoric and Image, and that they represented a variety of races, ethnicities, and countries of origin. It was a challenge to make African American culture relevant to the diverse group and to also demonstrate the ways that all cultures have rhetorical strategies that are equally valid and important. It was critical for all of the students (regardless of race, gender, sexual orientation, learning ability/style, or country of origin) to feel as if they could contribute to the conversation and provide needed perspectives on the materials. I borrowed the strategy detailed by Walker (1994) in the essay and book that inspired this edited volume, *In Search of Our Mothers' Gardens*:

> We must fearlessly pull out of ourselves and look at and identify with our lives the living creativity some of what our great-grandmothers knew . . . even without "knowing" it, the reality of their spirituality, even if they didn't recognize it beyond what happened in the singing at church—and they never had any intention of giving it up. (pp. 405-406)

Fearlessness. Identification. Creativity. Uncertainty. Spirituality. Walker's words helped me to discover that by finding the purposes and goals of those who have come before us, thereby understanding who we are and our own purposes and goals, we can also find empowerment. Though the class is officially over, a majority of students stay in touch to continue discussing certain issues raised in the class and in classes they are now taking. I consider this interaction a special honor as I watch them go on to graduate and professional schools, corporate America, the entertainment industry, and not-for-profit careers in media and political activism. I carry these successes with me as I make every effort to become a different kind of professor.

My first experience as a different kind of professor teaching African American Rhetoric and Image has spilled over into other classes I also teach such as Contemporary Communication, Rhetoric of Popular Culture, Rhetorical Criticism, Communication Theory, Fashion as Communication, and Argumentation and Advocacy. In these classes we focus on applying critical communication theories to real-world events and causes about which we are passionate, as well as to discovering the ways in which we are our own "walking arguments." As always, the primary focus remains teaching students how to connect the signs and symbols around them to their own identities and goals.

This focus is why the most important assignments in each of my classes, whether online or on ground, are weekly short essay responses to questions prompted by class discussion and material. For example, in my African American Rhetoric and Image course I ask students to compose responses to the following questions: When was the first time you realized you were a race? How, if at all, did it affect you? Engaging them in this way allows me to provide a space for introverted students to express themselves if they are uncomfortable speaking face to face in class. I also read a few of the responses aloud (anonymously), which makes the students more confident in their writing and critical thinking skills. And, perhaps most importantly, it provides a way to gauge whether the material is being understood fully. Sometimes I need to slow down or repeat part of a previous lecture so that all the students have a firm grasp of the concepts presented. This approach is highly successful. The students engage with the materials and demonstrate their capacities for becoming more aware and compassionate citizens. A number of them have been inspired to go back into their own communities and abroad to help educate others and work actively for political, cultural, and social change.

Perhaps my standpoint is best expressed as an answer to the questions I have asked myself throughout these pages: What do I have to say in my scholarship? Why am I in the classroom? Put simply, I hope to inspire powerful people who will produce artful and influential ideas. True education begins a continuing experience in which ideas and information can be tested in action and communicated as standpoints. Through the development of critical thinking skills, written and oral communication, engagement with technology, and an appreciation for new and different ideas, students are prepared to engage in meaningful ways with the people and situations they encounter. My goal is that they leave the classroom with a better understanding of our society, of themselves, and of the power they each possess to create positive change in the world. Working toward this goal allows me to mobilize my identity and standpoint for the common good by fostering an understanding of learning as a communal activity where, as March and Coutu (2006) described it so eloquently, "no one comes first; and no one stands alone" (p. 148.).

FIGHTING EXTINCTION

While I facilitate learning in the classroom, my most valuable lessons have come from my experiences outside the classroom—in faculty meetings, in office hours, on committees, working with academic presses, and in informal interaction with colleagues. When I landed my first academic job I thought I had gained access to an environment that valued critical thinking and social justice over budgetary restrictions and interpersonal politics. I have learned that the latter prevails much too often over the former. My experiences thus far reveal several predatory presumptions and perceptions that endanger my survival and success. These include the presumption that because of my background I am less competent or objective than a white male peer; the underlying perception that I am an outsider, which brings with it emotional stress and intrapersonal fear that I am an imposter; the imposed visibility that comes from an institutional logic that declares "we finally have one," and that one is sufficient, which means that I have unknowingly become either the fount of or repository for all things woman, multiracial, and under age 35; or the inability to check my own perceptions with mentors who may share my background, experiences, and communication styles. These kinds of presumptions and perceptions based on negative differences between people lead to nothing but paternalism. However, despite this state of affairs, I can say that hope is not lost. In learning to navigate these choppy waters I am changing my environment and charting a different course, a course that will make me a different kind of professor.

My scholarship and service, in addition to my pedagogy, are formulated with the objective of becoming a different kind of professor and fighting the predatory presumptions that make me part of an endangered species. As I hope to have demonstrated thus far, I strive to make clear the processes by which I have obtained my knowledge and to communicate clearly the relevance of the questions I ask. Recently, I have been a part of planning and implementing a research and advocacy program involving students and using experiential learning models to help them connect research and advocacy efforts. As a part of this program, I have applied for a grant through my institution and proposed a series of events designed to explore issues of identity and diversity; these events will also demonstrate prominent models negotiating a tenuous identity and leveraging their intrinsic resources to create sustainable change. The grant will fund proposed events that will take the form of formal presentations and informal luncheons. The presentations will first focus on the speaker's public identity and related issues of concern, such as advocacy for balanced racial and gender representation in media and encouraging young women to pursue graduate study. Speakers will also touch on the role of research in addressing these issues, how advocacy is a part of their lives, and obstacles they have faced in creating change. Outstanding students from related schools and departments will be chosen by faculty to attend an informal luncheon featuring the speaker, faculty, and representatives from related non-profit or advocacy groups. The purpose of these sessions will be to highlight specific programs of interest, and to allow meaningful conversation to take place about identity mobilization for advocacy and change. Ultimately, students will be empowered to understand themselves through exploring their passions and engaging in activities of significant impact.

Based on the small-scale success of this endeavor in other contexts, I have already expanded the scope of my scholarly work to reach a larger population of readers. To this end, I write for a variety of newspapers and magazines in addition to traditional scholarly journals and academic presses. I have also begun two projects and proposed two classes on multiracial self-concept and representation to meet the needs of the changing majority population at my institution. My goal is to develop a communication theory about the interrelations between mixed race identification and passing as they pertain to the field of rhetoric and to multiracial identity formation in the United States. For instance, in my book manuscript I introduce the concept of *(bi)racial passing* to argue that passing is a form of rhetoric that identifies and represents passers intersectionally via synecdoche, or taking part of their racial identities for the whole. Some of the key questions I ask in my research and pedagogy concern how racial identity is constructed, enacted, and encountered. Questions include but are not limited to: Where/What are the labels for multiracial individuals? When did you first realize you were a race and how, if at all, did it affect you? What are the effects of repeated exposure to the question: "So what are you anyway?" I am using this data to develop a model for communication that also accounts for the psychological violence and emotional responses such questions impose on the formation of a cohesive self. One emerging result is the reactionary identification strategies of mixed race individuals connected to Burke's (1966) guilt-redemption cycle—martyrdom, denial, vigor, or transformation. Another is the location of labels for mixed race individuals using historiographical content analysis—media, family, census documents, legal cases, and self. I am also charting significant differences among responses from males and females and across varying age groups. This type of research is triangulated, blending qualitative and quantitative methods, in order to ask new kinds of questions about multiracial identification and the ways in which it shapes the nature of communication itself.

Moreover, my service to the University seeks to offset past injustices by working to recruit more women of color to our departments, helping our faculty become more reflective of current demographics, and raising fiscal support and awareness for the needs of marginalized student communities. I currently serve on several departmental, college, and University committees in which I strive to enhance diversity outreach on the faculty and student levels. My service takes the form of guest lecturing, organizing events, and offering new ways of thinking about diversity and multiculturalism inside and outside of the classroom. I also make use of traditional networking tools such as national and international conferences for enhancing opportunities for recruiting and publication. However, in an environment of economic uncertainty I place an increased value on new media's social networking tools such as LinkedIn, del.icio.us, Twitter, and Facebook to stay in touch with and identify other women of color and scholars who share my interests. By taking the time to interact with my academic environment in these old and new ways I am better able to approach my work with a sense of purpose endowed by a more complete understanding of who I am, what I have to say, and for whom I speak.

CONCLUDING THOUGHTS

What I have attempted to provide in these pages has been a narrative about my experiences within the academy as well as the ways in which I keep my creative spark from being extinguished by the discrimination I face. What I have provided is a set of questions that have helped me to make sense of the academy and my place within it. In addition to asking what my standpoint is, I have also questioned my own capability, competence, and communicative effectiveness inside and outside of the classroom. Questions posed have varied from, "How do I simultaneously encourage dreams, spark imagination, and convey the message that success is as much about the journey as it is about the destination?" to "How do I communicate to my students, who are on the precipice of that next phase of life, how to find their passion or achieve success?" to "How do I communicate to the academic community that I am competent and that my methods are not chaotic but liberating?" The answer is simple. I rid myself of these anxieties and embrace my role as a different kind of professor.

What follows is my vision for this role. A different kind of professor is part of a paradigm shift that makes her decisive, responsible, and able to maintain her standpoint in an uncertain and anxiety-ridden environment. Her decisiveness allows her to understand that everything is done at the expense of something else, and that every choice to undertake a project or engage in a relationship will cost her in some way. Because of this, she manages her expectations and is not afraid to decline requests and opportunities that present themselves. Her sense of responsibility allows her to regulate the ways in which she reacts to her environment. She sees liabilities as assets, times of crisis as moments ripe for change, and focuses on the resources at her disposal rather than those she either does not have or has lost due to forces beyond her control. Since her standpoint is always under construction, she is more interested in asking new questions rather than answering old ones. Thus, she can rethink traditional dichotomies of academia such as logos-pathos, student-teacher, new-old, faculty-administration, online-offline, and intimacy-distance (not to mention majority-minority and woman-man). This kind of thinking demonstrates the playful resilience necessary for her imagination to flower in spite of the constraints she will face.

At the same time, a different kind of professor also demonstrates caring for, interest in, and love for others. This kind of professor understands that status and hierarchy are not as important as listening, learning, and teaching. She also finds real joy in serving her students, colleagues, institution, and world by finding her standpoint and connecting it to a vision larger than herself. In doing so she refuses to confuse self-interest with individualism or consensus with community. By communicating her standpoint and vision to others she foregoes intellectualism for its own sake and gives her knowledge away for the common good. By making herself available in these ways, both inside and outside of the classroom, she shuns selfish ambition and seeks to uncover the maximum of her own and others' potential. With a spirit of humility and relentlessness she addresses the emotional, physical, and intellectual needs of those she encounters. In so doing she addresses her own. The struggles she faces do not tempt her to retreat or quit. Rather, they inspire her to push forward, confident in the fact that she will make a difference and catalyze change.

Finally, a different kind of professor understands that personal experiences affect the facts that scholars, students, and laypeople choose to see. My hope is that I will borrow from my experiences and follow Sotomayor's (2001) lead in "extrapolating [the good] into areas with which I am unfamiliar" (par. 23). I also hope that I can harness the sense of adventure and imagination of those who have faced similar or worse constraints. From historical examples of my colleagues and scholars such as Alice Walker, I can learn to get over my need for perfection and control, recognizing that I cannot will myself into a different situation. Instead, I can engage the role of a different kind of professor and create new possibilities for myself, my students, and my institution. And finally, I hope that by raising the questions of difference and of what difference I can make as a professor that you, the reader, will begin your own evaluation of these questions. What should being part of the changing majority mean to you in your profession? For the fledgling professor, what will you do to keep your nerve and find your purpose while avoiding, as much as possible, anxiety, fear, and doubt? For the more seasoned scholar, what experiences and beliefs will help you realize that social identities, and the new media through which they are transmitted, are and will continue to be relevant variables by which to categorize and distinguish interpretive processes? For all of us, how can we negotiate our social and communicative differences without ignoring our emotional and psychological similarities? In other words, are we willing to challenge and respond to each other in order to recognize, refine, and articulate our standpoints? If you are like me, meaning that you want to be a different kind of professor, then your answer will be yes. Thank you in advance.

REFERENCES

Amato, J. (2009, June 3). Newt Gingrich backtracks on calling Sotomayor a "racist" updated. *Third branch.* Retrieved from http://thirdbranch. crooksandliars.com/john-amato/newt-gingrichbacktracks-calling-sonia-1

Babb, D., & Mirabella, J. (2007). *Make money teaching online: How to land your first academic job, build credibility and earn a six-figure salary.* Hoboken, NJ: Riley & Sons.

Bandura, A. (1989). Human agency in social cognitive theory. *American psychologist, 44,* 1175-1184.

Black, E. (1970). The second persona. *Quarterly Journal of Speech, 56,* 109-119.

Bow, L. (2004). For every gesture of loyalty there doesn't have to be a betrayal: Asian American criticism and the politics of locality. In L. F. Rakow & L. A. Wakwitz (Eds.), *Feminist communication theory* (pp. 121-138). Thousand Oaks, CA: Sage Publications.

Burke, K. (1966). *Language as symbolic action: Essays on life, literature, and method.* Berkeley, CA: University of California Press.

Cillizza, C. (2009, June 4). Gingrich retracts "racist" charge. *Washington Post,* A section: political digest. Retrieved from http://www.washingtonpost.com/wp-dyn/content/ article/2009/06/03/AR2009060304023.html.

Collins, P. H. (1998). *Fighting words: Black women and the search for justice.* Minneapolis, MN: University of Minnesota.

Crenshaw, K. (1989). Demarginalizing the intersection of race and sex: A black feminist critique of antidiscrimination doctrine, feminist theory, and anti-racist politics. In D. K. Weisberg (Ed.), *Feminist legal theory* (pp. 57-81). Philadelphia, PA: Temple University Press.

Faludi, S. (1992). *Backlash: The undeclared war against American women.* New York, NY: Doubleday.

Freire, P., & Ramos, M. D. B. (2002). *Education for critical consciousness.* New York, NY: Continuum Publishing Company.

Habermas, J. (1973). *Theory and Practice.* (J. Viertel, Trans.). Boston, MA: Beacon Press. (1971).

Haraway. D. (1988). Situated knowledges: The science question in feminism and the privilege of partial perspective. *Feminist Studies, 14,* 575-599.

Harding, S. (2004). Standpoint theory as a site of political, philosophic and scientific debate. In S. Harding (Ed.), *The feminist standpoint theory reader* (pp. 1-16). New York, NY: Routledge.

Hartsock, N. (2003). The feminist standpoint: Developing the ground for a specifically historical materialism. In S. Harding & M. Hintikka (Eds.), *Discovering feminist perspectives on epistemology, metaphysics, methodology, science* (2nd ed., pp. 283-310). Amsterdam: D. Reidel, Inc.

Mavin Foundation. (2009). Retrieved from www.mavinfoundation.org.

March, J. G., & Coutu, D. L. (2006). Ideas as art: A conversation with James G. March. *Harvard Business Review, 84,* 82-89, 148.

McGee, M. C. (1980). Movement: Phenomenon or meaning? *The Central States Speech Journal, 31,* 233-244.

Obama, B. H. (2009, June 4). *A new beginning: Cairo speech* [Video file]. Retrieved from http://www.youtube.com/watch?v=Cgn7_HlvkVo

Perspective. (n.d.). In *Oxford English Dictionary.* Retrieved from http://dictionary.oed.com/cgi/entry/

Race not 'overriding issue' in criticism. (2009, September 19). *CNN.com,* political ticker. Retrieved from http://politicalticker.blogs.cnn.com/2009/09/18/obama-race-not-overriding-issue-in-criticism/

Rosen, J. (2009, June 11). Where Sotomayor Really Stands on Race. *Time Magazine.* Retrieved from http://www.time.com/time/politics/article/ 0,8599,1903981,00.html

Sotomayor, S. (2001, October 26). *A Latina judge's voice.* Lecture presented at Judge Mario G. Olmos Memorial Lecture, Raising the bar: Latino and Latina presence in the judiciary and the struggle for representation, University of California Berkeley School of Law. Retrieved from *UC Berkeley News,* http://berkeley.edu/news/ media/releases/2009/05/ 26sotomayor.shtml

Taliaferro Baszile, D. (2006). In the place where I don't quite belong: Claiming the ontoepistemolgoical in-between. In T. R. Berry & N. D. Mizelle (Eds.), *From oppression to grace: Women of color and their dilemmas in the academy* (pp.195-208). Sterling, VA: Stylus Publishing.

Tasker, Y., & Negra, D. (2007). Feminist politics and postfeminist culture. In Y. Tasker & D. Negra (Eds.), *Interrogating postfeminism: Gender and the politics of popular culture* (pp. 1-26). Durham, NC: Duke University Press.

U.S. Census Bureau (2000). "Overview of Race and Hispanic Origin." Census 2000 Brief. March. p. 1-11.

U.S. Census Bureau (2001). "The Two or More Races Population: 2000." Census 2001 Brief. November. p. 1-10.

Walker, A. (1994). In search of our mothers' gardens: Womanist prose. In A. Mitchell (Ed.), *Within the circle: An anthology of literary criticism from the Harlem Renaissance to the present* (pp. 401-409). Durham, NC: Duke University Press.

Wander, P. (1984). The third persona: An ideological turn in rhetorical theory. The Central States Speech Journal, *35*, 197-216.

Chapter 5

Standpoint Theory and Discontinuing Denial of Racism, Sexism, and Ageism

Michele S. Foss-Snowden

Sandra Harding (2004), one of the earliest standpoint theorists, describes standpoint theory as a "seductively volatile site for reflection and debate about difficult to resolve contemporary dilemmas" (p. 13). As a young, female Assistant Professor of color, I recognize the dilemma created by my racial/gender/generational background and my current location (Assistant Professor) as being both contemporary and difficult to resolve. I also recognize the appropriateness of standpoint theory as a method for reflecting on how I got here and how I perceive and experience where and who I am.

The following exploration of the relationship between standpoint theory and the experiences of a young, female, Assistant Professor of color will ask and answer the following questions: What is my standpoint? How does my standpoint affect the way I communicate with my colleagues, including those who have acted unfairly toward me? How does my standpoint affect the way I communicate with my students? More frighteningly, does my standpoint cause me to deny the actual discrimination I encounter? I will consider the leading critiques of standpoint theory, especially those that frown at the potential essentialism encouraged by it. Finally, I will evaluate the effectiveness of the approach in my experiences in academia. What if I have used standpoint theory to help me survive in the overt/covert world of bias and prejudice in academia, but that same standpoint leaves me open to even more alarming dangers?

THE CREATION OF A STANDPOINT: YOUNG, BLACK, FEMALE, ASSISTANT PROFESSOR

Northern California is one of the most diverse areas in the United States. I grew up and attended high school, college, and graduate school in a place where no one kind of person stood out as different from anyone else. The first few days of school were always the same. I could look around and see different cultures, ethnicities, and lifestyles represented, but I would still try to identify those faces in the crowd that looked most like my own. As a high school student in Sacramento, a college student in the Bay Area, and a master's student in Davis (30 minutes southwest of Sacramento), I would begin my experiences with a search for those people who would understand my circumstances as a woman of color, who would empathize with me, and who would always have the time to hear a story that would begin with, "You won't believe the crazy racist thing my professor said in class today." It was not difficult to form these partnerships in my life as a student. I was never surrounded by other black women, nor was I ever the only black woman. I saw myself as *a* member of different minority groups, not *the* member. I did not feel that I was carrying the burden of representation alone.

The first part of my standpoint emerges from these early experiences. According to Collins (2005), "where you stand will shape what you see and, often, what you stand for" (p. 98). Even as a young black woman, I had been exposed to inequality and injustice. As a student, and without giving it conscious thought, I created links between what I had experienced in the social margins and what I chose to study, between what I thought about what I read, heard, and observed and how I interpreted my social and academic reality. I began my life as a student in a diverse setting, but it was not so diverse that it made me oblivious to various social and political power struggles.

I held my first teaching positions in several different institutions in that same diverse Northern California region, but noticed quickly the difference between finding others like me as a student and finding others like me as an instructor in these institutions. According to the National Center for Education Statistics (2009), in 2006 and 2007, females earned only 35 percent of all doctoral degrees awarded and African Americans earned just over six percent. Although more female than male African Americans earned doctoral degrees (66 percent female to 34 percent male), the number of African American females holding doctorates and working in academia was (and is still) disproportionately low. Even in my multicultural Northern California haven, these national numbers were represented. What these statistics indicate is the glaring underrepresentation of female faculty of color on college campuses in the United States. In each position at the various institutions at which I taught, I noticed right away that I was either one of two or the only black female professor in my department. I always noticed the lack of diversity right away—*of course I noticed*—but I hoped it would not be a significant problem. After all, every campus where I taught was diverse by national standards; each campus town in which I worked was known for and boasted about its diversity. In addition, the state of California is one of the most diverse places in the country, with three or more racial/ethnic groups each contributing at least 10 percent of the overall state population (Bean, Lee, Batalova, & Leach, 2004). How could people function (and how could instructors educate) in such a diverse environment without a healthy respect for the ways in which we are all different? It seemed unlikely that someone lacking that respect would choose the professorial profession in such an environment. In essence, the first part of my standpoint leads me to be cautiously optimistic regarding my experiences as a black female Assistant Professor. I give my colleagues the benefit of the doubt, but I also keep one eye open.

Perhaps the caution in my optimism is the result of the second part of my standpoint. If, as a result of the first part of my standpoint, I am an idealistic student of life who was educated in a multicultural and diverse semi-oasis, then as a result of the second point of my standpoint, I am a scholar of race, ethnicity, gender, discrimination, and social justice, and I am an activist who cares deeply about these issues. The second part of my standpoint has led me to approach my experiences as a black female Assistant Professor through a much more critical lens and has made the topics of culture and diversity common and comfortable in my daily life. It felt natural to study in these areas as a novice scholar. The more I committed myself to the examination of cultural differences, the more I realized how unique my upbringing had been. I saw, heard, and understood that the rest of the world continued to suffer from the sickness of inequality. More importantly, I started to notice the inequality even in my own backyard. My Northern California sanctuary was not as immune to the effects of institutionalized prejudice as I had thought. Thus, because I am a combination of both parts of my standpoint, I see my position in society, and I know that the evils of intolerance can reach me, even inside my inclusive bubble, but I was educated in an environment that inspired hope and suggested progress. As an educator, I remember those past experiences fondly, and I remain hopeful, but I am much more aware of how little progress has actually been made.

Thus, the combination of my experiences as a young, black, female student in a diverse environment and my critical (and informed) reflection upon those experiences shape the way I act, feel, and communicate today as an educator. Collins (1997) argues that a standpoint is informed by "historically shared, group-based experiences" (p. 375). For that reason, any individual experiences I might have (or might have had) with institutionalized racism, sexism, or ageism[1] will be my own, unique to me, but the types of benefits or constraints I might face will resemble the benefits or constraints faced by those of my race/ethnicity, age, or gender as a group (Collins, 1997). As I experience my world as a young woman of color, I interpret each moment during which I become aware of my position in the social hierarchy through a lens of group identification. For example, my knowledge of the existence of racism toward African Americans and my identification with African Americans as a group lead me to interpret certain situations through that lens. According to standpoint theory, "groups who share common placement in hierarchical power relations also share common experiences in such power relations . . . [leading] those in similar social locations to be predisposed to interpret these experiences in a comparable fashion" (Collins, 1997, p. 377). Thus, I share a common hierarchical power position with other African American women who have had experiences with racism, sexism, and ageism similar to what I have experienced. Our shared struggles and similar hierarchical position predispose us to interpret our experiences in a similar way.

Even with our comparable group identities and similar histories, my hypothetical hierarchical sisters and I are individuals. However, our experiences as individuals become the model for how we understand our group affiliations, the nature of group processes, and power structures in general (Collins, 1997). As a woman, I appreciate the struggle for gender equality, I recognize gender-based discrimination, I have looked into the eyes of true misogynists and because of my feminist standpoint, I am predisposed to see the world as a place where men (as a group) oppress women (as a group). As an African American, I know the history of my people; I see the long-standing effects of slavery in the United States, and because of my racial/ethnic standpoint, I am predisposed to see the world as a place where people of color continue to be forced to reside near the bottom of the power structure. As a young, female, African American faculty member, I understand the events that occur within the hallowed halls of the academy in a *different* way than my "majority" colleagues would understand them. I feel a certain responsibility (more than I ever did as bright-eyed student) to frame the moments in my life as being connected to my memberships in groups with a history of oppression.

Harding (1991) argues that women "start [their] thought[s] from the perspective of lives at the margins" (p. 269). Thus, using standpoint theory in considering my role as a young professor on a new campus, I started as an outsider while my majority colleagues started as insiders who did not need to think about their status at all. My minority status made me different; my difference made me an outsider. Collins (1986) refers to this condition as the "outsider within" (p. S14). I earned my place at the academic table and I was free to eat (I was within the social circle), but when it was time to clear the plates, my standpoint told me that everyone else at the table was waiting for me to put on my apron and retreat to the kitchen while they enjoyed their after-dinner drinks, a clear indicator of my outsider status "within" the group.

My position as a young woman of color has created a hesitant voice in the back of my head; this voice continues to whisper to me that when questionable moments occur at work between my majority colleagues and me, the motivations behind those moments are in fact bigoted or prejudicial in nature. Due to my standpoint, however, I find myself both questioning and denying the possible racist, sexist, or ageist intent prompting these moments.

Standpoint Theory and the Young, Female, Assistant Professor of Color

Though scholars have examined the perspectives of women in academia in general (Bell, Orbe, Drummond, & Camara, 2000; Collins, 1986, 1997; Dougherty & Krone, 2000; Houston 2000), exploring standpoint theory from the point of view of young, female, university/college professors of color is an area yet to be fully mined. Standpoint projects should create important additions to the body of knowledge about women, women of color, or young women of color, additions that would typically be missed or skipped in favor of work that is more supportive of the status quo (Harding, 2004). Those who use standpoint epistemologies accept the challenge of addressing social inequality in their work. As Collins (2005) states, "I do not do Black intellectual work because of academia—I do the kind of social theory that I do in spite of it" (p. 95). She adds that the black female intellectual does not have the luxury of being the "archetypal armchair intellectual who ponders and passes judgment on the issues of the day without taking any responsibility for [her] thoughts and inaction" (Collins, 2005, p. 95). Instead, these women have to expend large amounts of mental and physical energy to create academic spaces where standpoint critiques can exist (Collins, 2005).

Jacquelyn Mitchell (1983) defines the experiences of the minority professor as falling generally into three categories: visibility, vulnerability, and viability. Faculty of color, especially female faculty of color, face expectations, rules, and judgments from others based on physical appearance or visibility (Mitchell, 1983). Fortunately (or unfortunately, depending on one's proximity and perspective), most women and people of color come to the academy with extensive prior experience in dealing with being judged in this way. The minority professor might be warned to increase research and place less emphasis on committee work or other service obligations (so as to combat the assumptions that a visible woman of color is less competent than her male majority peers), while also dealing with the pressure of being asked or urged to get involved in "presenting a minority perspective in class or on a committee, counseling a minority student who has academic difficulties, or speaking to an outside group" (Mitchell, 1983, p. 21). Minority visibility thus creates an odd dichotomy, one where pressure to blend in coexists with pressure to "represent" one's group. Working within such a dichotomy can make a professor fatigued, both mentally and socially. Mitchell argues that community and campus reactions to visibility force the minority professor to "create and maintain a feasible balance and meaningful synthesis of self, ethnicity, and profession—no small task" (p. 22). Majority professors do not face a similar challenge.[2]

Visibility plays an important role in the creation of my standpoint. I have experienced the competing pressures of trying to overthrow stereotypes ("I will *not* be the minority professor who runs late to every meeting!") and still wanting to make a difference in my own ethnic and gender communities, both on and off campus. Assistant professors in general work very hard, and as a member of that group, I know I am not alone in feeling overwhelmed by my workload. However, my standpoint is colored by the fact that I know I carry the extra burden of trying to create the balance Mitchell (1983) describes. The thought that I am working harder than others influences my actions and feelings. My critical review of my past experiences tells me to exhaust myself in this way. I do not see another option; either I agree to carry the extra emotional/social weight not carried by my majority colleagues (because others in my group have carried far heavier loads and I do not wish to dishonor their struggles) or I validate the stereotypes and biases that those who came before me worked so hard to disprove.

The second area of experience discussed by Mitchell (1983) concerns vulnerability, especially "vulnerability to student-initiated evaluations of performance" (p. 24). Common sense suggests that feeling defenseless against students who come from the same diverse Northern California environment as I did amounts to paranoia. Why should I feel vulnerable around people who were born into an atmosphere of valuing diversity and multiculturalism? My standpoint, however, suggests that even in the Northern California climate of acceptance, I would be wise to keep those racial, gender, and age factors in mind as I present myself to my students. I know that prejudice exists, and not every student will join my cheerleading squad for the multicultural team. Students can easily lash out at me in their course evaluations about any perceived "injury" they think they have experienced on account of my interactions with them. Those evaluations, in turn, inform decisions about my retention, tenure, or promotion in the institutions in which I have taught. The student holding the pencil with which she/he will evaluate me thus holds considerable power over my future. I cannot expect students to remove their biases and subjective feelings about the instructor from the evaluation process. Students have the opportunity to evaluate an instructor based on her or his teaching, but they also use factors such as race, gender, age, language, and attractiveness to judge a professor's effectiveness or quality (Wachtel, 1998). In this way, being a member of multiple minority groups and a tenure-track (but not yet tenured) professor makes me vulnerable to the conscious and unconscious biases of my majority students; some students might give me low ratings because they have issues with my teaching. Some might give me low ratings because I am a young black woman. Some might have issues with my teaching because I am a young black woman. Even as the first part of my standpoint pushes me toward the calm, the second part of my standpoint pushes just as hard in the direction of anxiety. I do sometimes worry about being vulnerable when my fate is placed in the hands of my majority students.

I also know that I am vulnerable, in a different way, to my minority students, who might expect more from me as a minority professor (Mitchell, 1983). As a student, I approached my young black female professors with awe and admiration. I expected them to be just as smart and qualified as my older white male professors were, and more. I assumed that they would take special interest in me and my success. It is only now, as I look from the opposite side of the lectern, that I realize how much extra work and stress I might have added to my young professors' lives. Now, I fear that if I am unable to accommodate the black student who appears during times other than my regularly scheduled office hours, or to be exceptionally understanding when a female student's excuses roll like river rapids, then I should expect to see those students' disappointments with me reflected in my evaluation summaries at the end of the semester. Majority students are not the only ones who bring biases and subjective feelings to the evaluation process. When I think back to my own evaluations of my minority professors, I can admit that I carried my elevated expectations of my minority professors with me into the evaluation situation. Because I expected more from those individuals, I created a higher pedestal for them; should they fall from that pedestal, the results would be that much more destructive. Not only would they have "failed" me as instructors, but they would have also created negative precedents about the minority groups to which they belonged. Those academics who are on (or who remember) the track to tenure know how terrifying negative student evaluations can be. For me, the idea of low evaluation scores is *almost* as terrifying as the thought of creating a negative representation of my age, race, or gender.

This perspective changes the way I communicate with students. I treat students delicately, perhaps more delicately than an ideal application of my teaching philosophy would require. The first part of my standpoint (that of a student educated in a multicultural but still flawed environment) tells me that even though my students were raised in a country under the thumb of institutionalized racism and sexism, they will be more likely than others in less diverse environments than Northern California to base their evaluations of me on *just* my teaching. The first part of my standpoint tells me that my black female students have a good chance at being successful without my extra attention, and they will not evaluate me negatively if I am unable to give them more than I give my majority students. I water myself down. I censor my true thoughts on controversial topics that might arise, in an effort to deflect any chances that I might become the minority professor wearing a scarlet "A" (in this case, "A" stands for "agenda"). However, the second part of my standpoint (that of an educator who has been made aware of the inequalities present even in the most multicultural academic environments) asks me to bend over backwards and exhaust myself for my minority students, especially the young black females. I work hard for them because I know how much they need someone to work hard for them, and I know how much they are counting on me. They might not want to give me that negative evaluation, but the pain of disappointment is a powerful motivator. Because I am vulnerable as a female Assistant Professor of color, to protect my own survival in my career, I often find myself holding back the honest criticism or the "tough love" I might think a student needs.

The third and final area of experience discussed by Mitchell (1983) concerns viability, or the need to create a bicultural existence (the two cultures being the professor's racial or gender culture and her/his academic culture). Turner, Myers, and Creswell (1999) addressed viability in their study of the challenges of the academic professional; they identified several barriers to the success (measured as recruitment and retention) of minority faculty, including but not limited to, feelings of isolation, lack of mentoring, the devaluation of "minority" research (research conducted by minority scholars or research with a focus on minority populations, experiences, or representation), and the "token hire" misconception. If I think about my own experiences as a female faculty member of color, I can recall with great ease personal examples of my encounters with these barriers. However, in each case, the first part of my standpoint stepped in and played the role of a coping mechanism or strategy for my survival.[3] In other words, for each challenge that might have been the result of ageism, racism, sexism, or some combination of the three, I allowed the first part of my standpoint to override the second part. I convinced myself (in order to deal with the uncomfortable prospect of working for or with bigots) that the monster under my bed could not be real.

When I felt isolated and marginalized (Boice, 1993) as a result of being left out of social functions ("Oh, did you not get the email?"), I blamed my hypersensitive spam folder.[4] I used the first part of my standpoint to reach the conclusion that anyone who would choose to teach in such a diverse environment would never intentionally avoid a colleague of color due to that colleague's color. When a colleague disagreed with me about some guidance I had given a student *in front of that student*, I felt as if I had been publicly and passive-aggressively scolded by a peer. I was embarrassed and angry, but I swallowed both emotions and counted the experience as motivation for me to study up on advising policies, and not so much as an encounter with a colleague in possession of unfavorable ideas about young women or African Americans or both. I quieted the second part of my standpoint and allowed the first part to make my decision for me. I decided that this colleague could use a course on manners, but scheduling her/him for diversity training would be a premature move.

My standpoint is constantly shifting and changing, as new experiences add to or detract from where I stood previously. For example, when a colleague laughed out loud at a conference presentation of my research on representations of race in a reality-based television program, I felt puzzled by her/his reaction. I thought to myself, "Maybe she/he just doesn't like research on television." Or, "Maybe she/he subscribes to the philosophy that says an objective researcher must study the world outside her or his own backyard, so she/he doesn't like that I study race and gender."

The first part of my standpoint does not always prevail, however. Just as the first part of my standpoint represents my strategy for survival, informing the way I understand my career and what happens at work, the second part of my standpoint incorporates each new questionable experience and makes all the more critical my desire to write about what I write, to research what I research, and to call for action in the areas where I see inequality and injustice. Just as my scholarly agenda is formed by and forms my standpoint, it is likely that my standpoint contributed to the tension I felt in that moment during which I had to decide how to respond to my colleague's outburst. The first part of my standpoint might have prescribed a pass for my colleague, but the second part of my standpoint would not allow me to be satisfied with looking the other way. In this case, I justified the two parts by recommitting myself to research that "aims to empower those who remain relegated to the bottom of intersecting social hierarchies of race, class, gender, sexuality, and nation" (Collins, 2005, p. 95). The quality of that solution, however, and the dissonance it creates based on my current reflection of these events, remain open for discussion.

STANDPOINT THEORY CRITIQUES

This application of standpoint theory to my experiences as a female faculty person of color as narrowed by Mitchell's (1983) areas of experience reveals a surprising conclusion: I have used my standpoint to keep myself out of trouble, but in the process, I have created excuses for those who may not have deserved the free pass. Perhaps one or more of the individuals in the scenarios described above did possess racist, sexist, or ageist tendencies, and I did nothing to confront them. My use of my standpoint as a survival strategy has muted me, a prospect that the critical theorist in me finds both fascinating and frightening.

Perhaps the problem lies in the theory. Alison Wylie (2003) argues that because I belong to multiple populations (i.e., women and African Americans) that are systematically marginalized by society's structures of domination, I am able to "know different things, or know some things better than those who are comparatively privileged (socially and politically)" due to my awareness and understanding of my past experiences (p. 26). Critics of standpoint theory take issue with these ideas, arguing that the theory essentializes the groups in which standpoints are developed and that it also generalizes that those who belong to marginalized groups automatically know more or know better because of their marginalized social/political position (Wylie, 2003). Thus, standpoint theory critics would argue that even though I represent a combination plate of oppression, those group memberships alone do not mean I can create any knowledge that my majority colleagues cannot also create, and it does not mean I can create any *better* knowledge than that which could be created by my majority colleagues. Also, according to standpoint theory critics, my group membership does not mean that as an individual I have any greater ability to create knowledge because such an assertion would essentialize those minority groups to which I belong. However, if standpoints have the advantage of being able to "put the critically conscious knower in a position to grasp the effects of power relations on their own understanding and that of others" (Wylie, 2003, p. 34), then essentialization is unlikely because the critically conscious knower would be careful to avoid the negative effects essentialization could have on an already unbalanced power structure.

I do not assume to know better or know more than my majority colleagues; I only assume to know differently. I see the world and build my body of knowledge as a result of *my* standpoint. The way that I act, feel, and communicate in my academic environment is shaped by the fact that I know differently. The application of standpoint theory to the unique experiences of young female faculty of color still results in good knowledge, even in the face of logical criticism. However, the application might not result in good practice. In epistemological terms, the approach is valid. In practical or critical terms, the approach leaves room for concern. Perhaps my standpoint, my survival strategy, has allowed me to cover myself in discrimination denial.

Conclusion: Discontinuing Denial of Racism, Sexism, and Ageism

This process of revisiting the events of my past as an academician has been both cathartic and disconcerting. I have been able to use standpoint epistemology to help me understand how I have made it this far. I am not the first young African American woman to survive her first few years in the academy, but I might be among the first to use standpoint theory to help me understand exactly how I survived, especially during a time when the world seems to be particularly interested in and critical of matters of race, gender, and age. The ideas expressed here are only my own, and I do not speak for my entire community, but I can say with confidence that standpoint theory has (in this chapter) created an important and therapeutic piece of knowledge. This African American female Assistant Professor has navigated the roughest waters by calling on what she knows about race, gender, and age in the United States.

However, in those rough waters, I am upset by the knowledge that I appear to be only drifting instead of putting my paddles in the water and bravely pursuing a righteous direction. By calling upon the first part of my standpoint, my past experiences, and my critical reflections of those experiences, I have frequently given those around me the benefit of the doubt. In situations where I might have had every right to point an accusatory finger, I have instead turned the questions on myself: Am I being too sensitive? Am I missing opportunities to challenge real acts of discrimination because I am spending my time worrying about simple misunderstandings of the colorless, genderless, and ageless variety?

For the words here to hold any weight, they must be taken in the spirit in which they were formed: for the discontinuation of denial when *real* acts of racism, sexism, or ageism appear. Racism, sexism, and ageism exist, and they exist in the academy. Both parts of my standpoint tell me that this is true. When any one "ism" seems to rear its head, my standpoint makes me think twice ("Was that racism?"). In my experience, my standpoint has led me to believe that my ethnic, gender, and generational group memberships do make me sensitive and, especially in such a diverse area, most scenarios are probably not motivated by racism, sexism, or ageism. Only the most simple or blindly optimistic among us would believe that our society has made the full post-racial leap, or that similar complete progress has been made in terms of gender. Denying or excusing racism or pretending that sexism and ageism do not exist does not end the problems or even help them move closer to an end. The only possible solution to the problem is to continue the discussion.

Does my standpoint encourage my denial of the unholy trinity of "isms" (racism, sexism, ageism)? For this one researcher, the answer is a disappointing affirmative. To answer an earlier query (Wylie, 2003), the problem in this situation is not in the theory itself, but rather in its application. Just as the introduction of race complicates feminist standpoint theory (Collins, 1997), the introduction of region or geographic location complicates the theory even further. It is possible that in places less diverse than Northern California, my standpoint would still work as a strategy of survival, but not by encouraging denial. It is possible that my regional group affiliation and identity have enough momentum to change the parts of my standpoint that are formed through my national affiliations (race/ethnicity) and my global affiliations (age/gender).[5] Thus, my denial is both self-inflicted and externally motivated. I have agency over the consciousness I create in my own mind (Collins, 1997), so it is my choice to accept or deny. I also have questionable experiences that may or may not be tinged with bigotry, and if I wish to stay employed, I have to find a way to survive.

Perhaps future research could reveal a way to combine the redefined objectivity of standpoint theory (Harding, 1991) with the activism and purpose of critical theory. Could such a combination result in multiple benefits for multiple populations, not just educators, but also the students under their guidance? My standpoint leads me to believe that anything is possible, and my desire for change and equality in academia lets me know that I am not likely to end this line of research before I can answer in the affirmative (yes, the combination works and yes, the benefits are practical), with no disappointment.

Notes

1. The terms racism, sexism, and ageism are defined here as related to acts or practices that perpetuate inequality, based on membership in a minority or non-dominant group (Better, 2002). A racist act is one that perpetuates inequality based on racial group membership. A sexist act is one that perpetuates inequality based on gender. An ageist act is one that perpetuates inequality based on age (in academia, youth is the salient factor).

2. This assertion does not mean that majority professors, or professors who are in minority groups other than those discussed here, do not face discrimination or challenges at work. The ways in which the academy can be unfair to majority groups are many, and I do not intend to discount the importance of any of them.

3. Using denial as a coping mechanism is a common strategy for many African American women. Jones and Shorter-Gooden (2003) argue that Black women often choose to blame themselves for perceived mistreatment, finding it less painful than acknowledging the presence of actual racism or sexism. This strategy results in the possibility of a maintained sense of control and self-determination of fate (Jones & Shorter-Gooden, 2003).

4. To protect the identities of the actual players in this drama (and to protect myself as much as is possible), certain elements have been slightly modified. However, the spirit and feeling of each moment is unaltered, and even in their current "based on a true story" format, any person who has experienced a similar situation should be able to recognize the honest place where these stories were born.

5. It is important to add, however, that Californians are obviously not considered an oppressed group. So, under traditional application of standpoint theory, there can be no such entity as a Californian standpoint. My suggestion here is that there may be other factors that influence the creation of a standpoint, and regional differences are likely among those factors.

REFERENCES

Bean, F. D., Lee, J., Batalova, J., & Leach, M. (2004). Immigration and fading color lines in America. In R. Farley & J. Haaga (Eds.), *The American people: Census 2000* (pp. 302-331). New York, NY: Russell Sage Foundation.

Bell, K. E., Orbe, M. P., Drummond, D. K., & Camara, S. K. (2000). Accepting the challenge of centralizing without essentializing: Black feminist thought and African American women's communicative experiences. *Women's Studies in Communication, 23*, 41-62.

Better, S. J. (2002). *Institutional racism: A primer on theory and strategies for social change*. Lanham, MD: Rowman & Littlefield Publishers, Inc.

Boice, R. (1993). New faculty involvement for women and minorities. *Research in Higher Education, 34*(3), 291-341.

Collins, P. H. (1986). Learning from the Outsider Within: The Sociological Significance of Black Feminist Thought. *Social Problems, 33*(6), S14-S32.

Collins, P. H. (1997). Comment on Hekman's "truth and method: Feminist standpoint theory revisited": Where's the power? *Signs: Journal of Women in Culture and Society, 22*, 375-381.

Collins, P. H. (2005). That's not why I went to school. In A. Sica & S. Turner (Eds.), *The disobedient generation: Social theorists in the sixties* (pp. 94-113). Chicago, IL: University of Chicago Press.

Dougherty, D. S., & Krone, K. J. (2000). Overcoming the dichotomy: Cultivating standpoints in organizations through research. *Women's Studies in Communication, 23*, 16-40.

Harding, S. (1991). *Whose science? Whose knowledge? Thinking from women's lives*. Ithaca, NY: Cornell University Press.

Harding, S. (2004). *The feminist standpoint theory reader: Intellectual and political controversies*. New York, NY: Routledge.

Houston, M. (2000). When black women talk with white women: Why the dialogues are difficult. In A. González, M. Houston, & V. Chen (Eds.), *Our voices: Essays in culture, ethnicity, and communication* (3rd. ed, pp. 98-104). Los Angeles, CA: Roxbury.

Jones, C., & Shorter-Gooden, K. (2003). *Shifting: The double lives of Black women in America*. New York, NY: HarperCollins.

Mitchell, J. (1983). Visible, vulnerable, and viable: Emerging perspectives of a minority professor. In J. H. Cones, III, J. F. Noonan, & D. Janha (Eds.), *Teaching minority students: New directions for teaching and learning, no. 16* (pp. 17-28). San Francisco, CA: Jossey-Bass.

National Center for Education Statistics (2009). Fast facts. Retrieved from http://nces.ed.gov/fastfacts/display.asp?id=72

Turner, C. S. V., Myers, Jr., S. L., & Creswell, J. W. (1999). Exploring underrepresentation: The case of faculty of color in the Midwest. *Journal of Higher Education, 70*, 27-59.

Wachtel, H. (1998). Student evaluation of college teaching effectiveness: A brief review. *Assessment & Evaluation in Higher Education, 23*(2), 191-212.

Wylie, A. (2003). Why standpoint matters. In R. Figueroa & S. Harding (Eds.), *Science and other cultures: Issues in philosophies of science and technology* (pp. 26-48). New York, NY: Routledge.

Chapter 6

Negotiating Resistance
Challenges of a Female Faculty Member of Color from an Islamic Arab Background[1]

Ahlam Muhtaseb

In 2007, I wrote an essay (Muhtaseb, 2007) about my experience as a female faculty member of color teaching in a majority White institution, using expectancy violation theory and critical race theory to deconstruct students' resistance to my background as a female, Palestinian Arab, and Muslim[2] faculty member of color with an Islamic head cover. I received responses to my essay from several people, but one email in particular encouraged me to write the current book chapter expanding more on such an experience. This one came from another female, Arab, Muslim faculty member of color who wrote to me in May of 2009:

> I am glad that you have written about your experience as a faculty [member] of color and mainly as a Muslim with a head scarf in America because I identify with it so much and I have also had similar experiences. But as you say, not too many people would be able to understand our experience as Muslim female faculty of color because even Christian Arab-American women would have a relatively different experience from ours. I have also received some good

> evaluations and some harsh ones, I even had a student comment, "No comment on her appearance" and I knew that this person could just not get over my headscarf, and I am in a very white conservative area.

This comment hit home with me as three similar comments appeared on one of my class evaluations last year, which made me think that after two years of writing the original essay, I still face a similar (if not the same) dilemma in the classroom. In addition, two years ago, I was faced with a new challenge, namely, the unfair retention experience that I had to go through during my fourth tenure-track year. In comparison to the experience and accomplishments of a White colleague in his sixth year, my repertoire of achievements was more advanced, both in terms of the number of publications and academic service. Notwithstanding, my White colleague had what appeared to be an uncomplicated tenure process compared to mine, which was marked by a discriminatory retention evaluation. I was able to rebut that unfair evaluation, which was ultimately changed to my favor; however, the memory is still vivid.

As a result of the aforementioned email and recent discriminatory experiences, I decided to continue my story. Thus, in this chapter, I will attempt to deconstruct the resistance I face as a female faculty member of color who is Muslim, Arab American, and wears the traditional Islamic cover. I will do this at the institutional and student levels. I will begin with a discussion of my ethnic background, explaining the racism and discrimination that results from such a background, followed by a discussion of expectancy violation theory and a survey of some of the literature on discrimination against female faculty, especially those of color, while reflecting on my own experiences. In addition, I will provide some background information about my university, a Hispanic-serving institution, which I believe needs to establish a support system for female faculty of color who are left on their own to deal with these daily challenges.

Stereotypical Images of Arabs and Muslims in Mainstream U.S. Culture

I am the product of different trajectories that produce my unique teaching experience in the United States where race, gender, nationality, and religion matter. Two of the major elements of my background are my race and religion, which have been marginalized in the United States. The marginalization of Arab Americans, for example, which is well articulated by Abraham (1989) as the "political and cultural stigmatization of Arab Americans, and their related subjective experiences" (p. 36), is witnessed in almost all aspects of life in the United States. Abraham traced such discrimination and stigmatization in U.S. society's cultural, social, and political institutions, citing examples of discrimination and prejudice in three domains, namely U.S. foreign policies, domestic policies, and stereotypes prevalent in media coverage of Arabs, Muslims, and Arab/Muslim Americans. He mentioned several examples, including presidential candidates' refusal throughout the years to accept any donations by Arab Americans while campaigning; racial profiling by the Federal Bureau of Investigation and other governmental agencies against Arab and Muslim Americans, long before September 11, 2001; stereotypical and humiliating media coverage of Arabs; and hate crimes against Arab and Muslim Americans. Panagopoulos (2006) also stated that "the proportion of Americans who held 'very favorable' feelings toward Muslim Americans" (p. 609) before and after 9/11 never exceeded 15 percent, with the lowest percentage occurring immediately after 9/11. These perceptions of Arab and Muslim Americans are mainly the result of the stereotypical images that mainstream media in the United States perpetuate.

According to Domke, Garland, Billeaudeaux, and Hutcheson (2003), media's representations and framing of different races are usually accepted by audience members as common sense without any challenge. This results in stereotypical views of certain minorities by the public, which reinforce a racial hierarchy that benefits Whites more than any other group. Those stereotypes that are formed over the years play a critical role in informing people's expectations of "others," especially when they meet them for the first time. For example, Brennen and Duffy (2003) compared portrayals of Japanese Americans in the wake of Pearl Harbor and Arab Americans in the wake of 9/11 in *The New York Times* and found that the coverage in both cases was that of "otherness." According to the previous review of studies conducted to measure discrimination and stereotyping against Arabs and Muslims, there is a direct relationship between such stereotypical images in media and people's beliefs about these groups of people, both to which I belong.

As it pertains to the portrayal of Arab women in particular in American popular culture, Shaheen (1994) found that they are depicted in the media as either faceless housewives or belly dancers. In addition, Shaheen (1984, 2001) described how Arab characters in Western comics were portrayed using many degrading physical and behavioral features. He warned about the danger posed to the safety of Arab/Muslim Americans by these very negative stereotypes that are consumed by the over 150 million young people (including college students) who read these comics weekly. These stereotypes provide much of the background knowledge for my students, as they do for the majority of Americans, about my race, culture, and gender.

Even in 2009, things have not gotten better for Arab and Muslim Americans. The most recent poll on views of religious similarities and differences, conducted by the Pew Research Center for the People and the Press (2009), revealed that:

> Eight years after the terrorist attacks of 9/11, Americans see Muslims as facing more discrimination inside the U.S. than other major religious groups. Nearly six-in-ten adults (58%) say that Muslims are subject to a lot of discrimination, far more than say the same about Jews, evangelical Christians, atheists, or Mormons. In fact, of all the groups asked about, only gays and lesbians are seen as facing more discrimination than Muslims, with nearly two-thirds (64%) of the public saying there is a lot of discrimination against homosexuals. (para. 1)

Further, about 65% of non-Muslims see their religion as different from Islam, which is an indication of the "otherness" of Muslims in the United States. The most disturbing finding of the poll is that 38% of non-Muslim Americans believe that Islam encourages violence more than other religions do (Pew Research Center for the People & the Press, 2009). These perceptions and views, of course, affect students' and colleagues' attitudes towards professors who appear to belong to the Arab and Muslim population. It is normal for students and colleagues to have the same impressions and images of these groups as the rest of the American society.

In addition to discrimination based on race and religion, gender-based discrimination plays a part in my experience as an Arab Muslim female faculty. Using expectancy violation theory, the next section will explore research on the discrimination that female faculty, especially those of color, face in predominantly White academic institutions.

Facing Gender and Racial Discrimination in Academia

There have been a plethora of studies that provide evidence about the discrimination that faculty members face based on their gender, race, and even appearance (Fisanick, 2007; Nettles, Perna, & Bradburn, 2000; Samble, 2008; Trix & Psenka, 2003). However, there are not many studies that particularly investigate the experience(s) of female faculty of color who are Muslim and Arab. Further, with the exception of Muhtaseb (2007), an experience of a veiled Muslim Arab woman has not been an issue of discussion in past or current literature on the challenges facing female faculty of color in the United States. To help fill this void, in this section I first discuss the theory of expectancy-violation and link it to my experience in the classroom. I then focus on two major areas of my experience, namely the retention process and the resistance I faced from some feminist colleagues.

Violations of Stereotype-Based Expectations

According to expectancy-violation theory, developed by Burgoon in 1986, people usually evaluate others based on certain formed stereotypes of them. They also usually evaluate more extremely others who violate their stereotyped expectations (Bettencourt, Dill, Greathouse, Charlton, & Mulholland, 1997; Biernat, Vescio, & Billings, 1999). Expectancy violations also affect women of color in the academy. For example, Fisanick (2007) states that women are usually victims of unfair evaluations by students, colleagues, and administrators, especially those who violate certain gendered expectations of them. She adds:

> Therefore, women who fail to occupy typical gender roles are in double jeopardy of failure in the academic workplace. Female professors especially vulnerable to this second level of passing are often those who further occupy "othered" subject positions, such as women of color, fat women, women who are disabled, and lesbians. (p. 243)

As previously mentioned, there are many studies that have investigated the portrayal of Arab and Muslim Americans in U.S. mainstream media before and after September 11, 2001 (e.g., Shaheen, 2001). These studies concur that these depictions are usually very stereotypical and negative. With this in mind, I usually enter the classroom with the conscious realization that most of my students hold stereotypes about women like me similar to those mentioned by Shaheen and other researchers. This self-awareness usually makes the first meeting with my students a bit uneasy; however, I usually rise to this challenge by implementing several tactics to establish my authority as a professor to ensure teaching excellence (as will be discussed later). Realistically, this might not be the case with my students who still struggle to accept me as an authority in the classroom. The theory of expectancy violation states that sometimes, students form their judgments of my qualifications and credibility even before they have the chance to know me or listen to what I have to say. There were several encounters in which my students were severe in their judgment of me without even giving me the chance to prove to them my professionalism and teaching effectiveness. For example, a student went to the office of our department's chair asking about the procedure for dropping a class. When our student assistant asked the student whose teacher's class she wanted to drop, it turned out to be my class. The student assistant, who shared the incident to me later, expressed her astonishment and told the student that she thought I was a very good teacher, but the student's response was that she could tell she would not be able to understand my accent. This incident took place immediately after the first class meeting of the academic quarter. This example of prejudgment on the part of the student is explained further by expectancy-violation theory.

According to expectancy-violation theory, initial interactions and evaluations are usually based on preconceived stereotypes; however, the individual traits of those persons considered to belong to an "outgroup" prevail in the judgments of most, and the effects of the stereotypes fade away slowly (Bettencourt, Dill, Greathouse, Charlton, & Mulholland, 1997). The problem is, however, that usually the burden of proving those individual traits falls on the shoulders of the female faculty member of color when dealing with students' preconceived stereotypes and expectations—unlike their male and/or White counterparts who often take their privileged positions for granted.

For example, I have to work harder to assure my students that I am qualified to teach. Jackson and Crawley (2003) reached a similar conclusion in their qualitative study of White students' reactions to their presence and pedagogy as Black professors. The results of their study indicated that their White students were more critical of their Black male professors at the beginning, but were more accepting and trusting later on, though the students still kept their conservative views regarding intercultural communication. This process of negotiation between the students and female faculty of color can be exhausting and also unfair, to say the least.

The challenge of teaching becomes more complex when I have to prove that I am a good professor. My lesson plans and PowerPoint presentations are always prepared for my lectures. I put my syllabi, lecture notes, assignment instruction sheets, samples of assignments, and grades on Blackboard to ensure that there is no room for misunderstanding. I attend as many professional development workshops on and off campus that I can. Despite all of my efforts and hard work, I am usually evaluated more negatively than I expect. It is hard for me to compare my evaluations to colleagues with similar experience and rank, but from what I collect informally, my student evaluations, especially during the first two years, were lower than those of other assistant professors or even teaching assistants.

This issue of discrepancy in evaluations or judgment is discussed extensively by Biernat, Vescio, and Billings (1999). They state that judgment of a favorable (with perceived good qualities) ingroup member is usually more positive than that of a favorable outgroup member, a process they term "ingroup polarization" or "extremitization," which is explained by ingroup favoritism as a means of preserving positive ingroup qualities in comparison with outgroups. Since most of my students are either White or normalized to White professors, I usually represent the outgroup member.

There are several teaching issues that reveal the underlying, mostly unconscious, ingroup favoritism. One is the ability to discuss controversial or sensitive topics. In their self-reflective study about teaching race-related subjects to students, Williams and Evans-Winters (2005) noted that one problem they faced was students focusing on the messenger instead of focusing on the message. This is an issue that I encounter whenever I cover issues of race, gender, class, and sexual orientation. Here are two examples of students' notes in their evaluations of one of last year's classes:

> She always refers to her people when its [sic] not a part of class or appropriate.

> The class is titled 'Race, Gender, & Class in Media' but all we really ever talked about was discrimination of Arabs, especially, Palestinians.

A similar conclusion was reached by Jackson and Crawley (2003) who noted that:

> Anecdotal data reveal that many White . . . teachers (and, I suspect, other White non-education students as well) will challenge, debunk, and even question the credentials of faculty of color who discuss these taboo topics. This 'kill the messenger' syndrome may stem from guilt and/or anger at realizing their White privilege and the complicity of their racial counterparts in maintaining a racially stratified system. (p. 217)

In my Gender, Race, and Media class, it is hard for me to explain inequality in media representation of different segments of society based on gender, class, and race without my ethnic background being in the forefront of the discussion. It is very challenging for me to have students accept my criticism of U.S. mainstream media's portrayal of Arab or Muslim Americans, for example, which vilifies them and presents them as terrorists, violent, anti-American, etc. One of the major challenges that I face is discussing stereotyping; many students insist that stereotypes have "elements of truth" in them or that they must have started from a certain point in history. As I explain to students, some stereotypes have nothing to do with truth or statistics and are ideologically motivated, socially constructed, and related to the hegemonic narrative of the dominant group in society. Despite the evidence I provide, which contradicts their argument, students still resist and try to provide examples of stereotypes that they think are factual. Some White students take that class with the suspicion that such a class is White-bashing. My ethnicity is always in the foreground of any discussion that relates to ethnicity and race. Discussions of socioeconomic status and gender are somewhat easier because these issues are more open for discussion in the academic public domain.

It is worth noting here that although the classroom is the site of significant struggle for female faculty of color when dealing with expectations and violations of expectations, other sites of struggle in academia can be as harsh as the classroom. Stark discrimination by other faculty and administrators is still practiced against female faculty of color, which is an issue on which I will expand in the next section.

Gender and Race-Based Discrimination in Tenure, Retention, and Promotion

Eversole, Harvey, and Zimmerman (2007) state that despite the fact that more women receive their doctorates than men, less women get through the tenure and promotion process. They conclude that while mothering, for example, negatively impacts a woman's chance of getting tenure and promotion, having children actually helps a man during the tenure and promotion process. A similar conclusion was reached by Shope (2005) in her essay on what she terms "the no-uterus rule" based on her own experience of pregnancy—a rule that ignores the body in favor of the mind.

Nettles, Perna, and Bradburn (2000), in their analysis of the 1993 National Study of Postsecondary Faculty that focused on faculty at 2- and 4-year (and above) teaching institutions, wrote:

> There were several differences between male and female faculty members in the levels of faculty outcomes such as salary, tenure, and rank. Female full-time faculty averaged lower salaries than male faculty by about $10,000 in the fall of 1992. . . . They were also less likely to be tenured (42 vs. 66 percent) or to be full professors (15 vs. 39 percent). (p. v)

The report found similar differences between White and Black, non-Hispanic faculty; for example, in the fall of 1992, 58% of White faculty members were tenured, compared to only 48% of Black faculty members. However, the report indicates that these differences might be attributed to differences in human capital and structural characteristics, such as experience and research.

Even medical schools can be examples of stark discrimination against female faculty according to Trix and Psenka (2003), who conducted a discourse analysis of letters of recommendation for medical faculty at a large American medical school in the mid-1990s and found several gender differences in such letters between male and female faculty. For example, "the most common semantically grouped possessive phrases referring to female and male applicants ('her teaching,' 'his research') reinforced gender schema that tend to portray women as teachers and students, and men as researchers and professionals" (p. 191). The same authors concluded that in spite of the spike in the numbers of females attending medical school since the 1960s (reaching to 42% in the 90s), women's, especially those of color, access to positions of power in these schools (such as professorship, administration, etc.) is still very limited and obstructed by many gatekeeping techniques.

Comparing those experiences of minority faculty to my own, I find some similarities; however, an important difference lays in the fact that my racial *and* religious (Islam) backgrounds encourage discrimination against me and others who belong to these same categories. One of the major areas of such unfair treatment is usually the tenure (including retention) and promotion process. This was my retention experience two years ago, which I will revisit in the next section. I will start by explaining this process on our campus and then expand on my personal narrative.

REFLECTIONS ON MY PERSONAL EXPERIENCE

According to my institution's regulations, at the second and the fourth year of a faculty member's probationary period, she or he is to be evaluated through a full review process for retention purposes. This process includes a review of the faculty member's academic file by the chair and evaluation committee of the department separately (first tier), then the dean and evaluation committee of the college (second tier). The evaluation process is based on a thorough review of the accomplishments of the faculty member in three different areas: research/scholarship, teaching, and service. Since my institution is a teaching-oriented institution, more focus is usually placed on teaching. In addition, with the heavy load of teaching (3-3-3 for full-time tenure-track faculty), expectations of research are not supposed to be as high as research-oriented institutions. Therefore, two peer-reviewed and two non peer-reviewed publications are usually sufficient for granting tenure and promotion in our college if this is accompanied by good teaching and service evaluations. The tenure review should take place by the sixth year of a tenure-track faculty member's probationary period; hence, at the fourth year, a faculty member is expected to be close to having these four publications completed in addition to conference presentations, grants, an active research agenda, and other professional development and scholarly activities.

There was no justification for the no-retention decision provided to me at my fourth-year review except prediction that I would not be able to get peer-reviewed publications in two years for my tenure review. This prediction from one of the department evaluation committee members, a White male, came in spite of the fact that my 42-page, peer-reviewed journal article was accepted for publication in a communication journal after only two or three weeks of that prediction. I completed all, and even exceeded in some, of the retention requirements as outlined in our faculty manual. In response to the unfair decision of not recommending me for retention, I rebutted the decision with the help of my school's union and the decision was changed to a retention recommendation. Nonetheless, many female faculty members who suffer such clear discrimination might be intimidated into accepting such unfair and biased treatment without any resistance, which results in them losing their jobs. When reviewing some of the statistical facts about my institution, the numbers showed that such discrimination and tenure gaps also exist on a larger scale.

I teach at a medium-sized four-year college in Southern California. Its Fall 2008 Profile of Employees (The California State University Profile of CSU Employees, 2009) provides interesting statistics on the makeup of the institution's employees, including statistics of faculty analyzed by race and gender. After some calculations of the numbers of tenured and promoted faculty by gender and race, and comparing these numbers for 2008 and 2003, I found that although there was a slight reduction in the racial and gender gaps in terms of tenure and promotion in 2008, there was still a significant gap between White males and all other categories. In particular, the largest gap was that between White males and minority females. While 74% of White male faculty members were awarded tenure in 2008, only 58% of minority females were (compared to 67% of White females and 69% of minority males). In addition, 53% of all tenure-track White male faculty members were at the rank of full professor, while only 30% of minority females were (compared to 41% of White females and 47% of minority males).

My school provides protection to faculty in the tenure and promotion process by layering the review process and dividing it between several tiers, as mentioned previously. In spite of that, it does not necessarily provide clear enough criteria for tenure, retention, and promotion decisions and that sometimes open the door for discrimination. Such discrimination can be fought; however, the process is usually painful and draining for the faculty involved because she or he has to go through a time-consuming process of rebutting, filing a grievance if necessary, and potentially taking legal action. During this process, it is usually the faculty member who suffers increased levels of stress.

Part of the problem regarding unfair evaluation practices has to do with the heavy dependence on and confidence in students' evaluations. Of course, this is not a problem unique to my school or even the California State University system itself, for it is a national one. According to Fisanick (2007), research shows that in general, administrators (and even senior faculty) view students' evaluations as more authoritative than any other method of faculty evaluation. Not only are students' evaluations of faculty based on gender/race expectations, but so are faculty members' evaluations of other faculty, especially those done by White male faculty members. Several studies found evidence that senior faculty members (who tend to be White males) also act on their own stereotypical expectations of gender and race roles (Fisanick, 2007; Samble, 2008; Shope, 2005; Trix & Psenka, 2003). Therefore, female faculty of color are usually hostage to institutional cultural environments that might not be supportive at all.

Such discrimination is not necessarily practiced by White male faculty only; to the contrary, sometimes female faculty themselves are even more discriminatory than their male counterparts. Though there are several reasons for this, a significant one is ideological, such as feminists discriminating against other female faculty because of ideological reasons, which was one of the conclusions of Samble (2008). Similar to previous studies, Samble provides an extensive literature review of studies on the challenges and obstacles facing women's progress in academia. The author found a number of obstacles: biases against women in academia, overrepresentation of female faculty in service and teaching, the salary gap between male and female faculty, and the lack of transparency when it comes to the real reasons behind rejecting tenure (e.g., caregiving and motherhood could be perceived as having negative effect on a female faculty member's ability to succeed in academia). What is very interesting is the discussion on female faculty discriminating against female faculty (i.e., a feminist female faculty member might discriminate against another female faculty member who is not necessarily feminist).

The reason this is interesting for me is that in my own experience, some feminist faculty members who ascribe to a Western-oriented view of feminism see women like me with a headscarf as anti-feminist. This is in spite of the fact that I too am a feminist scholar and that in other countries and cultures, many feminists who adopt different worldviews may see me through a different lens than my institutional colleagues. El Guindi (2005) argued against a "universal" notion of feminism because it is grounded in culture; therefore, feminists should not evaluate the different experiences of women from their own cultural perspectives. In applying this argument to Muslim and Arab women in particular, she concluded, "some feminists are perhaps unaware of the hegemonic character of imposing their agenda upon women from different cultural traditions. If aware, then it becomes a situation not only of hegemony, but one of a false consciousness of dominance with a subtext of racist arrogance" (p. 54). This has been the predominant informant of my experience at my institution. For example, a male "colleague" from a different department, who considers himself to be the guardian of women's rights, more than once tried to humiliate me on our school's major listserv that is dedicated to political discussions and is subscribed to by hundreds of faculty and staff members. In one case, he took a comment that I posted to a private listserv of a group of activists on campus condemning attacks against illegal immigrants and reposted it to the major listserv of the school and attacked me personally—not my views—solely based on my religious background.

On a different occasion, another feminist colleague, also from a different department, attacked my activism for the Palestinian cause, describing my efforts as "religiously motivated." Despite the fact that this is a cause considered by many around the world as a human rights issue, she dismissed it as merely "part of our [Muslim] religious wars." Unfortunately, some feminists turn against other women who may also consider themselves feminists usually out of blind convictions that do not recognize the legitimacy of the "other's" views.

The backlash of Western feminists may also be informed by their impressions of others simply based on their appearance. Fisanick (2007) discussed the effect of appearance on the experiences of female professors in academic and popular culture. She argued that students and colleagues alike respond to what they perceive (and expect) to be the "normal" body of a faculty member and if that body looks different from what is expected, it will be "othered" in academia, usually resulting in a discriminatory evaluation by students, which ultimately affects the overall evaluation process of the faculty member. Of course, the issue of appearance applies as well to a head scarf that might be viewed as "out of the norm." A headscarf or "hijab" might symbolize the "internal oppression" of Muslim women for many in this country, which might not be the case at all in the views of women who choose to wear it.

It seems that the struggle of female faculty of color is still a long one, especially when they are from a racial/religious background like mine. However, narrating the experiences of these faculty and sharing the implications on their lives can be empowering to other female faculty of color who might feel alone in the world of academia.

CONCLUSION

In this chapter, I tried to open up the discussion of the obstacles that female faculty of color face in general in surviving academia, while shedding a special light on my own experience with my unique racial and religious background. I discussed the theory of expectancy violation and how it might explain the negative experiences of female faculty of color in predominantly White institutions, especially taking into consideration the effect of media's gender- and race-based stereotyping of those faculty.

During the research process in preparing for this chapter, I found out that up-to-date statistics on U.S. faculty members' tenure, promotion, and retention were lacking, which indicates that we need more quantitative data about the status of female faculty of color in academia. I also believe that more reflective qualitative essays on the experiences of female faculty of color could be valuable resources for not only other female faculty of color, which might help them in coping with their own frustrations, but also for other faculty members who should work on increasing their understanding of what female faculty of color go through in academia. Unfortunately, many White faculty members are not conscious about their role in perpetuating the long history of unfair treatment that female faculty of color have been enduring. Therefore, opening up the box of memories for female faculty of color might be therapeutic for all in academia. This might be a platonic view but one worth pursuing.

To my regret, three years after writing my original essay, my experience as a Palestinian, Arab, and Muslim female faculty member of color with distinguishable attire is very much the same. However, I believe that I am not the same person due to the confidence and skills that I have acquired throughout my years in academia that have enabled me to fight for my rights. Therefore, I suggest to all junior female faculty of color to first educate themselves about their rights in their respective institutions and to fight for these rights. It can be very helpful to get involved in their institution's unions if these are available, or at least get to know the major agreements their unions have with the administration of their institutions. Second, from several discussions with other faculty members with similar experiences, it seems that in many institutions, most senior faculty members and administrators, such as deans and provosts, do not usually consider service as a basis for tenure, even if it is on paper. Therefore, female faculty of color should be careful about balancing research and teaching with reasonable service required of junior faculty members. Junior faculty members might be excited about getting to know their institutions by serving them and their student populations, but this might affect their ability to focus on research in particular. This tendency might be true for all junior faculty members, but it is more serious when a faculty member is at a higher risk of being discriminated against, like female faculty of color. Lastly, junior female faculty of color should always remember to have confidence in themselves and their ability to be as competent as any other colleague, while being aware that their gender and color may be the reason students resist their authority in the classroom. They also should have the patience to survive in academic institutions that might not be equipped with the necessary tools to help them go through a very stressful academic environment. On the other hand, institutions themselves should provide the needed support for female faculty of color, not only in terms of written laws and rights on paper, but also through diversity training to all faculty members.

In a period of three years, I started attending a summer program that is sponsored by Cornell University and financed by several endowments and grants to ensure a nurturing environment for "minority scholars." The program is called "The Future of Minority Studies Research Project" and includes several activities and events throughout the year, including conferences, summer seminars, and summer colloquia. This project stemmed from the founders' conviction that faculty/scholars of minority studies are usually marginalized and discriminated against; therefore, they need support beyond whatever is offered by their institutions (if any is indeed offered). I am concluding with this synopsis of this unique Cornell program to emphasize the importance of providing support for female faculty of color by institutions that claim that their goal is to encourage diversity and equality. In the lack of such support, female faculty of color still have a long way for a fair and just entry and survival in academia.

NOTES

1. The author would like to acknowledge Ms. Basemeh Rihan's valuable input to this chapter.

2. Palestinian is my nationality, Arab is my ethnicity, and Muslim is my religion. I also use *Arab or Muslim American* to refer to Arabs or Muslims living in the United States.

REFERENCES

Abraham, N. (1989). Arab-American marginality: Mythos and praxis. *Arab Studies Quarterly, 11*(2), 17-43.

Bettencourt, B. A., Dill, K. E., Greathouse, S. A., Charlton, K., & Mulholland, A. (1997). Evaluations of ingroup and outgroup members: The role of category-based expectancy violation. *Journal of Experimental Social Psychology, 33*, 244-275.

Biernat, M., Vescio, T. K., & Billings, L. S. (1999). Black sheep and expectancy violation: Integrating two models of social judgment. *European Journal of Social Psychology, 29*, 523-542. doi: 10.1002/(SICI)1099-0992(199906)29:4<523::AID-EJSP944> 3.0.CO;2-J

Brennen, B., & Duffy, M. (2003). "If a problem cannot be solved, enlarge it": An ideological critique of the "Other" in Pearl Harbor and September 11 *New York Times* coverage. *Journalism Studies, 4*, 3-12.

Domke, D., Garland, P., Billeaudeaux, A., & Hutcheson, J. (2003). Insights into U.S. racial hierarchy: Racial profiling news sources, and September 11. *Journal of Communication, 53*, 606-623.

El Guindi, F. (2005). Gendered resistance, feminist veiling, Islamic feminism. *Ahfad Journal, 22*, 53-78.

Eversole, B. A. W., Harvey, A. M., & Zimmerman, T. S. (2007, February-March). *Mother and professing in the ivory tower: A review of the literature and a call for a research agenda.* Paper presented at the Academy of Human Resource Development International Research Conference in the Americas, Indianapolis, IN.

Fisanick, C. (2007, June). They are weighted with authority: Fat female professors in academic and popular cultures. *Feminist Teacher, 17*(3), 237-255. Retrieved from Academic Search Premier database.

Jackson, R. L., & Crawley, R. L. (2003). White student confessions about a Black male professor: A cultural contracts theory approach to intimate conversations about race and worldview. *The Journal of Men's Studies, 12*, 25-41.

Muhtaseb, A. (2007). From behind the veil: Students' resistance from different directions. *New Directions for Teaching & Learning*, Summer(110), 25-33.

Nettles, M., Perna, L., & Bradburn, E. (2000). Salary, promotion, and tenure status of minority and women faculty in U. S. colleges and universities. *Education Statistics Quarterly, 2*(2), 94-96. (ERIC Document Reproduction Service No. EJ613966) Retrieved July 22, 2009, from ERIC database.

Panagopoulos, C. (2006). The polls—Trends. *Public Opinion Quarterly, 70*, 608-624.

Pew Research Center for the People & the Press. The Pew Forum on Religion & Public Life. (2009). *Views of religious similarities and differences: Muslims widely seen as facing discrimination.* Retrieved from http://pewforum.org/docs/?DocID=436

Samble, J. (2008). Female faculty: Challenges and choices in the United States and beyond. *New Directions for Higher Education, Fall*(143), 55-62.

Shaheen, J. G. (1984). *The TV Arab*. Bowling Green, OH: Bowling Green State University Press.

Shaheen, J. G. (1994). Arab images in American comic books. *Journal of Popular Culture, 28*, 123-133.

Shaheen, J. G. (2001). *Reel bad Arabs: How Hollywood vilifies a people*. Brooklyn, NY: Olive Branch Press.

Shope, J. H. (2005). Reflections on the no-uterus rule: Pregnancy, academic, and feminist pedagogy. *Feminist Teacher, 16*, 53-60.

The California State University Profile of CSU Employees.(May, 2009). Retrieved from The California State University website: http://www.calstate.edu/hr/employeepro-file/ documents/Fall2008CSUProfiles.pdf

Trix, F., & Psenka, C. (2003). Exploring the color of glass: Letters of recommendation for female and male medical faculty. *Discourse & Society, 14*(2), 191-220. doi: 10.1177/0957926503014002277

Williams, D. G., & Evans-Winters, V. (2005). The burden of teaching teachers: Memoirs of race discourse in teacher education. *The Urban Review, 37*, 201-219. doi: 10.1007/s11256-005-0009-z

Chapter 7

PLAYING THE GAME

COMMUNICATIVE PRACTICES FOR NEGOTIATING POLITICS AND PREPARING FOR TENURE

Annette Madlock Gatison

For any faculty member, being promoted and awarded tenure is the most visible sign of accomplishment in academia and in order to reach this status, one must play by the rules of the institution from which it is sought. Teaching, research/creative activities, and service to the institution are the primary factors for evaluation when one is on the promotion and tenure track. Tenure refers to an arrangement by which faculty appointments continue until retirement age, although the faculty member is subject to dismissal for adequate cause or termination due to financial exigency (AAUP, 1973). Diamantes (2002) states that "tenure serves as a lifetime assurance that we will receive due process in higher education; it does not assure us lifetime employment" (p. 325). According to the American Association of University Professors' 1940 Statement of Principles (AAUP, 1973), tenure offers the freedom to teach and conduct research, do extramural activities, and have economic security. No other profession, except federal judgeships, awards tenure (Olswang, 2003).

Although the process of obtaining tenure is a designed to be objective, there is an additional factor embedded in the faculty tenure process that one must consider and that is collegiality. Collegiality is the ability to create and sustain meaningful working relationships with others, be a team player, and fit into the department or university environment (Cooper, 2006; Cooper & Stevens, 2002). Tenure has been won and lost based on a tenure committee's subjective judgment of an individual's collegiality (Lewin, 2002; Silverman, 2004).

Teaching, research/creative activities, service, and collegiality are the general evaluative factors for awarding promotion and tenure; thus, it is especially important for women tenure-track faculty of color to learn to navigate the process or, as I refer to it, play the tenure game. As one such tenure-track Assistant Professor of Communication at a predominately white institution (PWI), this personal narrative will explore the politics of tenure using co-cultural theory (Orbe, 1998a, 1998b) because it places the voice and worldview of the powerless at the center and not the periphery of inquiry. A junior faculty member beginning to navigate the tenure process has much to learn and do, while at the same time, is expected to maintain her sanity. Everyone wants a piece of that new Black professor on campus (Cooper, 2006; Alexander & Moore, 2008), which puts her in a place of having to make some critical decisions before she may be ready. She thinks, "I know I am not the only one, where is everyone else that looks like me?" "So now that I am here, how do I stay?" "How do I work and not get burnt out, step on toes, say the right thing to the wrong person (and then have my ideas stolen or words twisted in some stealthy political move of which I want no part)?" "How do I not put my foot in my mouth by saying the wrong thing to the wrong person in a moment of frustration?" Co-cultural theory suggests that I, and other junior women faculty of color, must negotiate my place in relation to others (including the dominant group) in my daily life, through communication and interaction.

Theoretical Framework

African-American women in the professoriate continue to face organizational and structural barriers in the promotion and tenure process that most of their White colleagues do not. Orbe's (1998a, 1998b) research in co-cultural communication provides the conceptual framework to better understand the power differential between dominant and non-dominant groups in the tenure process. *Co-cultures* refer to non-dominant groups that are part of a larger, dominant group or culture, such as African American women, while co-cultural communication is simply defined as interactions between "dominant" and "non-dominant" groups (Orbe, 1998a, p. 50).

Co-cultural theory builds upon the work of Kramarae's (1981) muted group theory and Smith's (1987) standpoint theory. Both theories recognize that societies are structured hierarchically, designating some groups as dominant, or centered, and other groups as subordinate, or marginal. Thus, muted group theory and standpoint theory acknowledge the operations of power relations in cultural life. Both theories also value the lives and the knowledge of subordinated groups. In addition, both theories are political—muted group in its attention to the power of naming and giving voice and standpoint in its recognition that power relations authorize designated social groups with privilege and others with a subordinate status. As such, standpoint theory calls attention to the fallacy of normality that is assigned to this designation process.

Building on these conceptual underpinnings, Orbe (1998a, 1998b) stated, "co-cultural theory works to create a framework that promotes a greater understanding of the intricate processes by which co-cultural group members (women, people of color, gays, lesbians, bisexuals, etc.) negotiate attempts by others to render their voices muted within dominant society structures" (p. 4). Orbe (1998a, 1998b) also identified the following communicative practices (some of which will be expanded on in the next section) used by co-cultural group members when interacting with dominant group members and within dominant group structures: avoiding, averting controversy, maintaining interpersonal barriers, emphasizing commonalities, exemplifying strengths, mirroring, dissociating, dispelling stereotypes, manipulating stereotypes, embracing stereotypes, developing positive face, censoring self, extensive preparation, overcompensating, communicating self, educating others, intragroup networking, strategic distancing, ridiculing self, using liaisons, increasing visibility, confronting, gaining advantage, bargaining, attacking, and sabotaging others (Orbe, 1998a, p. 55; see Appendix for an explanation of each). As Orbe (1998a) contends, "co-cultural theory seeks to provide a framework to gain insight into how those with little or no societal power communicate with those aligned with the power of dominant societal structures" (p. 9). Therefore, it is of extreme importance to correct the record of existing research and scholarship by providing space for differing voices and perspectives when it comes to life experiences (Orbe, 1998a, p. 10).

Communicative Strategies for Playing

Twenty-six communicative practices were identified by Orbe (1998a, p. 55) but not all were employed by this tenure track professor. As I reviewed my own work towards tenure and promotion, the following 12 communicative practices were identified: avoiding controversy, emphasizing commonalities, exemplifying strengths, dispelling stereotypes, developing positive face, censoring self, extensive preparation, overcompensating, communicating self, educating others, using liaisons, and increasing visibility. Each practice was used alone or in conjunction with another as a tool for working with the evaluative factors for awarding tenure and promotion, namely those of teaching, research/creative activity, service, and collegiality. The following sections provide broader contexts to discuss how I use these practices: learning the rules of the game; the classroom; service and research/creative activities; and collegiality.

Learning the Rules of the Game

From the very first day I joined the faculty, members of my department provided much needed information when it came to promotion and tenure (P & T). I was instructed on what information needed to be retained for the renewal file and how that file should be structured and organized so that it could later be easily transformed into a promotion and/or tenure file. One constant refrain was, "it's all about the file." The Department's P & T committee chairperson did a short workshop for the new hires (who included two White males) to make sure we knew what was expected as it related to teaching, service, and research. Interestingly, during this mini-contract renewal prep session, no direct mention of collegiality was made. However, throughout my first year, mention was frequently made by one of my colleagues about the importance of forming relationships and alliances outside of the Department.

The first three years have been quite an experience. Currently, I am one of 28 full-time Black faculty (14 women and 4 men according to the most recent data) in a state university in the Northeast United States that identifies itself as a teaching university and has a total of 438 full-time faculty members. This number includes tenured, tenure-track, and temporary appointments. I have a 4/4 course load as a tenure-track assistant professor and part of this load consists of holding the position of Basic Course Director for the all university required courses in communication, of which there are 3 courses and a combined 43 sections per semester.

Part of learning the rules was to understand where my role as Basic Course Director fit in the evaluation process for promotion and tenure. I learned that this role fits in multiple places, but specifically as a part of creative activity and collegiality. As Basic Course Director, I am responsible for supervising 19 adjunct faculty, 6 of whom I hired during my first year. I am expected to hold team meetings, develop online resources, and provide opportunities for part-time faculty development, all of which have been a challenge. Currently, collegiality and cooperation with my team of adjuncts has been successful, as they have had to make adjustments and buy into the standardizing of the curriculum across 39 sections for 2 of the basic courses. Part of this success was due to my obtaining a grant to develop and hold workshops for the part-time communication faculty. The workshops covered not only the changes to the curriculum and introduction to the new textbooks, but also assessment, scholarship of teaching, grading, classroom management, and technology in the classroom. This proved to be a positive experience as I was scared of failure and not sure if the well-established members of the adjunct faculty would accept me, some of whom hold the status of emeriti. The communicative practices employed in this context were a combination of using liaisons, extensive preparation, overcompensation, and developing positive face (Orbe, 1998a, Orbe, 1998b).

It was important for me to have the support of the department chair and other members of the full-time faculty as I assumed the role of Basic Course Director. They were the liaisons that served as intermediaries between the former course director and me, in addition to providing a show of confidence for the adjunct faculty. This helped to facilitate a transition that could have turned out to be disastrous due to the uncooperative nature of the former course director, which tainted the position and anyone filling it in the eyes of colleagues. *Using liaisons*, as described by Orbe (1998a, p. 77) is when members of the dominant group can be used for support, guidance, and assistance during interactions.

The next strategy employed a combination of two communicative practices, *extensive preparation* and *overcompensating. Extensive preparation* is a communicative practice that is carefully thought out, with all necessary information researched prior to the interaction (Orbe, 1998a, p. 69). *Overcompensation* is used when a member of a co-cultural group is in consistent face-to-face interaction with dominant group members. Examples of this include working longer hours, meeting deadlines early, and taking initiative on special projects (Orbe, 1998a, p. 71). In advance of meeting with any of the adjunct faculty, I researched other colleges and universities with basic course requirements, requested updated curriculum vitaes and teaching portfolios, and prepared a written survey to assess their needs in order to design the workshop and write the grant to fund it. Some colleagues felt this was going beyond what was needed; however, this strategy proved successful.

The final strategy employed was that of *developing positive face.* This communicative practice involves more than mere politeness for gaining favor. There is an extra measure of respect, attention, politeness, and graciousness when communicating with dominant group members to give the appearance of being less threatening and less assertive (Orbe, 1998a, p. 67). One stereotype that must be overcome, but will not be explicated here, is that of the overaggressive Black woman (for a detailed discussion on Black women stereotypes, see Collins, 2000). Therefore, this practice was used when meeting the adjunct faculty for the first time and when interacting with some senior faculty members.

THE CLASSROOM

The communicative practices necessary for classroom interactions will change from course to course and semester to semester simply because students change. For faculty of color at predominately White institutions, the classroom experience is tenuous at best when it comes to student evaluations (Germain & Scandura, 2005). My teaching evaluations for my first year were excellent. I was even surprised considering that the class discussions in the course on culture got passionately intense regarding topics such as racism, sexism, class, and White privilege. I considered embracing the *averting controversy* (Orbe, 1998a, p. 56) or *censoring self* (Orbe, 1998a, p. 68) communicative practices, but I felt that I could not teach a class on cultural communication without engaging in controversial topics that require comment.

However, the communicative practices I did embrace were those of *emphasizing commonalities*, *exemplifying strengths*, *dispelling stereotypes*, and *educating others. Emphasizing commonalities* focuses on human similarities while deemphasizing co-cultural differences and trying to ignore issues related to racism, classism, sexism, and other potentially controversial topics (Orbe, 1998a, p. 58). However, in the classroom, *emphasizing commonalities* is used as a reminder of shared humanity to deescalate emotional responses in hard conversations.

Exemplifying strengths is a communicative practice that focuses on the significant contributions of co-cultural group members to dominant society. This strategy is necessary to increase the awareness level of the dominant group as it relates to the experiences of co-cultural group members (Orbe, 1998a, p. 59). As a Black woman professor, there are many stereotypes that must be countered while interacting with predominately White students and students from other co-cultural groups. Some students come to the classroom with preconceived notions about minority quotas, feeling that affirmative action is used to "give" jobs to unqualified Blacks. For example, in the classroom, stereotypes related to the validity of my credentials and how I came to work for the university are addressed during conversations related to affirmative action. Using my work history and educational journey is just one way to correct student perceptions of how I "earned" my Ph.D. and competed against other applicants for the position of assistant professor and was not given the position simply because of my color or gender. Orbe (1998a, 1998b) calls this *dispelling stereotypes* (p. 64). In addition, *educating others* (Orbe, 1998a, p. 73) is a communicative practice that might seem obvious in a classroom setting; however, in conjunction with the previous practices, it becomes a strategy that moves beyond textbook materials and instruction.

For me, using the aforementioned communicative strategies in the classroom has had positive results. Classroom effectiveness is the quantitative basis for assessing one's quality of teaching based on student evaluations. My institution has 7,114 full-time undergraduate students, 832 of whom are Black. Each semester, I usually have between zero and five students of color out of twenty. Good teaching evaluations do not come easy, regardless of student demographics, and the challenge increases when none of the students looks like me. The department chair, P & T committee, dean, and provost were impressed with my evaluations, which was important as these are the players who have to recommend and approve my renewal for the next few years.

SERVICE AND RESEARCH/CREATIVE ACTIVITIES

Saying no to various "opportunities" to serve on committees, be interviewed, or serve on panels can help the junior, woman faculty of color avoid some of the mental and physical stresses that come with working on a predominantly White campus. I am keenly aware of what Harley (2008) calls "race fatigue—the syndrome of being over extended, undervalued, unappreciated, and just knowing that because one is the 'negro in residence' that you will be asked to serve and represent the 'color factor' in yet another capacity" (p. 21). Again, in creating a reputation of collegiality and relationship building, I am selective in the ways I serve. As a co-cultural group member, *increased visibility* is a communicative practice that provides an opportunity to make my presence known without being confrontational (Orbe, 1998a, p. 78). Therefore, it is important for me to be selective about committee work.

While serving, I have learned of a shift in the attitude of administration and faculty about the value of creative activities/research and publications; though I work at a teaching university, research and publishing are becoming increasingly important and the days of tenure without publication (for the select few) are drawing to a close. Alternative forms of creative activity will not carry as much weight in the future. A careful reading of the curriculum vitas of the faculty who have earned tenure without publications are few, but they do exist. I recognize, through informal channels, that P & T without publication at this university has become a thing of the past.

There are several areas that are important to me that qualify as service to the university outside of committee work; these include involvement with students beyond academic advising and teaching outside of the traditional classroom. For example, I worked with a multicultural group of students to establish a competitive speech and debate team. In addition, after much contemplation, I accepted an invitation to advise a non-African American service-oriented sorority. Young women from this organization sought my assistance as one of their members had been a former student and submitted my name as a potential advisor to the group. The decision to accept this position was done to avoid the label of only working with Black students on Black issues.

Further, working with students of color who seek me out because they heard I was approachable and helpful is an additional service that is provided, but not recognized, when it comes to the promotion and tenure process. Needless to say, students of all ethnicities seek faculty support for a variety of issues—from how to deal with a racist professor to being overburdened with managing family, work, and school responsibilities. One cannot solve every issue but referrals are made to appropriate counseling services. Finally, my service and teaching extend to my local community as I am a volunteer for a variety of youth-oriented programs and women's organizations. Harley (2008) discusses African American women in the academy simultaneously assuming the roles of "scholars, researchers, educators, mentors, service providers, and social change agents" (p. 24). I see these roles clearly being played out in my service activities. Varieties of co-cultural communicative practices are woven throughout these interactions and have influenced these roles. For instance, the communicative practice of *communicating self* (being genuine to myself) was used in conjunction with *educating others*, *overcompensating*, and *extensive preparation*, all of which were discussed earlier in this chapter.

COLLEGIALITY

Collegiality is viewed as the fourth evaluative factor for promotion and tenure, though it is not something that is easily quantified. It cannot be readily measured and reported. However, collegiality can influence the outcomes of other measurable areas that impact teaching, research/creative activity, and service. Collegiality is especially important for African American women junior faculty. Cornelius, Moore, and Gray (1997) state:

> Far too often African-American faculty are not aware of the 'implicit and unspoken' political environment that exists with regard to the issue of promotion and tenure because they are usually in the minority in terms of numerical representation on campuses and are not always part of the informational network system. (p. 150)

Keeping a low profile, focusing on my work, and minding my own business are not options or strategies that I can use to stay out of the way of racism and sexism. In the framework of co-cultural theory, this represents two communicative practices, *avoiding* and *maintaining interpersonal barriers* (Orbe, 1998a, 1998b). These strategies will be construed as standoffish, anti-social, and self-centered behaviors by the dominant cultural group, my White and senior colleagues. Part of playing the game is building positive, productive relationships with my immediate colleagues in order to be a member of the community. I have found that forming relationships outside of my department has been beneficial to gaining information that is necessary for getting things done administratively, in addition to acquiring travel funds and accessing grant and publishing opportunities.

Creating these relationships has created a space for me to serve on two high-profile university wide committees: the Faculty Senate and the University Strategic Planning and Resource Committee, of which I am one of two presidential appointments. These appointments are significant for me in the tenure process for the following reasons: first, they count as service to the university. Second, they provide an opportunity to build sincere relationships and collegial bonds outside of my department with some of the very individuals who serve or have served on the P & T committee; thus, I have the opportunity to listen and learn about these individuals. As a political process, one has to remember that people, not machines, grant tenure (Cornelius, Moore, & Gray, 1997, p. 151); therefore, it is important that people can place a name with a face.

According to Cooper (2006), institutional politics play an important role in the lives of academics, particularly women, because they often do not recognize that advancing in the academy is like a game. Cooper cited a report by Aisenberg and Harrington that concluded that one has to know the formal and informal rules in order to play the tenure game. This study suggested that the one primary rule most women do not know is that the tenure game is one of politics, not merit. Personally, I recognized it as a game right away and am willing to play and maintain my identity in the process. As I reviewed the literature for this essay, my thoughts and feelings related to the politics of tenure were confirmed, but at the same time I was disappointed to see that not much had changed since the research I reviewed from the 1980s.

Recommendations and Conclusion

The communicative practices that Orbe (1998a, 1998b) outlines in co-cultural theory can be used as strategic tools for negotiating and playing the promotion and tenure game. These co-cultural communicative practices provide implications for the woman, junior faculty member of color. To obtain promotion and tenure, she should be a team player and build and develop relationships with individuals inside and outside of her department and university. Also, she should understand that careful consideration is crucial when selecting the types of service activities she will participate in to maximize visibility, time, talent, and energy. Teaching and service activities should be seriously considered as a source for creative/research and publication. This combination maximizes time and resources towards earning promotion and tenure, but it also means that there must be room for flexibility in the research agenda. Ultimately, and consistent with co-cultural theory, communication and interaction with the dominant group is negotiated to fit the rules set for a game not meant for Black women to play. Recognizing that choices in research agenda, committee work, service to the university, collegiality, and all that goes with working towards tenure and promotion can underscore coming from a different social location (Collins, 2003).

REFERENCES

Alexander, R., & Moore, S. (2008). The benefits, challenges, and strategies of African American faculty teaching at predominantly white institutions. *Journal of African American Studies, 12*, 4-18.

AAUP (1973). 1940 Statement of Principles on Academic Freedom and Tenure. Retrieved from http://www.aaup.org/AAUP/pubsres/policydocs/contents/1940statement.htm

Collins, P. H. (2000). *Black feminist thought: Knowledge, consciousness, and the politics of empowerment.* New York; NY: Routledge.

Collins, P. H. (2003). Some groups matter: Intersectionality, situated standpoints, and Black feminist thought. In T. L. Lott & J. P. (Eds.), *A companion to African American Philosophy* (pp. 205-229). Malden, MA: Blackwell Publishing.

Cooper, J. E., & Stevens, D. D. (Eds.). (2002). *Tenure in the sacred grove: Issues and strategies for women and minority faculty.* Albany, NY: State University of New York.

Cooper, T. L. (2006). *The sista' network: African-American women faculty successfully negotiating the road to tenure.* Bolton, MA: Anker Publishing Company, Inc.

Cornelius, L. J., Moore, S. E., & Gray, M. (1997). The ABCs of tenure: What all African-American faculty should know. *The Western Journal of Black Studies, 21, 150-155.*

Diamantes, T. (2002). Promotion and tenure decisions using the Boyer Model. *Education, 123*, 322-325.

Germain, M., & Scandura, T. A. (2005). Grade inflation and student individual differences as systematic bias in faculty evaluations. *Journal of Instructional Psychology, 32*, 58-67.

Harley, D. (2008). Maids of academe: African American women faculty at predominately white institutions. *Journal of African American Studies, 12*, 19-36.

Kramarae, C. (1981). *Women and men speaking.* Rowley, MA: Newbury House.

Lewin, T. (2002). Collegiality as a tenure battleground. *New York Times (late edition, East Coast).* July 12, p. A12.

Olswang, S. (2003). The future of tenure. *Change, 35*, 36-37.

Orbe, M. (1998a). *Constructing co-cultural theory: An explication of culture, power, and communication.* Thousand Oaks, CA: Sage.

Orbe, M. (1998b). From the standpoint(s) of traditionally muted groups: Explicating a co-cultural communication theoretical model. *Communication Theory, 8*(1), 1-26.

Silverman, T. (2004). *Collegiality and service for tenure and beyond: Acquiring a reputation as a team player.* Westport, CT: Praeger.

Smith, D. E. (1987). *The everyday world as problematic: A feminist sociology of knowing.* Boston, MA: Northeastern University Press.

APPENDIX

CO-CULTURAL COMMUNICATIVE PRACTICES SUMMARY
(Orbe, 1998b, pp. 8-9)

PRACTICE	DESCRIPTION
Attacking	Inflicting psychological pain through personal attacks on dominant group members' self-concept
Averting controversy	Averting communication away from controversial or potentially dangerous subject areas
Avoiding	Maintaining a distance from dominant group members; refraining from activities and/or locations when interaction is likely
Bargaining	Striking a covert or overt arrangement with dominant group members in which both parties agree to ignore co-cultural differences
Censoring self	Remaining silent when comments from dominant group members are inappropriate, indirectly insulting, or highly offensive
Communicating self	Interacting with dominant group members in an authentic, open, and genuine manner; used by those with strong self-concepts
Confronting	Using the necessary aggressive methods, including ones that seemingly violate the "rights" of others; to assert one's voice
Developing positive face	Assuming a gracious communicator stance in which one is more considerate, polite, and attentive to dominant group members
Dispelling stereotypes	Myths of generalized group characteristics and behaviors are countered through the process of just being oneself
Dissociating	Making a concerted effort to elude any connection with behaviors typically associated with one's co-cultural group
Educating others	Taking the role of teacher in co-cultural interactions; enlightening dominant group members of co-cultural norms, values, and so forth
Embracing stereotypes	Applying a negotiated reading to dominant group perceptions and merging them into a positive co-cultural self-concept

(cont'd on next page)

(cont'd from previous page)

Emphasizing commonalities	Focusing on human similarities while downplaying or ignoring co-cultural differences
Exemplifying strengths	Promoting the recognition of co-cultural group strengths, past accomplishments, and contributions to society
Extensive preparation	Engaging in an extensive amount of detailed (mental or concrete) groundwork prior to interactions with dominant group members
Gaining advantage	Inserting references to co-cultural oppression to provoke dominant group reactions and gain advantage
Increasing visibility	Covertly, yet strategically, maintaining a co-cultural presence within dominant structures
Intragroup networking	Identifying and working with other co-cultural group members who share common philosophies, convictions, and goals
Maintaining barriers	Imposing, through the use of verbal and nonverbal cues, a psychological distance from dominant group members
Manipulating stereotypes	Conforming to commonly accepted beliefs about group members as a strategic means to exploit them for personal gain
Mirroring	Adopting dominant group codes in attempts to make one's co-cultural identity less (or totally not) visible
Overcompensating	Conscious attempts—consistently employed in response to a pervasive fear of discrimination—to become a "superstar"
Ridiculing self	Invoking or participating in discourse, either passively or actively, which is demeaning to co-cultural group members
Sabotaging others	Undermining the ability of dominant group members to take full advantage of their privilege inherent in dominant structures
Strategic distancing	Avoiding association with other co-cultural group members in attempts to be perceived as a distinct individual
Using liaisons	Identifying specific dominant group members who can be trusted for support, guidance, and assistance

Responding to 'Otherness'

Navigating Identity

Chapter 8

Barriers to Being Heard in a Majority Institution

Kamille Gentles-Peart

American universities, in response to global forces, have developed diversity objectives and have increasingly opened their doors to non-white, non-American faculty women from formerly colonized, developing nations, or the so-called "third world." However, being shaped by a Eurocentric and imperialistic history, these institutions foster ideological and material barriers that can coalesce to silence these new faculty members, limiting their contributions to the university. Employing feminist postcolonial discourses of neocolonialism and power, this chapter highlights some of the mechanisms at work in a predominantly white, American university that can suppress the voices of these immigrant black women from developing nations. Specifically, I employ Gayatri Spivak's (1988) concept of subaltern silencing to frame discussions of how prevailing discourses of equality and postmodernism, in addition to the valorization of dominant American cultural norms, can work to exclude immigrant black women from fully participating in and contributing to the intellectual and administrative life of the "majority" institutions in which they are situated.

Prelude: A "Third World" Woman in a Predominantly White American University

The arguments presented in this treatise are based on my experience as a "third world" immigrant, who is also a newly-hired, female, tenure-track faculty member at a predominantly white American university. Allow me to preface my analysis by sharing some of the experiences that shaped my opinions, and which are the catalysts for this chapter.

In a meeting during one summer break, the issue of racially-motivated acts of violence in our student body was raised, and one of my white colleagues asked if I had experienced any racism from my students. I was stunned by the question and the immediate attention bestowed on me from the other persons at the table. Prior to this moment in the meeting, my colleagues had not acknowledged issues of racial diversity (nor cultural or ethnic difference) at the university; that is to say, explorations of racially and culturally different perspectives, experiences, and problems were excluded from our discussions of plans and policies for the coming academic year. In fact, my own "otherness" as a black immigrant woman in the U.S. seemed unnoticed as my colleagues consistently drew on culturally-specific, mainstream knowledge—which they assumed everyone would understand—to explain and substantiate their comments. Furthermore, my perspectives and interjections, which were perhaps perceived as esoteric and quaint, were politely declined in favor of more mainstream points of view. So, to now be asked about victimization on the basis of my race was odd. It seemed as if the influence and validity of my difference was acknowledged only in relation to how others responded to me and not in relation to how my racial and cultural location could enrich our discussion and the university at large. It was as if as an "other," I could be recognized in the paradigms of oppression and victimization, but not as an agent with valuable contributions to make. Having acquiesced to the general suppression of racial and cultural difference in the meeting so far, I was surprised by this question that now made race in general, and my racialized body in particular, very salient.

Second, I did not know how to respond. Based on the preceding conversation, I knew that the question was in relation to my experience with classical and overt racism—that is, the use of racial epitaphs and stereotypes in my presence. During the time that I had been at the university, none of my students or colleagues had exhibited such behavior or used such language, so the easy answer to the latent question was no. Yet, I did have to contend with students challenging my authority, questioning the content of the class, and appearing in my office to offer "advice" on how to conduct the class meetings and structure assignments, all of which were perhaps reactions to my race. However, almost all of these challenges came from my male students, an indication of gendered power struggles. Furthermore, I have a discernable accent that marks me as "foreign," and my petite stature and youthful appearance are often mistaken for intellectual immaturity. These factors can also prime patronizing attitudes and behaviors. The simultaneous workings of these social symbols—young, black, female, immigrant—create a multiplicative effect that renders it impossible and futile to distinguish responses to each discrete element (Crenshaw, 1991).

Also, what about other forms of bigotry from other areas of the institution? Should I discuss what I felt were the underlying problems of the university of which the recent incidents were symptomatic, or should I mention the less overt and less socially-offensive forms of ethnocentrism that I had experienced? Would it be appropriate for me to talk about how I often feel like an outsider, even in this very moment in the meeting? Cognitively struggling with all of these arguments, and only having a few seconds to formulate an answer, I responded the best way I could: "I don't know. They could be responding to my race, the fact that I'm a woman and an immigrant, or all of these." My colleagues nodded in agreement, but did not pursue the topic any further. We returned to the business at hand.

I left that meeting with a familiar feeling, one that I had often experienced after so many other meetings throughout the school year: disheartened. There were so many things I wanted to express in these gatherings, but I did not know how to voice them, how to let myself be heard and understood. The organizers would often thank me (and others) for my contribution, but I knew that I had not significantly impacted the decisions that were made, or the plans of action taken. I was disturbed and discouraged by my lack of "presence" in these meetings, and equally bothered that my level of participation seemed fine to everyone else. While my raced, gendered, and foreign body posed challenges in the classroom, the most painful adversities came in these moments of dealing with being concurrently highly visible, yet intellectually absent and thus, silenced.

This problem was partially borne from the fact that, as a junior faculty member just out of graduate school, I was struggling to find confidence and my own voice in an unfamiliar personal and physical location. However, there were other exogenous factors that contributed to my muted existence at the institution. As an immigrant woman from the "third world" participating in an educational institution shaped by an imperialistic history, there are, as Spivak (1988) notes, limitations to speaking and becoming, and to developing subjectivity.

The Postcolonial Subject and Neo-imperialistic Silencing

According to Spivak (1988), Western intellectual spaces do not allow subalterns (women from formerly colonized nations) to realize and claim consciousness, voice, and subjectivity within their structures. Far from being neutral, these spaces embrace imperialistic discourses that tend to relegate women of former colonies to the margins and render them invisible. She states, "the subject of exploitation cannot know and speak the text of female exploitation even if the absurdity of the non-representing intellectual making space for her to speak is achieved" (p. 288).

Such silencing is evident among women of the geo-political "third world" participating in U.S. mainstream academia. They must function within interlocking axes of race, gender, and nation, systems that create complicated "outsider within" positions (Collins, 1998). As raced and gendered bodies, they necessarily contend with the white male epistemologies of their institutions, but as non-U.S. subjects, they also have to wrestle with American ideologies and ethnocentrism. Though much work has been done to debunk the exoticized images of women from formerly colonized nations, Americans generally perceive women from these countries as an essentialized, undifferentiated category, rather than complex social and cultural beings. They are seen as infantilized victims of their own culture, and as women who need rescuing. They are stereotyped as technologically and intellectually backward, and not productive members of society. Ultimately, they are perceived as different from and inferior to their Western counterparts (Lazreg, 2001; Ong, 2001). This tradition persists even in the face of increased "third world" presence in the U.S., or as Ruth Frankenberg and Lata Mani (2001) state, "the repressed" return "on the borders of the imperialistic center" (p. 486).

Black women emigrating from formerly colonized countries to Western nations are thus not entering an "ideological vacuum," but have to exist in spaces that historically have stereotyped them as "illiterate beasts of burden, bearers of many children, and the guardians of tradition" (Phizacklea, 2001, p. 323). Such women who choose to participate in Western institutions are required to speak and have their experiences interpreted within these standards (Lazreg, 2001; Ong, 2001). In other words, they are forced to "represent themselves in terms that already subsume and contain their representation" (Lazreg, 2001, p. 287). These naturalized ethnocentric, racist, and sexist thoughts within Western academia have symbolically silenced "third world" faculty women.

Even more pernicious than overt and explicit prejudice, however, are the Western discourses established to propagate subaltern voices, but which essentially reinforce their marginalization. Much of the so-called progressive rhetoric that is prolific in Western institutions and scholarship only recuperate imperialistic violence and serve to further silence the subaltern in academia. In fact, Spivak (1988) argues that the very discourses established in Western institutions to empower and engage women from this part of the world necessarily rehearse and reproduce subaltern silence and erasure. She asserts that,

> We should . . . welcome all the information retrieval in these silenced areas. . . . Yet the assumption and construction of a consciousness or subject . . . will, in the long run, cohere with the work of imperialist subject-constitution, mingling epistemic violence with the advancement of learning and civilization. And the subaltern woman will be as mute as ever. (p. 295)

I argue that discourses of equality and postmodernism, all ubiquitous on predominantly white American university campuses, can function in this manner. While parading as empowering, they collude in the silencing of black women from the "third world." In addition, I argue that latent expectations to acquiescence to dominant American cultural norms further contribute to the silencing of the subaltern. I discuss each in more detail below.

SUBALTERN SILENCING AND THE RHETORIC OF EQUALITY

A progressive discourse that ironically works to silence the voices of immigrant black women in predominantly white American institutions is the rhetoric of equality. Equality (that is, consistency in status, opportunity, and treatment regardless of gender, race, class, religion, etc.) is promoted in American universities and seems to create spaces within which immigrant black women may realize their voices. However, such women are often disappointed as they soon realize that the availability of opportunities parallel to their peers is contingent on their level of sameness. Western ideology seems to conflate difference and inequality (Jaipal, 2006; Weedon, 2002). In other words, Eurocentric societies tend to perceive as their equals only those who share their value systems and worldviews, so that those who are perceived as "other" and "foreign" are denied moral, cultural, and intellectual equality. Therefore, within American society, social and political equity can only be conceded and claimed when difference is renounced and sameness is embraced. In fact, many human rights movements in the U.S., such as the Civil Rights Movement and the first and second waves of mainstream feminism, have couched their demands in discourses of similarity (Weedon, 2002). However well-intentioned, the minimization of difference to promote equality is not always beneficial to the marginalized, because, as Christine Stanley (2006) suggests, it requires the erasure of their differentiating characteristics, indeed their subjectivities. This rhetoric of equality thus promotes ethnocentricism and assimilationism (Jaipal, 2006).

Nevertheless, such logic continues to prevail in American society, and is very prominent within academia. The institutions "talk a good game about valuing diversity among colleagues in the academy, yet [they] want to be able to maintain systems of power and privilege by asking those who are 'different' to walk the assimilation line and be like the majority" (Stanley, 2006, p. 337). This means that non-white, non-Western women (who are dissimilar to even minority, American-born women) have to downplay their cultural difference and become like "normal" faculty in order to be perceived as the intellectual equal of their white colleagues. They have to remain ethnically inconspicuous, refraining from adorning themselves in cultural garb and speaking with as little accent as possible, and they must become less vocal about cultural diversity. Therefore, this particular rhetoric of equality rehearses rather than dispels imperialistic silencing of postcolonial subjects in U.S. academia.

SUBALTERN SILENCING AND POSTMODERN THOUGHT

In addition to discourses of equality, discursive mechanisms that minimize difference and silence "others" in the academy have also emanated from postmodern ideas. Noted for its critical and rhetorical practices, the movement of postmodernism conceptually encourages reflexivity and self-consciousness in academic endeavors, the deconstruction of binary categorizations and essentialist subjects, and the celebration of difference and diversity. In spite of its significance in reframing scholarship and academia, however, several scholars, particularly in women's studies and postcolonial studies, have cautioned against the uncritical acceptance and application of postmodern tenets, some of which have negative implications for oppressed groups (see Butler, 2003; Parameswaran, 2001). Specifically, the postmodernist call for the deconstruction of the subject has meant that marginalized populations—who have just now begun to gain the power to speak and represent themselves—now have to announce the "death" of the subject, and thus reinforce colonialist and ethnocentric practices of the past (Parameswaran, 2001). Such a move has repercussions for scholarship (as it makes it unfashionable to study identity groups), but also has ramifications for diversity projects in the U.S. By fueling post-identity and post-ethnicity ideologies, it has erased platforms from which the inequalities based on race, culture, and gender can be presented because that which does not exist cannot experience discrimination and certainly cannot speak of it. Ethnicity and identity are depoliticized, and the subaltern experience is muted.

This discourse has also affected the collegiality among faculty on campuses, engendering a backlash against expressions of the marginalization of immigrant women faculty. Displays of non-whiteness and non-Westerness are encouraged on campus, but only in neo-liberal, exoticized ways that allow Western audiences to consume and "appreciate" it, shoring up their own cosmopolitanism and reinforcing imperialistic ideas of the female ethnic body as valuable for its ethnicity (hooks, 1992). For instance, cultural festivals are promoted on campuses, where ethnic cuisine, dances, and dress are displayed. However, these events are often staged exhibitions and spectacles of the ethnic, designed for white American members of the campus community to gaze at (and consume) the other.

Similarly, while discrimination against non-white and non-Western faculty is discussed, these discussions are often led by (well-intentioned) Western colleagues, viewed as progressive for championing the issue, but who fail to grasp the multiplicative effects of racism, sexism, *and* ethnocentrism (Crenshaw, 1991) on the experiences of immigrant black women within their midst.

Conversely, the culturally and racially different who try to address the real issues that stem from their "otherness," or who try to produce works that debunk stereotypes about their communities, are dismissed. So, revelations of my Jamaican nationality have been met with expressions such as "Oooh, Jamaica! It's so beautiful!" from my American colleagues. By making latent and overt references to the island's "paradise" and exotic image, these colleagues also inherently conjure the accompanying idea of the friendly, but backward and dull-witted, native. Meanwhile, my discussions of the social, political, and economical problems of Jamaica and its legacy of imperialism and colonization generate less interest than discussions of the music, food, and beaches of "di i'land." Furthermore, my attempts to explain to white American colleagues the challenges I face as a new faculty member have been frustrating, garnering responses of "I went through the same thing," which denies the distinctive effect of my otherness on my experiences. Thus, the deconstruction of the subject has not erased difference in universities per se, but has contained and depoliticized it, allowing it to be palatable for white and Western members of academia. Meanwhile, the ethnic subaltern is rendered mute.

SUBALTERN SILENCING AND AMERICAN CULTURAL NORMS

While the continued silencing of immigrant black women in predominantly white American institutions often comes from restraints imposed by the dominant culture, the incapacity—or disinclination—to speak may also be created by their own cultural norms and heritage, or rather, the conflict between their cultures and that of the institution. A major conflict is engendered by what Jaipal (2006) refers to as the "American style of communication," which privileges extroverted personality types (p. 192). Here, Jaipal (2006) expands on this notion:

> It seems that shyness and reserve are not appreciated. Instead one should be outgoing and friendly, with an open and frank style of communicating, even with strangers. If [one] does not talk or volunteer some general comments and observations at a faculty gathering, [one] is seen as unfriendly or uninterested in participating. . . . [T]he expected norm of workplace behavior is to put oneself forward and not be modest about one's accomplishments, and not to admit mistakes or put [one]self down, but to always put a positive spin on what one has done; that is, employ euphemisms. (p. 192)

Women in academia who emigrated from cultures that hold different views on public communications find expressing themselves within this mainstream American framework very challenging. This cultural difference does not merely create misunderstandings that may be rectified through acclimating to the new culture. Rather, it greatly impacts immigrant women's effective participation in and contributions to the intellectual and administrative life of a "majority" campus.

As an immigrant from Jamaica, where I was taught to speak when spoken to[1], and where garrulousness is deemed socially unacceptable, I still have difficulty voicing unsolicited ideas. My discomfort with "speaking up" among my colleagues pales in comparison only to the anxiety I feel with regard to networking, the practice of approaching strangers, introducing oneself, and engaging in the dreaded "small talk." In fact, I am still relatively unfamiliar with the rules of American banter: What are the right questions to ask? Which topics are proscribed? How much should one talk about oneself versus the other person? Talking about oneself is also frowned upon in Jamaican society, where it is more appropriate to be acknowledged and promoted by others. Therefore, in an environment where self-publicity is the norm, many of my accomplishments go unnoticed.

In addition, speaking the same language does not guarantee mutual understanding. Even though English is my native tongue, I often have difficulty communicating with my American colleagues as dominant American and Jamaican connotations of many words and phrases differ, and there are no American translations for several Jamaican expressions. The frames of reference once available for my use to ensure and increase understanding of my communiqués are of no effect in the American context. Furthermore, phonetical differences in American and Jamaican English have resulted in my "mispronunciation" of many words by American standards. On several occasions, my comments have generated blank and confused expressions, silence, and misinterpretations. Besides misunderstandings stemming from cultural difference, I also have to contend with my remarks and ideas being disregarded by my peers. When I express points of view and perspectives that differ from the dominant views, rather than being accepted as a standpoint shaped by a non-American, non-Western cultural heritage, they are often ignored. I am allowed to share my comments, but, though acknowledged as good points, they are often perceived as personal activism, bracketed as being outside of the scope of the discussion, or else referred to the appropriate "diversity" committee. This dismissal may be partially attributed to my perceived youth and my junior faculty status, but it is also evident that my opinions are not reflective of the mainstream or American perspective, and thus not "useful."

I have been frustrated and embarrassed enough times as a member of faculty that I am apprehensive and discouraged about expressing myself in American company and to American colleagues. I have begun to question myself and what I know, feeling that how I think, my perspectives, indeed, everything that allows me to make unique contributions to my field, are wrong, and in doing so I collude in my own silencing. Lucila Vargas (1999) comments on this phenomenon when she says, "Like other stigmatized individuals often do, the Other Teacher might begin to question her own legitimacy. Despite her educational capital, she may feel like an impostor . . . [and have] doubts about her self-worth, which are manifestations of internalized oppression" (p. 370). The subaltern thus silences herself.

CONCLUSION

American universities that serve predominantly white students have developed diversity objectives that include intentionally recruiting international faculty from formerly colonized nations of the world. Such a move should be appraised with caution, however, as these very institutions foster discourses that recuperate imperialistic violence. Specifically, I have argued that the rhetoric of equality and postmodern thought that are prolific on American campuses and that offer the promise of voice or subjectivity to subaltern women, can silence rather than empower these subjects. In addition, expectations to acquiesce to American cultural norms may serve to further marginalize and silence these subalterns who are not familiar with American mores.

The inclusion of immigrant black women in the faculty of predominantly white American institutions has important pedagogical and scholastic implications for the institutions, but only if the universities are willing to practice diversity rather than stage it. Often, organizations opt for cosmetic rather than substantive inclusion of subalterns (Collins, 1999). In fact, many choose black women for their faculty as the presence of their multiply-"othered" bodies can be used by the institutions to symbolize their commitment to diversity. Real progress can only happen when the administration and the faculty of these spaces of higher education promote an environment in which "others" are able and willing to speak, where they feel physically as well as psychologically safe. The growing self-reflexivity of white American faculty is a step towards fostering such an atmosphere, but that is not enough; efforts made by white American faculty on behalf of "other" faculty will keep the former at the center of the discourse, and will, as Ong (2001) says, result in them "speak[ing] without reducing the silence of the cultural Other" (p. 109). To avoid simply having conversations among themselves (dialogue that would only have patronizing and paternalistic results), the voices of "outsiders within" (Collins, 1998) must also be sought and encouraged. As Weedon (2002) says, it is possible to imagine a world where difference is embraced and celebrated, but "to move towards such a world continues to require the articulation of marginalized voices and the self-affirmation of oppressed groups as well as the recognition by white, Western, heterosexual, middle class women [and men] of their structural privileges" (p. 10).

Finally, to reduce their own silencing, subalterns must recognize the progressive possibilities of their "outsider within" positions (Collins, 1999). Rather than view their location with pessimism, immigrant black women on the faculty of predominantly white American institutions should use "the insights gained via outsider-within status" as "a stimulus to creativity" that can be rewarding for subalterns as well their institutional homes, and can be a platform to promote social justice (Collins, 1999, p. 88). Furthermore, rather than succumbing to assimilationist discourses, they should embrace their difference, knowing that their very presence in these institutions may be used to challenge and question mainstream Western ideologies. This is by no means an easy task; it will take courage—and a strong, supportive community—for subalterns to claim their voices in these ideologically hostile environments. Nevertheless, such bravery will take us one step closer to finding our "mothers' gardens" (Walker, 1983).

NOTE

1. Being a heterogeneous nation, not all Jamaicans were raised in this manner.

REFERENCES

Butler, J. (2003). Gender trouble, feminist theory, and psychoanalytic discourse. In L. Alcoff & E. Mendieta (Eds.), *Identities: Race, class, gender, and nationality* (pp. 201-211). Oxford, MA: Blackwell Publishing.

Collins, P. H. (1998). *Fighting words: Black women and the search for justice*. Minneapolis, MN: University of Minnesota Press.

Collins, P. H. (1999). Reflections on the outsider within. *Journal of Career Development, 26*(1), 85-88.

Crenshaw, K. (1991). Mapping the margins: Intersectionality, identity politics, and violence against women of color. *Stanford Law Review, 43*(6),1241-1299.

Frankenburg, R., & Mani, L. (2001). Crosscurrents, crosswalks: Race, 'postcoloniality' and the politics of location. In K. K. Bhavnani (Ed.), *Feminism and "race"* (pp. 479-491). Oxford, MA: Oxford University Press.

hooks, b. (1992). *Black looks: Race and representation*. Boston, MA: South End Press.

Jaipal, R. (2006). Anatomy of "difference": The meaning of diversity and the diversity of meaning. In C. Stanley (Ed.), *Faculty of color: Teaching in predominantly white colleges and universities* (pp.182-195). Boston, MA: Anker Publishing Company, Inc.

Lazreg, M. (2001). Decolonizing feminism. In K. K. Bhavnani (Ed.), *Feminism and "race"* (pp. 281-293). Oxford, MA: Oxford University Press.

Ong, A. (2001). Colonialism and modernity: Feminist re-presentations of women in non-Western societies. In K. K. Bhavnani (Ed.), *Feminism and "race"* (pp. 108-118). Oxford, MA: Oxford University Press.

Parameswaran, R. (2001). Resuscitating feminist audience studies: Colonialism, occidentalism, and the control of women. Presented at annual meeting of Association for the Education in Journalism and Media Studies. Retrieved from http://list.msu.edu/cgi-bin/wa?A2=ind0109A&L=aejmc&P=11475

Phizacklea, A. (2001). Women, migration and the State. In K. K. Bhavnani (Ed.), *Feminism and "race"* (pp. 319-330). Oxford, MA: Oxford University Press.

Spivak, G. (1988). Can the subaltern speak? In C. Nelson & L. Grossberg (Eds.), *Marxism and the interpretation of culture* (pp. 271-313). London, England: MacMillan.

Stanley, C. (2006). Walking between two cultures: The often misunderstood Jamaican woman. In C. Stanley (Ed.), *Faculty of color: Teaching in predominantly white colleges and universities* (pp. 328-345). Boston, MA: Anker Publishing Company Inc.

Vargas, L. (1999). When the "Other" is the teacher: Implications of teacher diversity in higher education. *The Urban Review, 31(4)*, 359-383.

Walker, A. (1983). *In search of our mothers' gardens: Womanist prose*. Orlando, FL: Houghton Mifflin Harcourt.

Weedon, C. (2002). Key issues in postcolonial feminism: A Western perspective. *genderealisations,1*. Retrieved from http://www.genderforum.uni-koeln.de/genderealisations/weedon.html

Chapter 9

Women of Colour in the Academy
The South Asian 'Corner'

Peruvemba S. Jaya
Rukhsana Ahmed

The story never stops beginning or ending. It appears headless and bottomless-for it is built on differences. . . . We—you and me, she and he, we and they—we differ in the content of the words, in the construction and weaving of sentences but most of all, I feel, in the choice and mixing of utterances, the ethos, the tones, the paces, the cuts, the pauses. The story circulates like a gift; an empty gift which anybody can lay claim to by filling it to taste, yet can never truly possess. A gift built on multiplicity. (Minh-ha, 1989, p. 2)

Using a communicative approach, this chapter focuses on a conversation between the authors about our experiences as two colleagues who are women of colour in a department of communication. The chapter situates us in a space and location that is built upon our strengths, similarities, and differences. We envelop and embed this in a theoretical frame informed by the intersection of gender with multiple facets of race, ethnicity, religion, immigrant status, and language (Denis, 2006; Tastsoglou, 2006). We find that the postcolonial feminist framework addresses and resonates with some of the challenges we face and the perspectives we share (Mohanty, 2003; Spivak, 1999). We approach this chapter methodologically using Bakhtin's (1981) dialogism.

Both of us are immigrant women of colour in a Canadian institution and have similar ethnic and racial attributes. Our standpoints, as we see ourselves, differ in terms of nationality or imagined nationhood (Anderson, 1995) and in religious belief systems: one is Hindu and the other Islamic. However, we feel that because of our common South Asian backgrounds, one from India and the other from Bangladesh, we are viewed as the common exotic "Other," a term coined by Said (1978) to refer to the opposition and duality between the colonized and the colonizer. The "Other" is also used to define the way history has constructed and shaped the dialectical relationship between the colonized self and the colonized Other to create the process of "othering," which results in exclusion. In the context of our chapter, we incorporate Said's use of the term to reference our experiences as women of color in academia. Said (1978) stated that Western writings about the Orient depict it as a weak, feminised Other, in contrast to a strong, masculine West. We therefore use the term to explain and situate ourselves as women from former colonized parts of the world who fall into the trap of being viewed as the Other in Western societies. This othering carries with it the connotations of being excluded, being seen as exotically different, and as possessing an aura of mystery and inscrutability. Most importantly, nuances that differentiate us in ways that are significant to us, such as language (Tamil and Bengali) are made invisible through this process of othering that we both experience in the academy.

While communicatively discussing our experiences in different arenas—the classroom, individual interactions, institutional meetings, and our scholarly and research activities—we use a two-pronged conversational approach. The conversation provides a space for us to present our common stories through an exchange that does not privilege one of us over the other. At the same time, we recognize our unique and separate identities and stories; hence, we give individual voice to our reflections.

We write this chapter acknowledging our very specific identities; that is, being Indian and Bangladeshi, being Hindu and Muslim, and having had separate life courses. However, we share certain underlying commonalities; for example, being South Asian and being women of colour. As such, our conversation creates synergy, shared subjectivity, and intersubjectivity, thus revealing our impressions in varied contexts. First, we present a conversation that has been part of an ongoing dialogue between us as colleagues, friends, and women of colour. In the second part of the chapter, we present our individual reflections as women of colour in the academy. In this way we present both our shared stories as well as our individual narratives, which facilitate the exploration of our interpersonal intersections and our self reflective and introspective aspects with the aim of "[connecting] the personal to the cultural" (Ellis & Bochner, 2000, p. 739). The common underlying concurrent and recurring themes that we find are the issues of voice (or lack of it in many instances), issues of power (or lack of it), and the ways in which we have to negotiate and renegotiate ourselves in the context of the academy so we can reclaim both voice and power, or at least attempt to do so.

THEORETICAL FRAMEWORK

We ground our discussion in the theoretical tradition of feminist scholarship as it provides an adequate framework for undergirding our shared and individual stories.

THE FEMINIST LENS

It is true that feminist scholarship embraces a variety of theoretical and disciplinary boundaries, and that an exhaustive survey of the infinite rainbow of opinions is not the central focus of this chapter (for varying opinions of feminist scholarship see Ghosh & Bose, 1997; Mills & Tancred, 1992; Shiva, 1988; Smith, 1987; Spivak, 1987). However, there exists a common core interlinking feminist writings, which is to question the assumptions of predominantly male-centered analysis. The discourse of feminist scholarship positions itself as the voice of the female "Other," even while there may be a diversity of issues being addressed. As Smith (1987) states:

> Being excluded, as women have been, from the making of ideology, of knowledge, and of culture means that our experience, our interests, our ways of knowing the world have not been represented in the organization of our ruling nor in the systematically developed knowledge that has entered into it. (pp. 17-18)

Smith raises a point about the exclusion of women's voices through a process of representing the authority of the male voice and institutionalizing it through time. This, argues Smith, forces women to treat their own experiences and feelings as irrelevant and even more disturbing, "to live inside a discourse that is not ours and that expresses and describes a landscape in which we are alienated" (Smith, 1987, p. 36). Further, this discourse uses that alienation to perpetuate the authority of the male voice and subdue the female voice.

The feminist voice cuts across other lines of difference such as race, ethnicity, nationality, colour, etc. As Mohanty (1991) explains:

> The relationship between "Woman"—a cultural and ideological composite Other constructed through diverse representational discourses . . . and "women" —real material subjects of their collective histories—is one of the central ques-

> tions the practice of feminist scholarship seeks to address. . . . It is an arbitrary relation set up by particular cultures . . . [that] . . . discursively colonize the material historical heterogeneities of the lives of women in the third world thereby producing/re-presenting a composite, singular "third world woman"—an image which . . . nevertheless carries with it the authorizing signature of Western humanist discourse. (p. 53)

Having considered the general spread of feminist theory, we now specifically examine postcolonial feminism and its relevance to our discussion in this chapter. We believe that this feminist approach is central to situate our experience, reflections, and conversation.

POSTCOLONIAL FEMINISM

The postcolonial feminist framework as embodied by Mohanty (1991) and Spivak (1987) is even more focused in terms of our experience. Postcolonial feminism posits that the effects of colonialism and the colonial experience have an impact on understanding and locating the experiences of women from non-Western societies. This historical caveat places these women's experiences in a context that is different from their Western counterparts. That is, postcolonial feminism does not universalize women's issues. Instead, one of its central arguments is to question the use of the term 'woman' as a universal group in Western feminism. Western feminism identifies women's experiences only according to gender and not by social class or ethnic identity (Min-ha, 1989; Narayan, 2000). Important nuances that differentiate women in various parts of the world in unique ways are lost when placing all women in one category. It is also believed by postcolonial feminists that mainstream Western feminists ignored the voices of non-white, non-Western women for many years (Mohanty, 2003; Spivak, 1988).

While we share with all other women in the feminist discourse the othering process, the exclusion as women, and being on the periphery of a male centric workplace universe, we also, as ethnic women of colour, have certain unique experiences that go beyond the universal female experience. The intersections of race, gender, and ethnicity that postcolonial feminism addresses and highlights, and the non-Western nature based in the history of postcolonial societies from which we both hail are very important as foundational constructs and theoretical building blocks for this chapter. In addition, along with other women of colour in the Canadian academic context (Agnew, 2003; Bannerji, 1995; Dhruvarajan & Vickers, 2002; Tastsoglou, 2006), we position ourselves in terms of the experiences of immigrant women of colour.

Thus, the feminist framework in general, and more specifically, the postcolonial feminist lens, as well as our positions as Canadian immigrant women scholars, provide us with the contextual background and setting to place our voices and our experiences as South Asian women of colour in the academy.

The postcolonial feminist theoretical approach is extremely relevant to situating and locating ourselves since we both belong to former colonized countries and have also moved from our countries of origin to the West. This gives us a vehicle to place our voices in a historical context, which enables us to give a contextualized account of our experiences as women of color in the academy, an account that is not representative of all women in the academy. We are women of colour from South Asia and so we privilege our unique space/s, place/s, and location/s and acknowledge our very specific experiences. The postcolonial feminist frame, as explained above, makes us appreciate our unique position as immigrant women of colour and not just as women in a universal sense.

Methodological Framework

Bakhtin's Dialogic Approach

We approach this chapter methodologically using Bakhtin's (1981) dialogism. Dialogue is discourse's desire for discipline and transparency, which is approximated to the extent that meta-communicative openings—communicating about current communication patterns, processes, and practices—are available to all participants (Hawes, 2003). It is in this context that Bakhtin's notion of language (i.e. dialogue) in the form of heteroglossia, or the multilayered nature of language, provides a useful framework for us to use our voices and opinions as evidence when we tell our shared stories and individual narratives.

In his seminal piece, *The Dialogic Imagination*, Bakhtin (1981) introduces the concept of dialogism, which refers to intertextuality, or linkages across texts. Dialogism can be defined as the necessary relation of any utterance to other utterances, using utterance in a very inclusive sense as referring to communicative phenomena or language ranging from bodily gestures and spoken phrases to artistic texts. According to Bakhtin, language is learned through contextualized social interaction, which brings us to the related notion of heteroglossia.

Bakhtin (1981) supports heteroglossia, a multiplicity of languages in a culture, over monologic language, language coming from a single, unified force. Heteroglossia, another name for the socially generated contradictions that constitute the subject, like the media, is the site of conflicting discourses and competing voices. A voice is never merely a voice; it also relays a discourse, because within the Bakhtinian perspective an individual voice is a sum, or a polyphony, of voices. Polyphony points to the juxtaposition of voices and how they are counterposed to generate something beyond themselves. Each cultural voice for Bakhtin exists in dialogue with other voices. A plurality of voices does not fuse into a single consciousness but instead generates dialogical dynamism.

Bakhtin (1981) also discusses two forces in terms of language use, namely, centripetal and centrifugal. Operating from a centripetal force, monologic language tries to push all the elements of language into one single form or utterance. Centrifugal forces, on the other hand, move language towards multiplicity, which creates heteroglossia—a multiplicity of languages in a culture. According to Bakhtin, heteroglossia and monologia, the centrifugal and centripetal forces of language, are constantly in operation in any utterance. He says that "every concrete utterance of a speaking subject serves as a point where centrifugal as well as centripetal forces are brought to bear" (Bakhtin, 1981, p. 272). However, Bakhtin is sensitive to the "reductive nature of monologic discursive frames," and privileges "heteroglossic [modes] of narrative discourse" (McIntire, 2005, p. 31) that enable dialogue and create opportunities for individuals to express themselves.

In this chapter, we describe heteroglossia as the collection of the various forms of social speech, or rhetorical modes, that we use in the course of our daily lives. For example, first, we engage in a dialogue between us inquiring into our lived academic experiences as Indian and Bangladeshi female scholars in the academy. Then, we engage in individual reflections. The Bakhtinian approach helps us advance the common goal of formulating a more nuanced, dynamic, and multidimensional framework as we use our voices and opinions as evidence while telling our shared stories and individual narratives. Bakhtin (1986) explains what he calls the inherent dialogism of the utterance:

> Utterances are not indifferent to one another, and are not self-sufficient; they are aware of and mutually reflect one another. . . . Each utterance is filled with echoes and reverberations of other utterances to which it is related by the communality of the sphere of speech communication. (p. 91)

Hence, the use of a Bakhtinian approach enables our collective conversations and individual reflections to emphasize less of a kind of one-to-one mimetic adequacy to sociological or historical truth than the interplay of voices, discourses, and perspectives.

The discussion now turns to the conversations between us and will be followed by our individual reflections on our experiences as women of colour in the academy.

LET'S TALK: SHARING OUR STORIES AND EXPERIENCES

This section narrates our personal and professional experiences as women of colour in the academy. We unfold our shared stories and our individual narratives that speak to our lived experiences as immigrant women of colour in a Canadian institution. More specifically, we reflect on our race, ethnicity, religion, immigrant status, and language as important factors in our scholarly and research activities in the Canadian context. In doing so, we examine the importance of stories, grounded in real life experience, in constructing identities.

Riessman (2002) argues that, "Storytelling is a relational activity that encourages others to listen, to share, and to empathize" (p. 697). By reading others' experiences, we are likely to become more accustomed to ask questions, seek advice, and learn to assert ourselves and communicate effectively. Thus, sharing personal stories is a collaborative process between the teller and the listener that bears significant practical implications for immigrant women of colour who are junior faculty members in Western institutions.

CONVERSATIONS

Bakhtin (1981) does not view language as a neutral, objective, or impersonal medium, but rather as carrying certain socio-ideological contradictions that find expression in dialogic exchange. Accordingly, we engage in the following dialogue that begins between two women exploring their lived academic experiences as Indian and Bangladeshi female scholars in a Canadian institution. Given that we had a shared understanding prior to the writing of this chapter, both as colleagues within the same department and, more specifically, as friends and "sisters of colour," we did not impose a structure or format on our conversation. The conversation evolved naturally as a flowing stream of consciousness. Particularly, we unpack how our interpersonal and intercultural relationships evolve and devolve through the ongoing interplay between the issues of voice and power (or lack of them). We digitally recorded our conversation and transcribed it. After the conversation we reread the transcript and through a collaborative process of consultation agreed on the following themes: hybrid women of colour, position/s in institutions, religious identity/ies, and the teaching experience. In the first theme, we use the term "hybrid" in the sense that Homi Bhabha (1990, 1994) defines "hybridity" to signify our mixed identities.

We explain our positions in the context of the institution: as full-time/part-time professors. Then, we examine our religious identities, one Hindu and the other Islamic, situated against the backdrop of mainstream faiths in the West. Finally, we talk about our teaching experiences, which is an important aspect of our shared lived reality in the academy.

HYBRID WOMEN OF COLOUR

> Rukhsana: I find it puzzling when people automatically assume my nationality to be Indian.
>
> Jaya: I understand. I have been mistaken by people to be a Hispanic woman, or a Mexican (they would come and speak to me in Spanish and when I did not understand and respond they would just turn away and leave as if disgusted), Native American, Egyptian, or a Tunisian.

The confusion of students, faculty, and administrators results in a construction of hybrid identity/ies and have to do with not just the construction of gender, but gender and nationality. Some people construct what a woman of colour looks like—she could be an Egyptian woman, a Hispanic woman, an Indian woman, or a Bangladeshi woman; this is a catch-all pool and we all kind of merge together. We become this one brown woman who belongs everywhere and nowhere. Look at the range: we could be Latin American, we could be North African, we could be South Asian, or we could be Native/Aboriginal.

Position/s in Institutions

> Rukhsana: Oftentimes I am asked for my student ID. I have been asked whether I am a teaching assistant or a part-time professor. Even after the fact has been established that I am a full-time faculty member, the question would come up: "So, you are a regular faculty member; but have you finished your Ph.D.?" This question leads me to wonder what a regular faculty member looks like?

> Jaya: I have had similar experiences. If you dress or look a certain way and if you are more casual in your approach or you are more accessible then you cannot be a full-time faculty member.

There is an implicit assumption that an immigrant woman of colour in a competitive workplace is unlikely to easily be part of mainstream academic life. This assumption is even more problematic in the Canadian context given Canada's leadership role in multiculturalism.

Religious Identity/ies

> Rukhsana: In the spirit of using lived experiences to enrich the learning environment for students, I explained to students when I am teaching during the month of Ramadan that I might not be speaking as loudly as I usually would. Unfortunately, my candid behavior would be considered as being unprofessional by some students.

> Jaya: Interestingly, during the month of Ramadan, people would assume that I too was fasting because they thought I am a Muslim. However, as you know, I am a Hindu.

These seemingly minor confusions become more critical because these are different facets of what define us: religion, language, and location. There is no awareness of the broad distinctions between different faiths. Given the fact that our academic environments are becoming more diverse all over in North America and moreso in Canada, it is important to recognize difference.

THE TEACHING EXPERIENCE

> Rukhsana: As a new professor coming as a fresh Ph.D. graduate, I had some ideals and expectations with regard to teaching and supervision of graduate students. Unfortunately, oftentimes because of a combination of complex factors, such as being a visible minority, woman of colour, being a new professor, I do not fit the norm; I look and sound different. On the other hand, I feel that students with diverse backgrounds tend to look for commonalities and are drawn to us based on the fact that we are females and females of colour. I feel that they see you as their mentor and they feel they can identify with you; they can share their experiences with you; oftentimes, they see you as a role model.

> Jaya: Speaking of students, I would like to share an experience I had with an undergraduate student. I was assumed to be the teaching assistant for a colleague who was an older South Asian male and had taught the same course or a similar course before. I had to make myself very clear that I am an independent person and that I had my own office and designation, et cetera and that I was an Assistant Professor. The student had a hard time believing it initially, but eventually, he came to terms with that. However, within the course of the semester the perception changed because of the class, the teaching, and the interaction. It is absolutely amazing to see how these issues of race, gender, and ethnicity can play out.

The way students view us is very much shaped by who we are. Race, gender, ethnicity, and religion are filters that influence the professor-student dyad.

Based on the above conversations, we are left to ponder how immigrant women of colour in a Canadian institution manage and create space within a given system. Being new to the Canadian culture and educational systems, we faced some challenges in terms of adjusting to the new culture, academic environment, and negotiating our separate identities as new professors who are also women of colour. We also felt challenged by the perceptions of such identities. Probing deeper, we now present our individual reflections.

INDIVIDUAL REFLECTIONS

This section highlights our own individual reflections as women of colour in the academy in a Canadian context focusing on the institution, students, and peers. As Canada becomes increasingly multicultural, there are more ethnically, linguistically, and culturally diverse academics than ever before. The impact of this diversity presents unique challenges to these scholars based on differences according to ethnic background, country of origin, primary language, religion, and immigration status. Consequently, certain questions arise: How do immigrant women of colour in a Canadian institution manage and create space within the system? How do these women negotiate their co-existence with their native colleagues? As communication scholars from South Asia, we feel the imperative to tell our stories so that we can create a space for dialogue for other individuals in similar positions and help convey the message that they may not be alone.

Below we will reflect on different experiences with respect to how our gender—which interacts with multiple facets of race, ethnicity, religion, immigrant status, and language—is perceived and used to attribute to us characteristics of a woman of colour who is a junior faculty member in a Canadian institution. To this end, we will discuss these experiences in terms of our institution, students, and peers.

JAYA'S REFLECTIONS

> The foreigner is the other of the family, the clan, the tribe. At first he blends with the enemy. External to my religion, too, he could have been the heathen, the heretic. Not having made an oath of fealty to my lord, he was born on another land, foreign to the kingdom or empire. (Kristeva, 1991, p. 95)

> The shock of arrival is multifold—what was borne in the mind is jarred, tossed into new shapes, an exciting exfoliation of sense. What we were in that other life is shattered open. But the worlds we now inhabit still speak of the need for invention, of ancestors, of faith. The old question, 'Who am I?' returns—I am what others see me as, but I am also my longings, my desire, my speech. But how is that speech formed, when what they see me as cuts against the grain of what I sense myself to be? Coming to America, I have felt in my own heart what W. E. B. Dubois invoked: 'two souls, two thoughts . . . in one dark body.' (Alexander, 1996, p. 2)

INSTITUTIONAL ASPECT. As an international female student in North America and as an untenured faculty member, it has been a challenge to give voice to my true feelings and opinions in the institutional context such as departmental, faculty, and committee meetings. The intersection of race, gender, and ethnicity gives me a heightened sense of awareness of a tension that plays out, which creates silences and absences. The expectation of fulfilling the role of the exotic, nice, South Asian woman, which has to be lived up to, and the fear of being seen as the submissive and invisible immigrant woman creates a barrier that gets internalized and that then needs to be fought against. There is an unwritten expectation of certain forms of behaving, so that if my opinions are strong or not in conformity with expectations, there is a sense of surprise from others. Also, when I speak strongly, it seems as if others think that 'these people' should be grateful that they are in a country like the United States or Canada and they have taken over here and have changed the face of academia.

WITH STUDENTS. A cloak of invisibility creates a sense of uniformity with many South Asian women faculty or 'other' women faculty, so that a confusion is created, real and imagined, in the minds and demeanour of the students with whom we interact. This is embodied in somewhat subtle and not so subtle nuances of behaviour, such as mistaking Jaya for Rukhsana, or for that matter, any other South Asian woman for the other, merging them into one inseparable, fused entity that is seen as that nice exotic teacher/professor. As a result, the student is absolved from the effort of remembering the "difficult" names that cannot be pronounced, or from having to make the effort to distinguish between the different and separate persons with their own subtleties and distinct personalities. Thus, students are let off the hook. Sometimes this is manifested in students stopping me on the way to work or from work in the downtown city area, remembering a class that they took with pleasure but always being careful to address me as "Professor" (not remembering the name). Sometimes it is seen in the classroom, through acts of trying to outsmart me, they try to pit me in a battle of wits, as it were, testing my expertise and knowledge, which is always open to question as an exotic woman of colour and immigrant. So there is a constant sense of being tested, of jumping in the eternal hurdle race, of trying to prove oneself to students.

In addition, I have recollections of teaching as a raw graduate student in my first class where students sense the vulnerability or fear and then work that to their favour through unacceptable behaviour, trying to "help" me learn the ropes as such, and/or trying to engage in a power game since they "know" they are right and I am wrong. As a graduate student who is not American but foreign, I was always seen as different and someone whom other students could not fully understand.

PEERS.

> The tolerated Others are by definition present within our "sphere of influence." They are part of our "world" (society, nation, neighborhood) but only insofar as we accept them. That is, the tolerated Others are never just present, they are positioned. Their belonging in the environment in which they come to exist is always a precarious one, for they never exist, they are allowed to exist. (Hage, 1994, p. 28)

Even as a doctoral student, it was brought home to me that I was different. It happened in the most innocuous of ways, seemingly. A group of us (fellow doctoral students in the same cohort) were talking about future plans, career aspirations, and the challenges of the job market. Suddenly one of my peers, a Caucasian male, turned to me and said, "Oh you have nothing to worry about, you will have no problems finding a job." Being puzzled by this remark, I asked why since I felt as we all did at the time—that the job market was very tight and we all would be facing challenges. Then it came to me in a flash even as my peer explicitly stated that it would be easier because I was a woman, a woman of colour and hence, employers or potential employers would see me as a way to fill their affirmative action quotas. This incident affected me deeply as I realized how I was being viewed by others and also put me in my place, so to speak. I realized that in America I was truly the Other and that this would define who I am and who I was regardless of how much I might try to deny it or overcome it.

The other aspect that I have noticed and come to understand is the essentializing of similar colleagues/women of colour as symbols or icons of diversity, which adds to the tokenization of diversity (Mirchandani & Tastsoglou, 2000); one is admired for one's exotic or colourful clothes, skin tones, jewelry, and/or hair. There is also an undertone of being different from other women; here lies the dichotomy between women as universal beings, and women as particular—brown women. Brown women by definition behave in a certain manner, dress in a certain manner, and therefore, think in a definitive way; they are viewed as being less liberated than their Western counterparts because they do not have the trappings of certain kinds of attire or ways of articulating. This then perpetuates a stereotypical understanding of such women and can create a space for various misunderstandings and miscommunications.

RUKHSANA'S REFLECTIONS

The discursive effort to make sense of what it means to be a woman of colour faculty member in a Canadian institution and what this identity means for the institution, my peers, and the students can create an ironic tension within self.

INSTITUTIONAL ASPECT. It was only when I allowed myself the time to consciously reflect on my individual experience as a woman of colour faculty member in a Canadian institution that I found myself negotiating multiple facets of my identity, such as race, ethnicity, religion, immigrant status, and language. I remember the sense of uncertainty in my first year as an Assistant Professor, especially after experiencing the privilege of having a committed mentor help me with my doctoral work, graduation, job search, and getting a job. I see myself as just another digit added to the increasing number of ethnically, linguistically, and culturally diverse academicians; often I am this invisible and silent flare to the desired multicultural campus. How much is known about how I enact and negotiate my identity as a woman and visible minority and how aware am I, for that matter, of such enactment and negotiation during my interactions with others? I do not recall how my attributed identity—a woman of colour junior faculty member—motivates me at work. Rather, I call to mind the extra pressure and the gaze that comes with being a South Asian woman faculty member. Sometimes my very existence, not as an individual, but as a woman of colour in the academy, appears to challenge and be challenged by traditional boundaries—faculty, departmental, disciplinary, or epistemological. It appears that I am being told:

> *You are not producing important work; I am not sure about your diverse scholarship and alternative methodologies for approaching scholarship; Your work is not part of what is seen as mainstream work in the social sciences; You did not publish in a leading journal; You are too junior to have a say about the direction of the department.*

As a woman of colour in the academy I feel constantly as though I am being judged—which, unfortunately, is not an isolated experience. Although many of these pressures may not be different from those that are shared by white men and women faculty members and by faculty members of colour in general, women of colour faculty members must prove that they are *truly qualified*.

WITH STUDENTS. I have come to realize that my woman of colour junior faculty member status creates a unique situation in the classroom. Often, I feel that my skin colour and my accent bear implications for my presence in the classroom. Sometimes I find myself being put to the test for my competency and legitimacy as scholar and educator not just because I am a new professor, but also because of the fact that I am *different*—I look different, I sound different. Unfortunately, when my "easy-going" personality is perceived as my weakness, I cannot seem to escape the label of "angry professor" who "treats students as high school kids" when attempting to assert control in a hostile classroom environment. Such scrutiny triggers a heightened sense of my woman of colour junior faculty member status, often resulting in the effort to be "perfect," and an extra effort to be *normal.* My otherness, that is, my visible minority faculty member status, creates the expectation that I will be an overly nurturing mother figure to students. However, if this expectation is not fulfilled, I am viewed as an abuser of power and student evaluations and complaints will result in an inverse power relationship.

Another unique challenge I must contend with in the classroom as a woman of colour in particular, is teaching issues of race, class, gender, and sexuality without being perceived as "unprofessional," *guilty* of using standpoint theory as a framework. Such greater consciousness regarding my identity often stifles spontaneity and sociability and thus translates into being tentative in my teaching.

PEERS. If I were to describe myself, my woman of colour faculty member identity would not be a salient aspect of who I am or how I see myself. However, when I am a faculty member who is the only person of colour and on certain occasions, the only woman of colour, in my collegial and collaborative interactions, it means that I am always standing for more than just myself. I am the *Other.* I remain on guard so as not to buttress the stereotype of being a woman academic, especially a woman of colour academic. I can pass with flying colours for being timid, unfailingly sweet tempered, and smiling.

Becoming acclimated to the academic life in a foreign land did not, however, result in a reduced level of consciousness of my woman of colour junior faculty member status. Being different resurfaces in my daily interaction with "others." It is often the special attention given, or the lack thereof, that contributes to the enactment of my "special" status in both positive and negative ways. Often, I find myself explicitly avoiding behaviours giving prominence to my woman of colour faculty member status especially when it becomes a point of contention with my peers who perceive my "special" status working in favour of my accomplishments. Apparently (and unfortunately), I do not have the free will (nor the discretion) to enact my woman of colour faculty member identity. What is more unfortunate is the guilty feeling that I find myself engulfed in for any accomplishment.

Upon reflection, I think I have to deconstruct my identity. I cannot only write about my ethnic identity. I am Bangladeshi, which is, indeed, one of the most important parts of my identity. But I should also mention my gender identity—I am a woman. I am also a junior faculty member. I am a Muslim. I could make a long list of the aspects constituting my identity. I would, however, like to defend the right to construct my own identity and disregard the elements, which distort my own sense of self. At the same time, I recognize that my identity is formed by my interaction with other people, just as Bruner's (1990) concept of "transactional self" is based on the notion of a narrative relationship between a "speaker and an Other" (p. 101). Such communicative practices can make space for a variety of cultures to continually evolve through narrating the historical and cultural experiences of self and Other.

SUMMARY

Bakhtin's dialogic approach permitted us to have an open communicative format to engage in our conversations and reflections grounded in the theoretical frame of postcolonial feminism. As revealed in our conversations and reflections, our location/s and position/s as women of colour from specific space/s and place/s put us in the niche of women from exotic cultures. Postcolonial feminism, with its emphasis on a non-universalizing and non-essentializing the experiences of women, gives us the perfect vessel to articulate our voice/s and exclusion/s. As women from formerly colonized parts of the world living and working in former colonies and interacting with former colonizers, it makes us painfully aware of the cracks and interstices that we fall into, being in the West but being seen as representatives of a particular, essentialized part of the world and the historical context of that. Thus, we are seen as the privileged few, fortunate enough to have made it from the undeveloped/developing former colonized parts of the globe into the camp of the developed/advanced former colonizer. Ironically, we live and embody the experience of the "Other" as exotic women of colour, even while we give voice to these silences and exclusions through the medium of this chapter.

DISCUSSION AND CONCLUSION

Communication is central to the initiation, development, maintenance, enhancement, and also termination of human relationships. Human communication is all-encompassing in our contemporary daily lives and helps us in creating better understanding in personal and professional relationships. As Tyler (1986) aptly said, "[communication is] a cooperatively evolved text consisting of fragments of discourse intended to evoke in the minds of both reader and writer an emergent fantasy of a possible world of commonsense reality, and thus to provoke an aesthetic integration that will have a therapeutic effect" (p. 125).

The academy provides a rich setting that can serve as the springboard for faculty members to dialogue about scholarship, teaching, and citizenship. We believe that we share with other women and women of colour the common platform that the feminist framework and feminist theory provides. As immigrant women of colour in the academy, we also share with other immigrant women of colour in the Canadian context the intersections of race, ethnicity, and gender that give us a space and place to explore our stories. In addition, given our respective backgrounds as women of colour from India and Bangladesh, we find that postcolonial feminist theory resonates with us. Thus, all these layers and aspects of the feminist approach provide an appropriate vessel for us to articulate our silence/s, absence/s, exclusion/s, as well as our experiences, and place our voice/s in a unique and very relevant contextualized frame of reference. In the academy, the postcolonialist feminist framework (Mohanty, 1991; Spivak, 1988), as well as the feminist writings of Canadian immigrant women scholars (Agnew, 2003; Bannerji, 1995; Dhruvarajan & Vickers, 2002; Tastsoglou, 2006), give us the theoretical and scholarly epistemological underpinnings and assumptions for placing our reflections and conversations. The feminist frame provides the foundation for us to explore our dialogue using a Bakhtinian exploration.

We believe that Bakhtin's dialogic approach, in this case, the two-pronged approach that we adopt in discussing our experiences and placing them in a communication format, allows us to explore our professional selves. Such explorations, as also underscored by Bakhtin (1981), grant us the space to present ourselves as unique individuals—women of colour in a Canadian institution with multiple facets of race, ethnicity, religion, immigrant status, and language. We also argue that Bakhtinian dialogism, as a pragmatic theory of language use, promotes recognition and respect for *doing* difference. Bakhtin showed interest in mundane everyday talk—the dialogic properties of everyday communication. Accordingly, considering language as a dialogic phenomenon, in this case, by using language from the perspective of those doing the othering (by sharing our lived experiences), we focus attention on the interrelationship between language and society as this is where the issues of power/disempowerment, inclusion/exclusion, silence/voice etc. are manifest. In doing so, we call for the need for the academy to be the place that permits and respects sharing of the canonical stories of professional selves. In order for us to carry through this culture, we must share insights and experiences, ask questions, articulate contentions, and, in turn, risk transforming or reinforcing our viewpoints through such dialogue.

Through the synergistic process of sharing our stories and reflecting upon our experiences, we hope to have created a new reality common to us and to others like us, South Asian immigrant women junior faculty members. By doing this, we also hope to open doors for further discussion among like-minded scholars and provoke thought within the larger academy as to how we can be aware of the impact of the different facets of race, ethnicity, gender, religion, and all these intersections of identity on individuals and institutions.

REFERENCES

Agnew, V. (2003). *Where I come from.* Waterloo, ON: Wilfrid Laurier University Press.

Alexander, M. (1996). *The shock of arrival: Reflections on postcolonial experience.* Boston, MA: Southend Press.

Anderson, B. (1995). *Imagined communities.* New York, NY: Verso.

Bakhtin, M. M. (1981). *The dialogic imagination: Four essays* (M. Holquist, Ed., C. Emerson & M. Holquist, Trans.). Austin, TX: University of Texas Press.

Bakhtin, M. M. (1986). *Speech genres and other late essays* (C. Emerson & M. Holquist, Eds., V. W. McGee, Trans.). Austin, TX: University of Texas Press.

Bannerji, H. (1995). *Thinking Through: Essays on Feminism, Marxism, and Anti-Racism.* Toronto, ON: Women's Press.

Bhabha, H. J. (1990.) *Nation and narration.* New York, NY: Routledge.

Bhabha, H. J. (1994). *The location of culture.* New York, NY: Routledge.

Bruner, J. S. (1990). *Acts of meaning.* Cambridge, Mass: Harvard University Press.

Denis, A. (2006). Developing a feminist analysis of citizenship of Caribbean immigrant women in Canada: Key dimensions and conceptual challenges. In T. Evangelia & Alexandra, D. (Eds.), *Women, migration and citizenship: Making local, national and transnational connections* (pp. 37-59). London: England: Ashgate Publication Limited.

Dhruvarajan, V., & Vickers, J. (2002). Gender Race and Nation. In V. Dhruvarajan & J. Vickers (Eds.), *Gender, race and nation: A global perspective* (pp. 25-63). Toronto, ON: University of Toronto Press.

Ellis, C., & Bochner, A. (2000). Authoethnography, personal narrative, reflexivity: Researcher as subject. In N. Denzin & Y. Lincoln (Eds.), *Handbook of qualitative research* (pp. 733-768). Thousand Oaks, CA: Sage.

Ghosh, B. & Bose, B. (Eds.). (1997). *Interventions: Feminist dialogues on third world women's literature and film.* NY: Garland Publishing, Inc.

Hage, G. (1994). Locating multiculturalism's other: A critique of practical tolerance. *New Formations, 24*, 19-34.

Hawes, L. (2003). Double binds as structures in dominance and of feelings: Problematics of dialogue. In R. Anderson, L. A. Baxter, & K. N. Cissna (Eds.), *Dialogue: Theorizing difference in communication studies* (pp. 175-189). Thousand Oaks, CA: Sage, 2003.

Kristeva, J. (1991). *Strangers to ourselves.* London, England: Harvester Wheatsheaf.

McIntire, G. (2005). Heteroglossia, monologism, and fascism: Bernard reads the waves. *Narrative, 13*(1), 29-45.

Mills, A. J., & Tancred, P. (1992). *Gendering organizational analysis.* London, England: Sage Publications.

Min-ha, T. T. (1989). *Woman, native, other: Writing postcoloniality and feminism.* Bloomington, IN: Indiana University Press.

Mirchandani, K., & Tastsoglou, E. (2000). Toward a diversity beyond tolerance. *Studies in Political Economy, 61*, 49-78.

Mohanty, C. T. (1991): Under western eyes: Feminist scholarship and colonial discourses. In C. T., Mohanty, A. Russo, & L. Torres (Eds.), *Third world women and the politics of feminism* (pp. 51-80). Bloomington, IN: Indiana University Press.

Mohanty, C. T. (2003). *Feminism without borders: decolonizing theory, practicing solidarity.* London, England: Duke University Press.

Narayan, U. (2000). Essence of culture and a sense of history: A feminist critique of cultural essentialism. In U. Narayan & S. Harding. (Eds.), *Decentering the Center* (pp 80-100). Bloomington, IN: Indiana University Press.

Riessman, C. (2002). Analysis of personal narratives. In J. Gubrium & J. Holstein (Eds.), *Handbook of interview research* (pp. 695-710). Thousand Oaks, CA: Sage.

Said, E. W. (1978). *Orientalism.* New York, NY: Pantheon Books.

Shiva, V. (1988). *Staying alive: Women, ecology and development.* London, England: Zed Books.

Smith, D. E. (1987). *The everyday world as problematic: A feminist sociology.* Boston, MA: Northeastern University Press.

Spivak, G. C. (1987). *In other worlds: Essays in cultural politics.* NY: Methuen.

Spivak, G. C. (1988). Can the subaltern speak? In C. Nelson & L. Grossberg (Eds.), *Marxism and the interpretation of culture* (pp 271-313). Urbana, IL: University of Illinois Press.

Spivak, G. C. (1999). *A critique of postcolonial reason: Toward a history of the vanishing present.* Cambridge, MA: Harvard University Press.

Tastsoglou, E. (2006). Gender, migration and citizenship: Immigrant women and the politics of belonging in the Canadian Maritimes. In E. Tastsoglou, & A. Dobrowolsky (Eds.), *Women, migration and citizenship: Making local, national and transnational connections* (pp. 201-230). London, England: Ashgate Publication Limited.

Tyler, S. (1986). Post modern ethnography: From document of the occult to occult document. In J. Clifford & G. E. Marcus (Eds.), *Writing culture: The poetics and politics of ethnography* (pp. 122-140). Berkeley, CA: University of California Press.

Chapter 10

STRANGERS IN THE IVORY TOWER

FRAMING INTERNATIONAL FEMALE FACULTY IDENTITY NEGOTIATIONS IN A 'MAJORITY' ACADEMIC INSTITUTION

Elvinet S. Wilson

Whenever a teacher enters a classroom, she or he is not free to act on the basis of consciously chosen principles. The teacher is constrained by factors of history and biography. Symbolically, teaching is a culturally and politically loaded term. Materially, the teaching act is embedded in the organizational setting of a particular school, in the occupational norms of the profession, and in the social climate of the times. (Sprague, 1992, p. 182)

My mother didn't have a garden. Instead, she fashioned a yard full of fruit trees that blossomed well in the subtropical climate of the island nation where I grew up. When I was hungry and there was no food to eat in the house, I could go onto the front porch, make my selections with an easy glance and collect ripe joo-joos from the sweetest tree in our neighborhood. A little to the left of the porch was a cherry tree, which was a little harder to climb and riskier because of the wasps' nests, but the prizes were always worth it. A little farther back on the left side of the house was a sapodilla tree, two steps back from which was a sugarcane patch. Another two or three steps and there was a guava tree and next to it a scarlet plum tree. The plum tree shaded the woman-made pump that brought fresh rainwater up from the well my mother dug herself. A few feet from the pump was a mound of dirt surrounded by a square of stones, on which stood the proudest avocado pear tree I ever saw. When I walked across the back yard I would pass our clothesline, an aloe vera patch, and the garbage heap where we burned junk. At the Southeast corner of our little abode was a wash stand, where my father once scrubbed the household laundry until he was as wet as the clothes in the steel tub. No, my mother wasn't the gardening type; at least not the type that fashioned foliage and pretty flowers for others to view. My mother cared more about providing the fruits that would sustain her six children when we were surrounded by cultural famine. Perhaps, those fruits that I ate back then still sustain me as I search for a place to plant my own trees.

I tell this story to demonstrate the nature of my own cultural difference from what I conceive as a social norm that dictates a particular way of being a woman and of being a mother. I do not come from a typical North American family. I grew up in The Bahamas, a small place with less means than most. But ironically, my graduate education and current position as Assistant Professor have at times left me feeling starved for intellectual fruit that might nourish my soul the way tropical fruits once did. Perhaps, if I can find such fruits on the U.S. mainland, I can also nourish the souls of students, colleagues, and administrators with whom I interact throughout my career as a Communication Studies professor.

In my effort to create a research agenda that can help me survive on the tenure-track, I have continued to search for safe spaces in which to discuss issues related to the experiences of difference and the political and material struggles of others defined as such. I am often relieved to find scholars who describe experiences similar to my own. In this process, when I scanned the pages of the National Communication Association convention program in November 2008, I found such a group. I found a description of a panel on the experiences of new, Black, female tenure-track professors in Communication. I was both saddened and excited upon arrival at the session. Saddened by the stories of struggle and pain some of the African-American and international women of color on the panel described and, at the same time, excited that such issues were being discussed in the setting of our national forum. The conversations I had with panelists and the panel respondent after this session morphed into the current book. I remember thinking at the time of our conversation that perhaps the truth about race in the academy continues to be as hooks (1989) suggested, i.e. university hiring has indeed shifted to accommodate a more diverse U.S. society, but the presence of "more Black professors in predominantly White universities . . . only mediates in a minor way, the racism and sexism of White professors" (p. 56).

My intent here is not to discuss the construction of racial differences in the academy per se. The central objective of this chapter is to highlight national origin as an important but less-researched identity category intersecting with gender in faculty experiences. I argue that women's particular geopolitical positionalities are the bases for significant distances, which separate us from centralized academic discourse and privilege. Such discourse and privilege prescribe a particular way of being a university professor. This chapter will draw from the personal narratives of four international female faculty members, including me, in order to demonstrate how we each frame our multifaceted identities in the academy and how such framings might indicate something about the nature of power relations at institutions where we find ourselves as minorities. First, I will discuss how the chapter is theoretically grounded, review scholarship that examines issues significantly related to the experiences of international female faculty, and detail the process of data collection. This will be followed by a presentation of data and a discussion of insights yielded from our narratives.

LITERATURE REVIEW

This chapter is grounded theoretically in feminist standpoint theory. Standpoint theory provides an excellent starting point for recognizing and understanding the experiences of international female faculty. The theory foregrounds the value of understanding women's distinct social and cultural experiences and suggests that it is impossible to generate knowledge about women's experiences without studying how we interpret those experiences. The theory also asserts that an individual's experience, knowledge, and communication behaviors are shaped largely by their membership in various social groups (West & Turner, 2010). Feminists like Haraway (1988), Harding (1991), and Harstock (1983), all proponents of feminist standpoint epistemologies, argued that while reality could be observed by the elite of a given society, those observations and the resulting interpretations are always partial views of reality. It is therefore incumbent upon scholars to approach any study of society from where we are actually situated, within the particularities of our lived worlds. In this chapter, I situate myself as a new, international faculty member. I have direct knowledge of what it is like to be a U.S. immigrant, Black, and a relatively young woman employed at a majority institution in the Midwest United States, and I use that knowledge and my situatedness to interpret the narratives of other international female faculty similarly situated.

Feminist scholars and other education professionals have successfully used critical theories like standpoint theory to deconstruct some of the inequities in U.S. higher education. Communication researchers have more recently joined these groups of scholars in addressing the very ways we think about diversity in the academy. Shome (2000) observed a paucity of critical perspectives on power, ideology, and privilege, particularly in cross-cultural communication literature. Describing an application and theory-driven field of cross-cultural study, Shome asserted that at the time of her graduate education, researchers interested in this context of communication study emphasized hard and fast rules about intercultural competence, principally focusing on successful communication with non-White subjects or "Others." Shome wrote:

> Titles such as *Communicating With Strangers* or *Bridging Differences* seemed to be informed by an assumption that 'strangers,' and those with 'difference,' were those from another culture or nation, and that intercultural theory could be a route through which to 'master' the Other and her or his difference. Rarely were the 'voices' and experiences of pain, struggle, and disempowerment of Others represented; rarely were the issues of systematic racism, neocolonialism, and imperialism that inform the ideologies embedded in various communicative interactions between Anglo Americans and those from 'Other worlds' addressed. (p. 170)

Shome (2000) encouraged communication scholars to examine their positionalities and power, particularly in relation to the production of knowledge about colonized others. Her research bears significantly on the subject of international female faculty identities. Similarly, Keane-Dawes (2004) explained how the popular intercultural theme of host-stranger communication sets up guidelines for how newcomers should adapt to host culture communication practices. She argued that current theories of cross-cultural understanding often accommodate rather than question the privilege and power of the host culture over the discourse surrounding immigrant bodies and identities. A Jamaican-born immigrant and communication professor, Keane-Dawes asserted that processes of delegitimation in everyday interactions continually work to disempower those who are "different."

Education researchers have a much longer tradition of examining faculty diversity issues in the U.S. academy. Turner (2000), for example, highlights the importance of having an ethnic minority faculty presence, emphasizing the benefits of developing global perspectives in the U.S. teaching and learning environment. Higher education diversity scholarship often provides useful strategies for institutional recruitment, retention, and support of women and minority faculty (Aguirre, 2000; Erickson & Rodriguez, 1999; Rai & Crizer, 2000). But most of this research tends to focus on single, simplified, or monolithic identity categories. Monroe, Ozyurt, Wrigley, and Alexander (2008), for example, assert that gender equality is still a major issue in the academy and that the outlook for female faculty is dismal. These researchers suggest that all women, regardless of race, ethnicity, or class can expect "[a] rigid system of rewards that makes scant allowance for deviation from the traditional male model . . . continuing unconscious and deep-seated discrimination and stereotyping by male colleagues, and a remarkably unbreakable glass ceiling" (p. 217).

Such studies tell us a great deal about the problems related to diverse faculty, but few researchers examine the multiple jeopardy inherent in the experiences of individuals who do not fall neatly within the boundaries of more commonly used identity categories—those who may be uncritically labeled "faculty of color," or listed in affirmative action records as domestic minorities (African-American, Asian-American, etc.). At times these uncritically labeled types may also be women and first-generation immigrants whose national origins or other aspects of their multifaceted selves are erased by racialized category systems. Even fewer articles and books provide information on what faculty of different national origins can do to strategically empower themselves and realistically navigate the dominant culture of the U.S. academy that researchers still find alive and well.

The intricacy of the matter is also amplified by the fact that present-day immigrants are not like those of a past generation that sought to integrate fully into American society. For example, a study of Afro-Caribbean immigrants in Phoenix, Arizona indicated that they made a special effort to maintain distinct cultural identities at the same time as they understood the instrumentality of becoming U.S. Americans through the naturalization process (Wilson, 2008). Other migration studies have also indicated that newer immigrants seek to maintain connections to their home cultures and identities (Schiller, Basch, & Blanc-Szanton, 1992; Waters, 1999; Waters & Jimenez, 2005). Based on these trends in scholarship and a need to more fully address the complexities of power, ideology, and privilege suggested by communication scholars like Shome (2000) and Keane-Dawes (2004), uncovering the voices of female, non-native, ethnic minority faculty holds much potential. Narrative research is perhaps best suited to do this and narratives like the ones in this chapter and in this edited text may help institutions develop more equitable academic environments that reflect the very real, global dimensions of contemporary life experience.

METHODS

Narrative research is a form of interpretive and qualitative scholarship that allows the researcher to deconstruct the relationship between self and society. Narratives denote much about the ways in which we order our experiences, and in so doing, also reveal a great deal about culture and society. Through focus on the 'self,' narrative research highlights how a person's experience mediates and is mediated by the social contexts in which she/he exists. Women's narratives in particular, continue to correct centuries of androcentric analyses that either silenced or distorted women's experiences. Feminists have thus encouraged the use of narrative to highlight how power relations manifest themselves in individual women's lives (Bloom, 2002).

The narratives presented in this chapter are positioned within scholarship related to two concepts: *multiple jeopardy* (King, 1988) and *primary frameworks* (Goffman, 1986). First, the idea of multiple jeopardy springs from feminist standpoint epistemology. It is sensitive to issues of intersecting, marginalized identities, and also allows me to situate myself within the research itself. Many international faculty members lack privilege in an academic environment. It is my contention that many of us are often distanced from certain aspects of participation in the cultures of our institutions and in the dominant culture of the U.S. academy as a result of immigrant status, ethnic classification, gender, and class, which help to determine the exact nature of those distances from full participation in the production of knowledge in the classroom, research, and academic service. As a new tenure-track faculty member at a majority institution and a former student at two majority institutions, I continue to experience what feminists refer to as *multiple jeopardy* (King, 1988): I am an immigrant, I am Black, I am a woman, and I do not come from a privileged economic background. But the way in which I am immigrant, Black, woman, and underprivileged and the ways in which I may perform and understand those aspects of my multifaceted self, are different from the ways in which for instance, a Black U.S. native may perform or understand self.

Goffman (1986) suggests that *primary frameworks* allow individuals to "locate, perceive, identify, and label a seemingly infinite number of concrete occurrences defined in its terms" (p. 21). A *primary framework* is equivalent to an interpretive schema that allows one to reduce perceived phenomena into simplified but meaningful fragments "by selectively punctuating and encoding objects, situations, events, experiences, and sequences" (Snow & Benford, 1992, p. 137). By applying Goffman's idea of framing within the parameters of this study, I suggest that international female faculty actively contribute to the production of meaning surrounding their own participation in the academy. Typically, Goffman's framing is used as an analytical tool in media studies, but here I utilize the concept as it is often used in conflict resolution studies in order to understand how international female faculty negotiate their identities within majority institutions.

With the concepts *multiple jeopardy* and *primary frameworks* in mind, I combine personal narrative (Ellis & Bochner, 2000) and interviewing methodologies (Ellis, 2004; Kvale, 1996) to present qualitative cases of my own experiences and the experiences of three other international female faculty members at a majority Midwestern university. Such a combination of interpretive methods and concepts is aimed at illuminating experiences and arousing critical thought about diversity rather than generalizing and confirming a particular hypothesis.

Research Journey

Joining the group of scholars I met during the 2008 National Communication Association convention, I set out to review literature on diversity in the U.S. academy and received approval from my university's human subjects research review board to begin collecting and interpreting qualitative data about how international female faculty framed their academic experiences at a majority institution. Eventually I was able to locate three participants willing to be interviewed, but recruiting proved challenging. I learned through the process of recruiting research participants that there was a major disconnect between the social identity categories used by the university to gather data on faculty diversity and the ways in which individual faculty members actually described themselves. More specifically, both the immigration status categories and the racial categories in university records were inconsistent with some faculty members' views of themselves. Hence, terms like "faculty of color," which are often used in diversity scholarship and which I used in my recruitment e-mail and initial questionnaire, were somewhat problematic.

The term "faculty of color" assumed that all international faculty members fell within some kind of ethnic minority category, which was likely to be true. However, it did not mean that those who were ethnic minorities necessarily viewed themselves as Black, Hispanic, Asian, or Native American. I sought to include both native and non-native English speakers, so it was not my intent to exclude ethnic minorities who were recognized racially as White. Further, some potential research participants were listed in employee records as legal resident immigrants with country of birth clearly indicated in their profiles, while others were labeled domestic minorities. The problem was that there was no way to tell, based on how personnel records were kept, if those faculty members listed as domestic minorities were naturalized U.S. citizens or native U.S. citizens. In my own case, I found my name under the category, domestic minority, i.e., as African American, even though I do not identify as such and have not yet become a naturalized U.S. citizen. Such terms as "faculty of color" or "people of color" are loaded U.S.-based historical terms that refer to ethnic minorities but connote the exclusion of many first-generation immigrants. For example, after sending out my initial recruitment message to locate interviewees, which referred to potential participants as "faculty of color," I received messages like the following: "Hello Elvinet, Your study sounds very interesting, but I don't qualify as a subject because I am White. Good luck" or,

> Dear Dr. Wilson, I am a foreign-born female, but I do not feel that I am of 'color.' . . . All my ancestors are from Spain and my skin is White. I would be willing to participate in your study if it does not take too much time, but I think I am not eligible.

Not long after the send button was pressed on my recruitment e-mail, I realized that many of the women designated as Hispanic in university records actually self-identified as White. Additionally, many of the women I identified based on their foreign visa status were labeled in records as White but self-identified as ethnic minorities. The term "faculty of color," or rather, according to Turner (2000), "people of color," references African Americans, American Indians, Asian Americans, and U.S. Americans of Latino or Chicano heritage. I found further evidence of such labeling or identification issues indicated in a document developed by the Faculty of Color Caucus in the College of Arts and Sciences at Western Michigan University. Their mission statement in 2003 read:

> To increase the presence of native-born faculty of color in the College of Arts & Sciences through institutional practices, procedures, and programs that recruit, retain, and enhance the productivity of African American, Asian American, Hispanic American/Latino, Native American, and Multiracial American faculty members. (Fuller, Orbe, & Potter, 2003, p. 1)

The identity category consistent in this service group's mission is obviously *American*. At the time, the Faculty of Color Caucus argued that it was inappropriate to count international faculty in historically underrepresented categories, as institutional benefits from federal affirmative action policies were designed to help create equality for domestic rather than international minorities (Orbe, 2004). I learned that the language I used to identify potential research participants could be highly politicized but it also had to be based on perceived and very real differences between native and non-native referent groups. While I do not know the outcome of the Caucus' efforts, I found it necessary, as my investigation progressed, to utilize the term *ethnic minority* rather than "people of color" or "faculty of color" in order to direct my focus on a variety of international female faculty.

To gather initial data I used an electronically distributed questionnaire in which I asked respondents to describe their communication with students, faculty, and administrators at a predominantly White institution. At this early stage, I also inquired about experiences in which respondents felt discriminated against. The questionnaire was not intended to measure data in quantitative terms, but was a springboard that helped me identify important aspects of respondents' experiences, which I could make further inquires about in semi-structured interviews. The three participants who chose to be interviewed were international female faculty from Argentina, Jamaica, and Russia. All participants were employed by a common Midwestern, majority institution. Three of us, the faculty member from Jamaica, the faculty member from Russia and the principal investigator, had not yet achieved tenure at the time of the study. The faculty member from Argentina had previously been promoted to a position of Full Professor. Stories of the successes of diverse faculty are lacking in the current literature on diversity in higher education and because of this, I included the experiences of a Full Professor in order to share a model of success on the tenure-track. In addition, I wanted to relate how she thought her identity as both woman and ethnic minority at a majority institution might have affected her tenure case. Each woman chose a pseudonym to shield her identity. I conducted individual 90-minute interviews both by phone and face-to-face over a period of two months in an effort to investigate how each of the women framed her identity as an international faculty member.

FRAMING ONE'S INSTITUTIONAL IDENTITY

Few things in my graduate education and in my current tenure-track position have wholly sustained me like the fruits from the yard my mother made for my siblings and me. An eye-opening experience during my studies gave me pause to consider my identity and identification as a non-U.S.-national. One day, when I was a graduate student in a classroom at a majority institution in the Midwest, I engaged in an open argument with other graduate students about U.S. American foreign policy and its relationship to the events of 9/11. In that moment, a White male student accused me of being a fraud. Arguing against U.S. foreign policy, I had identified myself as "not-American." I sought to denote that I represented a perspective that was different from the norm in our Midwestern environment. This I thought was true; I was born and raised in The Bahamas and had been in the U.S. only about five years then, still on a student visa. This White male student told me in front of the class, that I was just as American as everyone else. I was deeply troubled by his remarks. Not only did he fail to acknowledge the Middle Eastern and European graduate students as well as the Asian professor and graduate students in the classroom that day, he went on further to erase my Caribbean heritage by arguing that perhaps it was not obvious enough. Did he know the trouble, the struggle I went through to leave my country and get here? Perhaps I had become an expert at hiding the inner pain of culture shock, isolation, and frustration as I grew tired of waiting to become eligible to even apply to legally adjust my immigrant status. Believe me, I did not feel like a U.S. American, but I was good at being professional—at speaking the "Queen's English" in academic settings. It was what I had been taught to do growing up in The Bahamas. Perhaps my performance had gone over too well. I thought the ability to adapt to certain aspects of American professional life was important, but I never thought I had completely assimilated, nor did I feel the need to. Now I was confused. I thought, "What was I doing that prevented people from seeing or appreciating where I came from?"

Out of my confusion grew a strong interest in the experiences and negotiations of other internationals in the U.S. academy. I was particularly interested in what forms of discrimination, if any, other women in similar positions might suffer. In my conversations with three other international, tenured and tenure-track, female faculty members at a common Midwestern university, I learned that some had not experienced prejudice the way I thought I had and that they framed their experiences as academics in significantly different ways. Next I present some of the data drawn from their interviews that relates to how each woman framed herself.

IRENE: THE SCIENTIST

Irene had a slight Spanish accent over the phone but I knew from her responses to my questionnaire that she was from Argentina and 52 years of age. At the same time, she had previously sent me an e-mail message noting that she was unsure that she qualified for the study because she saw herself as White and not a person of color. So the first thing I asked was for her to tell me how she identified. Her voice steady and sure, Irene began:

> Well, I'm an American citizen but I was born in Argentina. Particularly when I fill out papers I put my [ethnicity] as Hispanic, but I can't tell I'm different than other people anyway. I think I'm White, but people see me probably as a different color.

Irene explained that her grandparents moved from Europe in the 1920s to South America and that before she came to the United States she never understood herself as different from any other White individual. She described herself as having brown hair and brown eyes as opposed to being blonde and blue-eyed and specified that her heritage was not Northern European. Even though she identified as White, she recognized that many in American society might see her as a person of color, although she preferred not to label herself this way. Irene thought that her accent rather than skin color was primarily what caused her to be recognized as an ethnic minority. As Irene described how she saw herself, she talked about her privileged upbringing in Argentina and how she continued to feel privileged in the U.S. professoriate. At the same time, she described herself as lucky, having been hired as a Full Professor for her first academic appointment in the United States. She noted, "Some of us may be lucky because we had a good mentor or it's just that we were able to take advantage of the opportunities. You have to be aware of where you are needed."

"Go where you are needed," was Irene's refrain. Although she thought she had been in a unique position with her first U.S. academic appointment, she felt she had seized opportunities that were in front of her and made the best of them. More importantly, Irene framed her institutional identity as a scientist and explained that she found acceptance in her department because of her commitment to science, despite stereotypes held by many U.S. Americans:

> I think I just tried to show ... to the other professors who wanted to work with me, to my director, to my mentor that I could contribute greatly to their research. And I showed that I had good ideas, I had good training from my country, although we're not in North America, but its South America. . . . They had to accept it. . . . Because, although she comes from you know the southern-most country in the world and she has strong accent, she still . . . has valid points. I was discussing things, we had meetings and I had good things to say and then the results. . . . I was doing experiments and I was successful and getting results. And even if I wasn't, I was repeating the experiments or changing my approach until I got it. . . . Perseverance I think, I just showed them that you know, accent and race and gender, sure this is part of yourself but science should really be independent of that. . . . At some point people . . . forget that I have an accent—they may like it or they may not like it . . . if you have interesting things to say, they will like it.

On numerous occasions Irene framed herself in terms of her geo-political positioning as a native of Argentina. She continually made reference to the global South, to the fact that her ancestors were *not* from Northern Europe, and that she was *not* from North America. So, while she identified as White and perhaps privileged in American terms, she also seemed to assert an underprivileged position in a more global sense.

COREY: THE RESEARCHER

For Corey, a 33-year old Jamaican immigrant, it was important that I understood that she identified as Black, but not as a person who felt underprivileged because of her Blackness. She framed herself in terms of her research as she explained that her Blackness was an attribute that gave her an advantage in terms of being better able to connect with African American students and teachers in the local public schools that served as her primary research sites. This narrative emerged when I asked her, "How do you experience yourself as different, as a person of color at your university?" She responded:

> I think I don't really; I mean it's clear that I'm Black and I identify as Black and this is a predominantly White institution and community. I was quite aware before I came here that this was a predominantly White institution and it was within a predominantly White community. I mean the Black population in

> [name of Midwestern city in the U.S. omitted] is quite small. Coming here I was aware of all that so there were no surprises so to speak. And I don't really differentiate myself from my colleagues in some ways. I mean clearly our education was different. I think in some ways our outlook is different. But I don't deal with a lot of issues of race and ethnicity in my research, so I find that I'm not really a part of that conversation overtly when I deal with my colleagues. And I don't think I'm treated differently because I'm Black. I've never had any experiences where I felt like I was singled-out or not provided with opportunities because I was Black. As a matter of fact, I think that I have had greater success gaining entrance into particular communities because I'm Black. And the teachers and the students can identify with me over my colleagues who are White. So I would say it was [more] advantageous than it's been non-beneficial.

Corey also explained that she has had positive relationships with her students and that many of them who also identified as Black found solace in her office. She stated that some of the students who visited her office were also from the Caribbean and that they primarily expressed frustrations about acclimating to living in a small Midwestern town. Most of them had come from bigger cities and more urban communities. She emphasized that their complaints were never about racialized issues. I delved deeper into Corey's relationships with her students by asking her to tell me more specifically about how students interacted with her in the classroom. Again, she explained her interactions in positive terms, but at the same time she drew attention to her accent as a noticeable difference that she felt she had to explain.

> Well, I make it clear when I'm introducing myself on the first day that I have an accent, I'm Jamaican. And there are some times when I speak, the words will not be clear, go ahead and ask me to repeat, I won't be offended. So I really introduce myself in that way and I talk about differences between us and differences in our educational experience, which I think is really pivotal in preparing them for the differences that will exist between them and the students in the classroom. So I really use that as the basis for talking about a lot of things that we deal with in the course: differences in economic status, differences in race and ethnicity, differences in learning styles, a lot of the kind of differences that they'll have and how you have to really be open to listening to your students and dealing with them on their level. Which I think puts me in a really good place to talk about that because we are different.

In this instance Corey discussed how she introduces herself and frames her identity when she is teaching a course that prepares education majors to teach Math in elementary classrooms. Corey explained that Math is a subject the students dislike in general and that they bring much of those anxieties, fears, and such dislike to her classroom. "It has nothing to do with me," she said. She described herself as being uniquely prepared to address student anxieties and noted that it was part of her responsibility to help to change their negative views of Math.

But when I asked more specifically how she thought the students perceived her, she said that they seemed to feel less relaxed and acted more cautiously around her, offering that perhaps they were afraid of being culturally insensitive:

> A lot of them they probably are far more cautious because we're in such a racially sensitive time. But I think maybe they're less open because they're possibly fearful that I may be offended. I haven't had any overt experiences but I think it's just sometimes the way that I see they approach me and I have to really be clear and try to get them to relax.

Corey's narrative illustrates that she felt empowered and confident in her position as a researcher and as an instructor in the university classroom. At the same time, her narrative reveals that she also bears a great deal of responsibility for making students feel at ease in her presence.

KIKI: THE TEACHER

Kiki is a 32-year old professor from Russia who had switched jobs from one Midwestern institution to another. Framing her faculty experiences at her previous university were distinct recollections of how she felt she was perceived by students, faculty, and administration. Kiki thought students and colleagues alike were prejudiced by her youthful appearance, feminine identity, and Russian accent. In addition, the handling of her application for an immigrant work visa, which would allow her to continue her tenure-track faculty appointment at the university, developed into a conflict with the university's administration. These issues combined were part of her rationale to submit an employment resignation. Her account of such prejudice came when I asked her to describe how she negotiated her identity at her previous institution:

> I don't know if it is characteristic or a feature of me being born female or not. But it was hard for me to be there. And I don't know how to explain that because I have this feeling that I'm a tiny little thing that brings something different. And they looked at me as I would always say, as a talking monkey who knows some things that they don't know. Sometimes people talk to me like that. I felt like a tiny little thing especially when I compare myself with my husband who is much taller and he looks his age, maybe older, and I look younger. I try to produce the impression of a softer person, more negotiable. And he's stricter, he's maybe stronger sometimes. Maybe I'm stronger sometimes. But when he enters the classroom nobody doubts that he is a professor. When *I* enter the classroom sometimes people don't notice me. And I have to use other power, you know, like occupy the space that a professor would occupy at the front; I have to speak louder, I have to write on the board, I give instructions and only after that, people take me as a professor.

Kiki's age and gender identity perhaps put her in a distinctive position as a faculty member, especially when added to the fact that she has a strong Russian accent. She also indicated that she uses a very accommodating communication style when she said, "I try to produce impression of a softer person, more negotiable." In this instance, perhaps her choice of communication strategy was intended to put her colleagues and students more at ease. She struggled therefore with trying to balance an accommodating communication style with the formal authority she found necessary in the classroom. Interestingly enough, Kiki later described her former work environment as one that did not include very many international faculty members, but the intersections of age, gender, and geopolitical facets of her identity seemed even more striking as she went on to describe her former department chair's reaction to her:

> And then during the first faculty meeting, the chair introduced me as, 'This is Kiki and she's not 14 years old.' That's what he said. And I was like shocked. He was making a joke, but it's kind of a[n] [in]sensitive joke. And another guy who was hired with me, he was a guy like some grey hair, about 40 or 45 and he was not introduced that way.

Kiki made it clear to me that she took offense to the joke. Further, her comparison between her own introduction and that of an older, White male colleague indicated that she was acutely aware of her chair's perceptual bias.

DISCUSSION

How international female faculty members express their multifaceted identities is centrally dependent upon primary frameworks they use to make sense of themselves but is also dependent upon the frameworks of others with whom they interact. Our interactions with students, colleagues, and administrators are embedded as Sprague (1992) suggests, "within the organizational setting of a particular school, in the occupational norms of the profession, and in the social climate of the times" (p. 182). The fact that the women in this study described such different experiences and feelings during their academic tenure is symbolic of the specific organizational contexts in which we each find ourselves. Irene described her successful tenure case as being based on her ability to contribute to the kind of research in which her colleagues were interested and invested. This is a sign of the established norms of our academic profession. Corey described her White students as being ill at ease and conscious of her potential sensitivity to racialized comments or questions. This is a sign of the social climate in which we now live. At the same time, our situatedness tells something valuable and different from the dominant narrative in the U.S. academy. Kiki described her colleagues as perceiving her as a "talking monkey." Her need to "produce [an] impression of a softer . . . more negotiable" person, is symbolic of how her gendered oppression interacts with her ethnicity, age, immigrant status, and language. Irene on the other hand, felt lucky to have been granted tenure. She was deeply conscious of how her accent and place of origin were perhaps set aside for her tenure approval. Irene's situation demonstrates how her ethnicity, language, and Argentinean origin provided a distinctive context for her tenure case. That Corey felt it was necessary to address her accent on the first day of class illustrates that she is mindful of how her "difference" is likely perceived by her students. In my own case, my ability to perform professionally and adapt my speech style to the academic-organizational context in which I was present at the time, caused others to identify me in a way that was incongruous to the way I self-identified. In other words, my accent did not match what Whites in my environment expected to hear when I spoke as an Afro-Caribbean woman. In each case, different aspects of our experiences and identities interacted with our gender to create a larger, unique context for international female academics as a unit of analysis for research.

These experiences confirm *multiple jeopardy*, where different forms of oppression interact to affect our lives in distinctive ways. Obstacles to full participation as faculty members in our distinctive disciplines, departments, and university campuses may also be more intensely aggravated by the linguistic and cultural differences we each express in separate ways. The dominant culture in the U.S. excludes and subordinates many immigrants' cultural expressions through a complex system of norms, practices, and beliefs. That central cultural framework organizes experiences into gendered and racialized semiotic indicators that most, if not all, social actors in U.S. society are aware of at some level. Hidden within our narratives are indications of how power relations in U.S. society are reproduced and maintained within the university setting. Next, I highlight additional insights from our narratives.

GEOPOLITICS AND RACE

Both Irene and Corey did something interesting as they told their individual stories. Their intent was to help me understand that they did not see their racialization as a barrier to their successes. In so doing, they inadvertently exposed how they understood the ordering of experiences and identities in their profession and in the U.S. context. Irene and Corey made every effort to indicate that they had not experienced racism in the academy. But at the same time, they framed their identities in hegemonic terms. For example, Irene felt she had successfully made a case for how she could contribute to scientific research in which other professors at her university were also interested. But in recognizing the strength of her tenure case, she repeatedly highlights her underprivileged geopolitical location and racialization: "I had good training in my country, *although we're not North America;*" " . . . *although* she comes from . . . the *southern-most country in the world and she has [a] strong accent*, she still . . . has valid points;" and "accent and race and gender, sure this is part of yourself, but science should really be independent of that." Irene described the logic that she thought her colleagues used in deciding her tenure case when she was hired. She recognized her racialization within the university system and within the dominant cultural structure of the U.S and in fact reproduced it, even as she framed herself as being a privileged, White professor. In effect, Irene played an active role in othering herself as she interpreted how her body is read by the dominant culture. Irene also made reference to the polarization between the global South and North and identified herself as belonging to the under-privileged South. Geopolitical discourses like U.S. national identity discourse are racialized and dependent on a confluence of factors from history to economics to demography to foreign policy. The systematic arrangement involved in Northern states and countries being viewed as more advanced and Southern states and countries being viewed as needing development is evidence of this redundancy.

LANGUAGE ATTITUDES

Just as Irene unconsciously reproduced the racial ordering of experience in the framing of her identity, Corey too maintained power relations in framing her experience through highlighting how she thought her White students would perceive her Jamaican accent. She recalled how she framed herself in front of the classroom by telling her students on the first day of class that she was aware she had a Jamaican accent and that if they had difficulty understanding her speech, they should ask her to repeat herself. While on the surface, this seemed like a fair way to describe herself, Corey not only invited her White students to pay attention to her accent, she exposed an American cultural predisposition; the way she speaks can affect the way students evaluate her competency as a professor. Corey's language style in effect confirms her position as "Other" and delegitimizes her role as professor. Her communication strategy is to pre-empt any issues students might have with the way she speaks English. But the mere fact that she found it necessary to explain her accent means she was compensating for a cultural attitude that was already there. Yet, Corey does not feel as though she is a major participant in the general social conversation about race/ethnicity: "I don't deal with a lot of issues of race and ethnicity in my research, so I find that I'm not really a part of that conversation overtly." By projecting an image of how she thinks the students will see her, Corey, perhaps unconsciously, reproduces and maintains relations of power between White and Black and citizen and foreigner—where dialect or accented speech signifies lower social standing than standard American speech.

Cargile (2003) discussed discriminating attitudes toward non-standard speech, noting the way U.S. Americans have consistently prejudged individuals who speak English with an Appalachian, Spanish, German, or African-American vernacular accent. These ways of speaking are perceived as "less intelligent, poorer, less educated, and less status possessing" (p. 217) than "standard American English." When international faculty members enter the college classroom, these attitudes are often reflected. Cargile also observed that Americans tend to overlook or minimize language-based prejudice and that much research still needs to be done on this issue.

In addition to Cargile's (2003) work, an earlier study by Johnson and Buttny (1982) suggested that, "[W]hite listeners may selectively bias their responses to a speaker who 'sounds [B]lack' and speaks about abstract and intellectual content" (p. 45). However, the researchers found no bias was expressed by research subjects when speakers who sounded Black spoke of their own experiences. The researchers concluded that abstract and intellectual expression, which are of high value in educational settings, are distinctly reserved for representatives of the dominant U.S. culture and that their subjects demonstrated "linguistic prejudice toward sounding [B]lack in the intellectual register" (p. 45). Hecht, Jackson, and Ribeau (2003) reiterate similar points in discussing Black identities and their relationships to language systems.

INTERSECTIONS OF FEMININITY, AGE, AND ETHNICITY

Unlike Irene and Corey who are identified by others as Hispanic and Black respectively, Kiki identified as a White woman, as she is European. However, Kiki highlights her feminine features as they intersect with ideas about being Russian in her professional experience. Stereotypes about Russian women as beautiful, domesticated, long-suffering, and effeminate are prevalent in U.S. culture. Kiki's narrative illuminates the ordering of her identity and experience as she constructs a narrative of how she thinks she was perceived at her former university: "And they looked at me . . . as a talking monkey who knows some things that they don't know."

Kiki attempts to subvert the dominant cultural arrangements by emulating a traditional White male professor and compelling students to see her as a formal authority in the classroom:

> And I have to use other power, you know, like occupy the space that a professor would occupy at the front; I have to speak louder, I have to write on the board, I give instructions and only after that, people take me as a professor.

At the same time, she struggles to balance that formal authority with an accommodating communication strategy. The two orientations that Kiki espouses, one of formal authority and the other of accommodation, can at times be incongruous. But it is perhaps her students' and colleagues' perceptions of her age and language style that aggravate stereotypes already associated with her femininity. These aspects of her identity played a central role in the incident where her department chair made an insensitive remark about her age: *"This is Kiki and she's not 14 years old."* The chair's remark in effect, was an attempt at a public "outing." It was as if he were saying, "Yes, Kiki is different from the rest of us—but not in a good way." This is an example of what Keane-Dawes (2004) refers to as delegitimizing through everyday interaction. It is a way of saying, "This person does not deserve the status associated with the position she is in." Performing as an effective faculty member in this kind of environment is additionally taxing.

CONCLUSION

While some international female professors may enjoy privileges extended to us through our membership in academia, there are many, like myself and the other women I include in this chapter, who perhaps still struggle to feel powerful in our positions as university faculty. The projections we four women share of how the majority culture views us do not appear out of thin air—they come from experience and from recognizing the grand narrative in U.S. culture. In each case, we tried to utilize communication strategies that would put majority group members more at ease: Kiki wanted to be seen as soft and negotiable, yet project formal authority in the classroom; Corey did not want to participate in the conversation on race but implicated herself as a racialized subject in order to compensate for her students' language attitudes; Irene reasoned that the goals of science trumped the perception her colleagues held of her as a racialized subject, but consistently reproduced dichotomies of White privileged/Hispanic underprivileged and North advanced/South backward, in her narrative. Prior to my graduate school experience, I was under the impression that my ability to adapt to certain aspects of U.S. professional culture would be welcomed. Unfortunately, I underestimated the personal risk involved in adjusting my speech code and not fully projecting a stereotypical Afro-Caribbean image. Each of us has a personal and professional interest in representing ourselves in ways that make majority group members more comfortable. So, how do we empower ourselves as professors, researchers, and women of service to our communities and professions?

As a new, international professor on the tenure-track, I can offer few clues to what might work. Perhaps, building personal relationships with students, other faculty, and administrators to demonstrate the inaccuracy of stereotypes might be the most effective option. I would also suggest that new, international faculty members not suffer in silence. Educate others on what you need. Ask for the kind of mentoring you need to be successful. Ask for additional support in your teaching and research. When conflicts arise, communicate with senior faculty to determine how to proceed. Locate allies who care enough about you individually and who respect and understand your cultural differences. Search for the kind of fruit (research topics, personal relationships, etc.) that will sustain you. However, to identify other strategies for international faculty, further research is necessary.

There are significant implications inherent in the narratives described here. First, it is difficult to measure the extent to which we project stereotyped images on ourselves against the extent to which those stereotypes are manifested in our experiences. But it is clear that there is a relationship between the two. Second, our narratives demonstrate the discursive capacity of language to disguise what is going on in intercultural moments. Perhaps, there is a need then to call out, to name, to formulate new phrases that describe the perceptions inherent in cross-cultural interactions as they occur. Third, it is evident that labels such as *faculty of color*, which some institutions use to identify faculty employees, are problematic, especially when such identifications are tied to institutional benefits. Finally, there are contextual implications related to differences of national origin in that, each of us as subjects experiences the intersections of race, gender, immigrant status, and class in diverse ways. Each of us has a distinct standpoint, shaped by our membership in various social groups. The narratives of international faculty experiences in other regions of the United States would probably be quite different from those found here. I make no attempt to generalize international female faculty experiences, but by strategically grouping ourselves as a unit of analysis, we can confirm the distinctiveness of our experiences. What is presented here is only part of the story of American and academic identity politics. What is important is that we recognize that such diversity can help universities expand their global reach, expose students to more global experiences, and increase the capacity of scholarship to address problems the dominant culture does not see. Such contributions from international female faculty in particular, can level the playing field of the professoriate and plant trees that bear fruit and bring nourishment to everyone's souls.

REFERENCES

Aguirre, Jr., A. (2000). *Women and minority faculty in the academic workplace: Recruitment, retention, and academic culture.* (ASHE-ERIC Higher Education Rep. No. 27-6). San Francisco, CA: Jossey-Bass.

Bloom, L. R. (2002). From self to society: Reflections on the power of narrative inquiry. In S. B. Merriam (Ed.), *Qualitative Research in Practice: Examples for Discussion and Analysis* (pp. 310-313). San Francisco, CA: Jossey-Bass.

Cargile, A. C. (2003). Language matters. In L. A. Samovar & R. E. Porter, *Intercultural Communication: A Reader* (pp. 239-246). Belmont, CA: Wadsworth/Thompson Learning.

Ellis, C. (2004). *The ethnographic I: A methodological novel about autoethnography*. Walnut Creek, CA: Alta Mira Press.

Ellis, C., & Bochner, A. (2000). Autoethnography, personal narrative, reflexivity: Researcher as subject. In N. K. Denzin & Y. S. Lincoln (Eds.), *Handbook of Qualitative Research* (pp. 733-768). Thousand Oaks, CA: Sage.

Erickson, C. D., & Rodriguez, E. R. (1999). Indiana Jane and the temples of doom: Recommendations for enhancing women and racial/ethnic faculty's success in academia. *Innovative Higher Education, 24*(2), 149-168.

Fuller, S., Orbe, M., & Potter, L. (2003, March). College of Arts & Sciences Faculty of Color Caucus. [Mission Statement Document]. Western Michigan University, Kalamazoo, MI.

Goffman, E. (1986). *Frame analysis: An essay on the organization of experience*. Boston, MA: Northeastern University Press.

Hecht, M. L., Jackson II, R. L., & Ribeau, S. A. (2003). *African-American communication: Exploring identity and culture*. Mahwah, NJ: Lawrence Erlbaum Associates.

Haraway, D. (1988). Situated knowledges: The science question in feminism and the privilege of partial perspective. *Feminist Studies, 14*, 575-599.

Harding, S. (1991). *Whose science? Whose knowledge? Thinking from women's lives*. Ithaca, NY: Cornell University Press.

Harstock, N. (1983). The feminist standpoint: Developing the ground for a specifically feminist historical materialism. In S. Harding & M. B. Hintikka (Eds.), *Discovering reality: Feminist perspectives on epistemology, metaphysics and philosophy of science* (pp. 283-310). Dordrecht, The Netherlands: Reidel.

hooks, b. (1989). *Talking back: Thinking feminist, thinking black*. Cambridge, MA: South End Press.

Johnson, F. L., & Buttny, R. (1982). White listeners' responses to "sounding Black" and "sounding White": The effects of message content on judgments about language. *Communication Monographs, 49*, 33-49.

Keane-Dawes, J. (2004). Positioning the postcolonial subject as illegitimate: Narrating the experiences of being black, foreign, and female in US academia. In M. Hall, J. Keane-Dawes, & A. Rodriguez (Eds.), *Embodying the postcolonial life: Immigrant stories of resistance* (pp. 87-99). New York, NY: Humanity Books.

King, D. K. (1988). Multiple jeopardy, multiple consciousness: The context of a black feminist ideology. *Signs: Journal of Women in Culture and Society, 14*, 42-72.

Kvale, S. (1996). *Interviews*. Thousand Oaks, CA: Sage.

Monroe, K., Ozyurt, S., Wrigley, T., & Alexander, A. (2008). Gender equality in academia: Bad news from the trenches, and some possible solutions. *Perspectives in Politics, 6*(2), 215-233.

Orbe, M. (2004, April). Communicating self and the negotiation of multiple co-cultural identities. Guest lecture presented at Arizona State University, Tempe, AZ.

Rai, K. B., & Crizer, J. W. (2000). *Affirmative action and the university race, ethnicity, and gender in higher education*. Lincoln, NE: University of Nebraska Press.

Schiller, N. G., Basch, L., & Blanc-Szanton, C. (1992). Transnationalism: A new framework for understanding migration. *Annals of the New York Academy of Sciences, 645*, 1-24.

Shome, R. (2000). A response to William Starosta's "On the intersection of rhetoric and intercultural communication." In A. Gonzalez & D. V. Tanno (Eds.), *Rhetoric in intercultural contexts* (pp. 169-173). Thousand Oaks, CA: Sage.

Snow, D. A., & Benford, R. D. (1992). Master frames and cycles of protest. In A. D. Morris & C. M. Mueller (Eds.), *Frontiers in social movement theory* (pp. 133-155). New Haven, CT: Yale University Press.

Sprague, J. (1992). Critical perspectives on teacher empowerment. *Communication Education, 41*, 181-203.

Turner, C. S. (2000). New faces, new knowledge. *Academe, 86*, 34-37.

Waters, M. C. (1999). *Black identities: West Indian immigrant dreams and American realities*. Boston, MA: Harvard University Press.

Waters, M. C., & Jimenez, T. R. (2005). Assessing immigrant assimilation: New empirical and theoretical challenges. *Annual Review of Sociology, 31*, 105-125.

West, R., & Turner, L. H. (2010). *Introducing communication theory: Analysis and application*. Boston, MA: McGraw-Hill.

Wilson, E. S. (2008). *Anywhere under the sun: Afro-Caribbean immigrants' perspectives on U.S. citizenship and experience of cultural transition* (Doctoral dissertation). Arizona State University, Tempe, AZ.

Chapter 11

My Brown Body as Strange and Suspect
Painful Moments and Powerful Realizations

Rachel Alicia Griffin

"It is a part of our deepest and most precious integrity that we should speak (if we wish) for ourselves." (Berry, 2000, p. 80)

I remember the day well. It was June 11, 2008 and I had successfully defended my dissertation at the University of Denver (DU). As my committee signed the final paperwork, I was swimming in a celestial space, overcome by joy and literally trembling at the possibility of getting a full night's sleep. Their gift to me at the end of my defense was the official permission to move forward into my new faculty position at Southern Illinois University at Carbondale (SIUC) without the pressing weight of a dissertation. I was filled with an insurmountable sense of pride as my committee members congratulated me as "Dr. Griffin." I had done it. I had worked through fear, fatigue, and tears to achieve a goal that had been ten years in the making, with the support of many. As a first-generation college student of color who was raised in a single-parent home in the lower working class, becoming "Dr. Griffin" seemed nothing short of a hard-earned miracle.

After my defense, I sat on the steps of the academic building that I had practically lived in during the previous six months with a slideshow playing in my mind. Triumphant tears slid down my cheeks as I remembered all of the moments when I had questioned whether or not I could in fact become "Dr. Griffin." I felt proud and even slightly invincible, given the cloud nine effect of my successful dissertation defense. In hindsight, I wish I could go back to that day for just a moment to truly remember what it felt like. I already long for the feelings of pride, peace, and strength that wrapped around me that day.

Since then, I have shared great moments with compassionate folks at my new institution. I have colleagues and allies here, some of whom I imagine in time will become close friends; however, the cloud nine effect has passed since I have also been steadily reminded of the ways in which my biracial Black, [1] female body is viewed as strange and suspect. I use the word "strange" as in a cultural "Other;" an inferior body that is not read as cerebral and as such, is suspect in academic spaces. Speaking to the ways that Black female professors are positioned as strange and suspect in the academy, bell hooks (2010) opines that, "we are still likely to be seen as intruders in the academic world who do not really belong" (p. 101).

The purpose of this chapter is to share the challenging and triumphant experiences I have encountered during my first year as a new female faculty member of color at a traditionally White institution.[2] Operating from a Black feminist (Collins, 2000; hooks, 1981) and womanist (Walker, 1983) standpoint, which positions Black women at the center of inquiry as vibrant, intellectual, and compassionate "cultural workers" (West, 1999, p. 119), I engage personal narrative to confront the stereotypical assumptions ascribed to my brown, female body in the ivory tower.[3] Given the rarity of visible perspectives provided by women of color in the grand narrative of the academy, I move forward in this chapter to fulfill part of my promise to my dissertation committee—I promised that I would mirror for others the caring support that they had offered me. Likewise, mindful of those whose shoulders my access to higher education rests upon and those whose access rests upon my shoulders, I seek to continue in Alice Walker's tradition to write "all the things *I should have been able to read*" (emphasis in the original, Walker 1983, p. 13).[4] In this vein, I will work through what I consider to be painful and powerful "critical incidents" (Sikes, Measor, & Woods, 1985, p. 57), i.e. the pedagogical moments during my first year when I learned hard lessons as a woman of color about the ways that systems of oppression are overtly and covertly thriving in higher education—the lessons that I wish I had anticipated. Rooting myself in Black feminist thought as a means to voice, I will describe each critical incident from memory and notes to myself that were often scrawled in the margins of whatever I had with me to write on when I felt marked as strange and suspect. As I move through each critical incident, I will unpack the pedagogical offerings of my encounters as a biracial Black woman who is discursively positioned as "Other" in the academy. Lastly, I will close with reflections rooted in hope and everyday praxis.

Black Feminist Thought as a Means to Voice

As an epistemological and methodological framework, Black feminist thought, hereafter referred to as BFT, provides a means to explore my experiences as a new female faculty member of color on a traditionally White campus. The shared foundational thread among Black feminist thinkers, activists, and writers is that Black women provide unique, experiential, and meaningful insight into the ways that "gendered racism" (Mutua, 2006) works in U.S. American society based upon their social locations as Black women (Collins, 2000; hooks, 1981; Reynolds, 2002). Paying close attention to the intersections of identities (i.e. race, sexual orientation, ability, nationality, class, gender, age, etc.), BFT highlights the ways that Black women endure what scholars have termed "double jeopardy" (Beal, 1970), "multiple jeopardy" (King, 1988), and "multiple marginality" (Turner, 2002) as members of multiple oppressed identity groups. From an intersectional approach, the intricacies of identifying with more than one form of oppression become visible in that the oppressive forces that Black women encounter are not simply "racism + sexism" (King, 1988, p. 51). Rather, our experiences are multiplicative and layered, which gives rise to nuanced forms of oppression (Beal, 1970; Bowleg, 2008; King, 1988; Turner, 2002).

Combined with the embrace of a strategic essentialist approach (Wing, 2003) that names and resists oppressive group treatment without dismissing the heterogeneity among Black women, intersectionality allows me to speak to the realities of being simultaneously raced and gendered while housed within the Black/White binary. This intersectional perspective is essential since, as a biracial Black woman, I do not "fit" in the Black *or* White binary nor can I speak from a Black *or* White positionality since my reality as a woman of color is shaped by being Black *and* White. Furthermore, as a critical scholar activist, I believe that my marginalized identities (biracial, female, lower working-class roots) and privileged identities (heterosexual, U.S. American, able-bodied, middle-class status) jointly shape my experiences in the academy.

By utilizing BFT to theoretically and methodologically create an oppositional space, I can speak openly as a biracial Black woman to the politics of institutional vulnerability, "endurance labor" (Cuádraz & Pierce, 1994), and "impostor syndrome" (Clance & Imes, 1978) at the intersections of my marginalized and privileged identities. In this context, I position my access to voice as a privilege. Thus, although women of color within and beyond the academy are clearly constrained by macro, meso, and micro (Kirk & Okazawa-Rey, 2004) forces of oppression, to give voice to my experiences is a privilege since many women who look like me have no space at all to speak to their experiences.

Drawing upon the historical roots of Black women in the academy, I am reminded that I am not the first who has taken this journey nor am I alone. Black women have been earning Ph.D.s since 1921 when Eva Dykes, Sadie Tanner Alexander, and Georgianna Simpson became the first African American women to earn doctorates (Perkins, 2009). Following in their footsteps, in recent years, Black female scholars have utilized elements of BFT to make powerful contributions to the defiant discourses that render the academy's oppressive practices visible. For example, Patton (2004) calls out the severe lack of foundational change in higher education despite the rhetoric dedicated to the importance of diversity. Similarly, via a classroom discussion addressing students' perceptions of Black female teachers at a traditionally White school, Brandon (2006) concludes that students identify her as a threat to "institutionalized conventions of truth" (p. 194). Narrating her struggles as a Black woman in higher education, Carter-Black (2008) contributes by posing stereotype threat (Steele, 1997) as a means of deconstructing the academy as an unwelcoming space for women of color. According to Steele, stereotype threat occurs when a person of color feels that she/he may "be judged or treated in terms of a racial stereotype" (p. 616). Addressing the individual and collective challenges that Black women face, Trotman (2009) asks a profound question that many Black female scholars have sought to answer:

> In the white male dominated ivory tower, how does the ebony woman manage to survive the constant assaults on her academic contributions, her intellectual capacity, and her humanity without doubting herself and feeling like the imposter that many in the academy seem to perceive? (p. 79)

Mirroring the critical insights and questions provided by those who have come before me, I often feel as if I am wading through an ocean of expectation without the relief of land in site. Hence, the academy stubbornly remains a space where those who do not embody, or at least affirm, dominant norms are discursively positioned as "Other" (Allen, Orbe, & Olivas, 1999; Berry & Mizelle, 2006; Bernal, 2002; Collins, 1986; Cuádraz & Pierce, 1994; Johnsrod, & Sadao, 2002; Turner, 2002). As someone rendered the Other, BFT serves a dual purpose for me as a life preserver and a means to "talk back" (hooks, 1989) to the academy. As a life preserver, BFT offers a validating space where my experiences, concerns, and interests as a biracial Black woman are positioned at the center of concern as significant and meaningful, rather than being silenced and dismissed in accordance with dominant cultural norms. Describing the essence of "talking back" as a means to self-determination through the resistant act of speaking truth to power, bell hooks (1989) says:

> Moving from silence into speech is for the oppressed, the colonized, the exploited, and those who stand and struggle side by side a gesture of defiance that heals, that makes new life and new growth possible. It is that act of speech, of "talking back," that is no mere gesture of empty words, that is the expression of our movement from object to subject—the liberated voice. (p. 9)

A defining feature of BFT, "the liberated voice" (hooks, 1989, p. 9), or what critical race scholars refer to as counter-narrative, can "shatter complacency and challenge the status quo" (Delgado, 2000, p. 61). For example, Frederick Corey (1998) reminds us "that the personal narrative is one way of disturbing the master narrative, and through the performative dimensions of the personal narrative, the individual is able to disrupt—and dare I say *rewrite*—the master narrative" (emphasis in the original, p. 250).

Counter-narrative creates a space for Black women rendered the strange and suspect Other to contradict dominant discourses in higher education that strategically labor to entrap brown female bodies in the subject positions of mammy, jezebel, sapphire, matriarch, and the more contemporary welfare queen, hoodrat, crazy Black bitch, superwoman, or a combination thereof (Collins, 2000; hooks, 1981; Hull, Scott, & Smith, 1982; Neubeck & Cazenave, 2001; Reynolds-Dobbs, Thomas, & Harrison, 2008). Within these predetermined discursive subject positions, there is not any room for intellectual Black women who are passionate, determined, and committed to social justice. Rather, our intellect is questioned, challenged, and ignored when lodged against the prolific backdrop of these negative, stereotypical representations.

Personal/Academic[5] Experiences and Private/Public Pain

As a biracial Black female faculty member, I have come to learn that my body in the ivory tower simply does not make sense to most folks. It is as if dropping a Ph.D. into the mix at the intersections of my identities is a baffling social mystery. In other words, "[my] brown skin and my Ph.D. appear to be oxymorons in this place" (Solórzano & Yosso, 2002, p. 486). For example, I have often been assumed to be a student and introducing myself as "Dr. Griffin" is frequently met with looks of surprise accompanied by an ascending "Really?" Then, the person who made the assumption of who I am (and who I am not), usually follows her or his "really?" with a quick apology and a comment about how young

I look and how my young appearance will serve me well in years to come. On the surface, these interactions may seem innocent and even complimentary and yet to me, they are constant, often daily, reminders of my "outsider-within status" (Collins, 1986, p. S14) as a woman of color in a traditionally White, patriarchal space. More specifically, the stereotypical assumptions and comments about who I am (and who I am not) serve as microaggressions, which undermine the legitimacy of my presence on campus. Microaggressions are defined by Sue et al. (2007) as subtle insults directed toward members of ethnic minority groups that are both intentional and unintentional. From my perspective, each stereotypical assumption serves as a microaggressive act that sends stern (although understated) messages that I do not belong. As such, these acts clearly mark me as a strange and suspect professor, always questionable and never commonsensical.

During my doctoral program, my mentors of color were generous with their time and energy in that they often transparently shared their thoughts about what they wish they would have known when they made the transition from student to faculty. In hindsight, I now understand that they were trying to prepare me for the microaggressions that I would encounter despite my beliefs that I was completely prepared for my new role as a female faculty member of color. I remember mentally contemplating my game plan, knowing that I had to learn how power worked at my new institution in order to survive. I knew that I needed to network within and beyond my department to find a community of critical scholars/activists. I knew that undergraduate and graduate students of color would inundate me quickly. I knew that my first year would be exhausting since the learning curve would be astronomically high, while safe spaces and places to reenergize would be far and few in between. I listened closely to their narratives and also sought out the research of scholars of color who described isolation, alienation, devaluation, lack of respect, fatigue, and exclusion as customary characteristics of the experiences of faculty of color (Calafell, 2007; Johnsrod & Sadao, 2002; Turner & Myers, 2000).

Brimming with this knowledge, I felt prepared for my transition from student to faculty member. However, the embodied experience of being faculty, having completed my dissertation, having *e-a-r-n-e-d* my Ph.D., and *still* having my brown body rendered strange and suspect was more painful than what I had ever experienced before. The uncertainty and seeming interrogation that flows beneath the surface of many of my everyday interactions with students, staff, and faculty seem to carry an additional sting. Moving forward, I will *always* remember the "critical incidents" (Sikes, Measor, & Woods, 1985, p. 57) that follow as powerful, pedagogical moments of my first year as faculty.

Sikes, Measor, and Woods (1985) refer to critical incidents as "highly charged moments and episodes that have enormous consequences for personal change and development" (p. 230). Processing these incidents through BFT, I endeavor to speak for myself, contradict the assumptions that have been made about who I can (and cannot) be as a brown female, work against the everyday (re)production[6] of the discourses of domination that mark me as strange and suspect, and counter the forces of internalized oppression.

CRITICAL INCIDENTS

CRITICAL INCIDENT #1: NEW FACES

I taught two undergraduate sections of intercultural communication during my first semester at SIUC. The critical incident that follows took place early during the fall semester immediately following one of my class periods. This conversation occurred between me and an older gentleman who I perceived as White who taught in the classroom right after I did. On this day, I was packing up to leave and saying goodbye to my students while he was coming in and greeting his students. Upon entering the room:

> *He said: Hey, you must be the new graduate student that they hired around here!*
>
> *I said: No, my name is Dr. Griffin, I am a new faculty member in Speech Comm.*
>
> *He said: Oh! You keep gettin' younger and younger!*

From my perspective, a surface view of our interaction indicates that it was brief and kind-natured, a few comments exchanged in a friendly moment of passing. However, I felt my body viscerally react to the sting of his words; my ears got hot and my stomach dropped to my knees while the credibility I had been working to earn with my new students surely took a nosedive. Already having to work harder to earn the respect of my students as a Black female professor (hooks, 2010), I was devastated at the loss. In less than 30 seconds he had announced to a room full of students (I imagine with the intent to be friendly) that, based on how I look, I did not make sense according to his assumptions. This experience marked my first "silent revolution"[7] (Solórzano & Yosso, 2001, p. 483) at SIUC. My painful-to-swallow-my-pride silence was strategic yet internally humiliating. Like Joni Jones (2003) in "Sista Docta," renditions of what I wanted to say/wished I could say/wished I had said flowed through my mind both during and long after our conversation. I wanted to react with a sharp correction of his assumption and explain to him that from my perspective, his interpretation of who I could possibly be at this institution was rooted in centuries of racist and sexist oppression (Collins, 2000; hooks, 1981; hooks, 1990). I wished I could tell him that my age was irrelevant because I had unquestionably earned my Ph.D., yet I held my tongue. In my mind, it was quite likely that the older White gentleman had a great deal more cultural capital at SIUC than I did as a brand new female faculty member of color. Was he tenured? Was he a Department Chair? Was he a Full Professor? I had no idea who he was or what the consequences of my reaction to him might be, so I chose not to problematize our interaction and to remain calm and friendly.

After this day, I saw him weekly for the remainder of the semester as we exchanged "hellos" on my way out of the classroom and his way in. Each time I saw him, I reflected on the humiliation of having been and continuing to be silent. I felt guilty for letting a teachable moment pass by and swallowing my own desire to "talk back" (hooks, 1989, p. 1). Although I still do not know who he is, I am sure that I could easily figure it out and conceivably broach a conversation with him about our initial interaction. Perhaps a teachable moment can be recovered. Yet to be honest, I feel hostile toward giving him more of my time and there is a part of me that fears he probably will not even remember our initial interaction, even though I have remembered it every time I have seen him since.

To ease the mental and emotional weight of carrying moments like these with me, I have since devised new ways of addressing assumptions about who I am and who I am not. As I mentioned earlier, rarely do people assume I am a faculty member and if they do assume that I teach, they typically assume that I am a graduate student. In response to the commonplace surprise, shock, and disbelief, I have started naming the ways that I feel racism and sexism play a role in their assumptions. For me, this has become a strategy that allows me to assert my perceptions while simultaneously (hopefully) creating a teachable moment. For example, I have used a touch of sarcasm to deflate the tense moment when they realize that I am offended by saying, "I know it's hard to imagine given the lack of positive representations of Black women, but here I am, Ph.D. and all, in the flesh!" Or without sarcasm (depending on the day), I might say, "I contextually understand your assumption. At the intersections of race, gender, and age, we are not socialized to perceive young Black women as intellectual, nor have many folks had a professor who is Black and female." By exercising agency to move myself "from silence into speech" (hooks, 1989, p. 9), I often feel a sense of relief, coupled with satisfaction, at having marked my distress and frustration.

Directly addressing the assumptions made concerning who I am (and who I am not) provides an outlet for the tension and humiliation of constantly being "defined out" (Turner, 2002, p. 74) of my well-deserved faculty position; yet this is not to say that I am not irritated by the constant call to (re)define myself back into my faculty position. However, my partner offered a compassionate reminder that has helped to soothe my frustration—although it is unfair that I have had the conversation a hundred times, there are 100 people who have only had the much-needed conversation once.

Critical Incident #2: "As in Colored People?"

At all of my previous educational institutions, beginning in elementary school, the use of the word "colored" to describe people of color was clearly demarcated, at minimum, as politically incorrect if not deeply offensive.[8] On a trip to SIUC's library dressed in jogging pants and a hooded sweatshirt, I was standing at the circulation desk when I overheard two young women who appeared to be White chatting at the next desk (they were approximately two feet from me). Overhearing their conversation, I heard one young woman make a reference to the "colored girl" that lived on their floor. Surprised by the ease of the use of the word "colored," I questioned whether or not I had heard her correctly until I heard the other young woman respond with, "You mean the colored girl who . . ." Then I was sure that they were indeed talking about a woman of color who lived on their floor. Despite feeling personally offended, I did not interrupt their conversation. In reflection, there were a number of reasons I chose not to interject. One, I was taken aback. I simply was not thinking quickly enough on my feet to create a teachable moment. Two, I felt as though I had been eavesdropping and three, I did not think I would be all that convincing in jogging pants and a hooded sweatshirt. By the time I had taken a couple of minutes to process and decide that I should speak up anyway, they were already gathering their belongings to head out the door. Clearly, a teachable moment had been missed. In hindsight, I am reminded of Collins' (2000) discussion of internalized oppression in which she recounts the infinite number of ways that Black women are socialized to discredit, doubt, and silence themselves in U.S. American society. Personally, I find myself deeply troubled that as a biracial Black woman with a Ph.D. in a public educational setting, I did not feel instantaneously strong enough to confront two White students casually tossing around "colored" as a harmless adjective. While BFT calls me to task for keeping my mouth shut, it simultaneously contextualizes my silence—granting me the crucial space to continue nurturing the process of coming to voice.

A few days later, the word "colored" made a second startling appearance in my undergraduate intercultural class that proved to be even more shocking. In a class discussion about the history of racism in a nearby town, a White male student said, "I don't think that colored people have it that bad anymore, not after Civil Rights and all that." I paused for a moment and was actually more surprised by the lack of verbal and nonverbal responses from other students in the classroom than by hearing "colored" casually tossed around again. Taking a quick look around the room, it seemed as if no one was visibly upset by his use of the word "colored" and the student who had made the comment had done so making direct eye contact with me without any detectable hesitancy. I was truly astonished that no one (in this class I had several White students and several students of color) raised their hand, sat up straighter, or even glanced his way. Feeling hurt and confused, I opted to address his assertion that people of color do not "have it that bad anymore" as an example of how perceptions likely differ across racial identities since being White is accompanied by racial privilege, rather than address his use of the word "colored." In the mere seconds that I had to decide how to react, this seemed to the most pedagogically effective road to take. More specifically, my desire not to alienate him interrupted my critical inclination to critique his assertion with a double-whammy of: (1) the use of the word "colored" can be deeply offensive; and (2) part of becoming socially conscious is to remember how privilege can shape our perceptions.

After this class period, I felt as if I had been jolted into a raw sense of contextual awareness about my new institution. Immediately afterward, I went to the main office to heat up my coffee and a trusted and respected colleague had her door open. Bewildered and disturbed, I opted to stop in for a chat.

I said (knocking on her door): Can I interrupt you to ask you a hard question?

She said: Sure!

I said: Is the use of the word "colored" socially acceptable here?

She said (taking off her glasses and orienting her body completely toward mine): As in "colored" people?

I said: Yes, as in "colored" people.

She said: What happened?

After listening to my descriptions of the two separate instances in which I had heard "colored" casually used, she kindly explained that from her experiences, "colored" is often the "best" word that some of our White students have to talk about people of color and that albeit unacceptable, she was not surprised by the lack of reaction from the students who had been present in the room. We chatted for a few additional minutes about the history of southern Illinois and how I might work in a teachable moment during class about the use of the word "colored" without alienating the White male student who made the comment.

I have spoken of this incident often as a means to help friends, family, and colleagues understand my experiences as a biracial Black female professor. For me, this incident serves as a striking illustration of how a supportive and conscious departmental climate can help alleviate some of the stress and tension that accompanies being a scholar of color. It is equally important to recognize that a supportive and conscious departmental climate does not remove the sting of an institutional climate that has yet to foster widespread social consciousness among students. Hence, the student in my class was nearing the end of his academic career at SIUC and clearly had not learned (or perhaps did not care if he had learned) that the contextual use of the word "colored" from a White male toward a Black female could be both hurtful and disrespectful. To be fully transparent, there is a part of me that felt bitter toward the added pressure of finding a way to help him understand the history of the word "colored" and the added complexity of my being the one to do so. This is not to even remotely hint that I cannot handle myself or my students in the classroom, but rather to recognize the emotional "endurance labor" (Cuádraz & Pierce, 1994) that it required to create a moment to explain to the entire class why a word utilized interchangeably with "nigger" throughout U.S. American history by Whites could be offensive. In essence, I did not want to risk embodying the Black female professor as mammy role (hooks, 2010) by gently confronting him to challenge the racism embedded in his use of "colored." However, there was a part of me that wanted to be as publicly angry as I felt and insist that he enlighten himself. I realized though, that revisiting the word "colored" was absolutely essential since the rest of the students in the class had learned something (albeit implicit or explicit) in that moment as well—so revisit we did. Reading the use of "colored" in both instances described above through the lenses of BFT, I am reminded of the ways that Black women in the academy are constantly called upon to address and refute the workings of White patriarchy (Collins, 1986; hooks, 2010; Patton, 2004).

Critical Incident #3: Replenishment

The last critical incident that I will share in this chapter revolves around a moment that I hold close to my heart. This is one of the memories that I turn to when I feel ready to run as far away from the academy as I can to dodge the angst of impostor syndrome (Clance & Imes, 1978). Trotman (2009) describes impostor syndrome as "an internal experience of intellectual phoniness" (p. 77; Clance & Imes, 1978). More specifically, imposter syndrome entails strong feelings of unworthiness, self-doubt, insecurity, and anxiety accompanied by low self-confidence and frequent second-guessing that women in general, and women of color in particular, often experience in organizations and institutions steeped in White patriarchy (Clance & Imes, 1978; Trotman, 2009). These feelings surface despite one's intelligence, potential, value, significant contributions, and previous accomplishments (Carter-Black, 2008; hooks, 2003). Offering a description of impostor syndrome from a Black feminist perspective, Carter-Black (2008) says:

> I second-guess myself much more than I like to admit. I question my potential as a junior faculty member who is capable of achieving tenure at a research university. These doubts, fears, and misgivings seem to surface at each new juncture, and as a novice in the world of academia, there are lots of junctures. Logic suggests that my past academic achievements—particularly the hard-won victories—should bolster my feelings of confidence and sense of self-efficacy. . . . It seems illogical to me as well, but the raw truth is that the qualms, the worries, and the reservations persist. (p. 119)

During my first year as a faculty member at SIUC (and still now at times), I too felt inundated by imposter syndrome. I wondered if I chose the right career path and if I belong here. Time and again, I have come quite close to convincing myself in a puddle of tears to out myself as a "fraud" because I felt as though I was living a professional life that could not possibly be my own in the context of where I come from. Day by day, I felt like I was cranking the handle on a jack-in-the-box and when the clown finally popped up, the joke would be on me. Despite feeling like an impostor, I have had moments that have fiercely combated my insecurities. For example, one day after class, a Black female student lingered behind while I was packing up and offered me an endless gift.

> *She said: You know Rachel, I think it's real cool to have a Black—I mean biracial and Black—woman as a professor. Before you, I had never had one before.*
>
> *I said: You know what? It is cool because I never had a Black female professor or even teacher either.*

After class that day, I walked back to my office proud and thankful. I was proud to be her first Black female professor and I was thankful that she had shared her feelings with me. Until that moment, I had not fully recognized that my students will have had a Black female professor even though I did not, nor had I fully recognized that that my students will know who bell hooks, Gloria Anzaldúa, and Cornel West are much earlier than I was introduced to their socially conscious work. Furthermore, of immense significance to me is that my Black female students in particular will be told and shown by example that they matter, which is arguably the most powerful aspect of my presence in higher education that BFT has helped me to understand.

Whenever I feel overcome by personally and institutionally imposed waves of uncertainty, I return to that student's gift and remind myself that my presence as a critical scholar activist does matter here. Students who look like me can do something that I did not get to do until the third quarter of my Ph.D. program:[9] they can look to the front of the classroom and see someone who looks like them. Students who do not look like me can look to the front of the room and for perhaps the first time, see a woman of color in a position of authority. My presence may not always matter to all of my students or in the ways that I institutionally want it to, but it mattered to her and that is replenishing.

Concluding Thoughts

In reflection on my first year as a faculty member in the academy, the most heart-wrenching questions that surfaced internally were, "What am I doing here?" and "Does my presence matter here?" I also struggled with paralyzing surges of self-doubt and grappled with whether or not I was "good enough" to be among the phenomenal scholarly company I keep in my department. By processing through three critical incidents ("New Faces," "'As in Colored People?'" and "Replenishment") that both confirmed and contested my struggles, I have sought to (re)articulate, via a space shaped by BFT, the imposed status of dismissal and invisibility that women of color often experience in higher education. In doing so, I feel strengthened by the realization that teaching as a biracial Black female at a traditionally White institution renders me a token in that my presence will be counted for the university to forefront its commitment to diversity; however, I will not succumb to being only a token. Gripping tightly to the hope entrenched in Patton's (2004) assertion that "we are both transformed by and transform the organization" (p. 192) and Jones' (2003) belief that "the work can be transformative" (p. 240), I am both optimistic and afraid. I am optimistic that institutions of higher education will continually work toward a genuine commitment to inclusive excellence (Milem, Chang, & Antonio, 2005) with far more than unwavering lip service. Likewise, I am confident in the enduring determination of "tempered radicals" (Meyerson, 2003) who will continue to call out the academy's shamefully oppressive conditions.

Despite my optimism, in the quiet pockets of nighttime when I ask myself, "What are you afraid of?," answers pour outward breaking down the dam that I build up every morning when I enter the performative space of "Dr. Griffin." I am afraid that working in a traditionally White institution will change me beyond personal recognition. That is, having earned all of my formal education in traditionally White schools, I fear that the process has already begun. I am afraid that as a biracial Black woman, the politics surrounding notions of Black authenticity (Leverette, 2009) will hinder the reprieve and protection I can seek among people who look like me. I am afraid of being shrugged off as an Angry Black Woman (Collins, 2000; hooks, 2010), regardless of my intelligence, integrity, and commitment to social justice. Nevertheless, I want to mark my own agency in serving as a faculty member at a traditionally White institution:

> I am here because I have earned my position and I belong here.

I am here because students who look like me need to see me here.

I am here because students who do not look like me need to see me here.

I am here because I believe that we can do far better when it comes to raising social consciousness and building positive relationships across difference.

I am here because SIUC is a space and a place where I can do my part to get us there.

Over time, I have come to terms with the reality that I will struggle in the academy as a woman of color for as long as I remain. At first I met this realization with a sense of hostility since I worked so hard to earn a Ph.D. but remain strange and suspect. Looking back, I think that part of my mistake was the flawed expectation to be humanized, unmarked as the "Other" by my Ph.D., when in fact I must move myself from a token object to a speaking subject (hooks, 1989). For me, this chapter is one step toward doing so; it is a journey that I imagine will span my entire career. For comfort, I return to the notion that I am not alone and neither are you.

NOTES

1. I choose to identify as a biracial Black woman to mark both avowal and ascription in regard to identity performance. Hence, I identify myself as biracial to mark both my African American and White cultural roots; however, my body is often read solely as Black.
2. Tuitt (2008) advocates utilizing "traditionally" opposed to "predominantly" White because "PWI [predominantly White institution] would not include those higher education institutions whose campus populations have been predominantly White but now have students of color in the numeric majority. I argue that even though institutions like MIT and Berkley have more students of color than Whites on campus, the culture, tradition, and values found in those institutions remain traditionally White" (p. 25-26).
3. Throughout this chapter, I use the word "brown" interchangeably with "Black" at times in reference to my lived experiences as a person of color. I do so purposely as a means not only to describe the color of my skin but also to signal the shared realities among multiple marginalized racial groups that are characterized by different skin tones.
4. It is important to recognize that Black women have built an incredible genre of insightful scholarship that speaks to the experiences of Black women at the intersections of their identities. However, despite the existence of this material, they were rarely incorporated into my formal education. Thus, the majority of my knowledge about womanism and Black feminism is self-taught, which has served as an inspiration to write from the intersections of my identities and to include the works of women of color in my course syllabi, discussions, publications, etc.
5. "Personal/Academic" is inspired by Ono (1997).

6. Working from Diamond (1996), "(re)" is utilized to acknowledge "the preexisting discursive field, the repetition—and the desire to repeat—within the performative present, while "embody," "configure," "inscribe," "signify," ["insert verb"] assert the possibility of materializing something that exceeds our knowledge, that alters the shape of sites and imagines other as yet unsuspected modes of being" (p. 2).

7. Describing the essence of a "silent revolution" via a composite and data-driven character named Esperanza, Solórzano and Yosso (2001) offer the following narrative example: "In my classes, because I didn't have a strong grasp of the many languages of the institution, the challenges I raised against the liberal ideas of social justice that ignore Chicanas/os fell on deaf ears. So at that point, I felt that a silent revolution was better than a clamoring battle cry quickly stifled" (p. 482-483). In this context, Solórzano and Yosso's notion of a silent revolution marks the ways that people who represent marginalized identity groups often choose to remain silent to prevent having their experiences explicitly and implicitly dismissed. However, silence does not necessarily indicate complicity. Rather, like Esperanza, the oppressed may strategically choose to keep their critiques of oppressive practices to themselves to protect their physical, emotional, and mental safety.

8. I am reminded by Kennedy (2008) that the interpretation of the word "colored" as a derogatory term is a contentious debate, much like the debates surrounding the use of the word "nigger." For the purpose of this discussion, my interpretation is that the term was used in a derogatory and socially unconscious manner given the contexts in which it was used. This is not to speak to the intent of the White students who used the term (unknowingly and knowingly) in my presence, but rather to speak to my interpretation of the effect of the term.

9. Whenever I talk about the power of positive representation in the classroom for students of color in particular, I am compelled by gratitude to name Dr. Frank Tuitt from DU as the first teacher, instructor, or professor that I ever had who looked like me.

REFERENCES

Allen, B. J., Orbe, M. P., & Olivas, M. R. (1999). The complexity of our tears: Dis/enchantment and (in)difference in the academy. *Communication Theory, 9*(4), 402-429.

Beal, F. (1970). Double jeopardy: To be Black and female. In R. Morgan (Ed.), *Sisterhood is powerful: An anthology of writings from the women's liberation movement* (pp. 340-353). New York, NY: Random House.

Bernal, D. (2002). Critical race theory, Latino theory, and critical raced-gendered epistemologies: Recognizing students of color as holders and creators of knowledge. *Qualitative Inquiry, 8*(1), 105-126.

Berry, T. R., & Mizelle, N. D. (2006). *From oppression to grace: Women of color and their dilemmas in the academy*. Sterling, VA: Stylus.

Berry, W. (2000). *Life is a miracle: An essay against modern superstition*. Berkeley, CA: Counterpoint.

Bowleg, L. (2008). When Black + lesbian + woman ≠ Black lesbian woman: The methodological challenges of qualitative and quantitative intersectionality research. *Sex Roles, 59*, 312-325. doi: 10.1007/s11199-008-9400-z

Brandon, L. T. (2006). Seen, not heard: A conversation about what it means to be Black and female in the academy. In T. R. Berry & N. D. Mizelle (Eds.), *From oppression to grace: Women of color and their dilemmas in the academy* (pp. 168-194). Sterling, VA: Stylus.

Calafell, B. M. (2007). Mentoring and love: An open letter. *Cultural Studies <=> Critical Methodologies*, *7*(4), 425-441.

Carter-Black, J. (2008). A Black woman's journey into a predominately White academic world. *Journal of Women and Social Work*, *23*(2), 112-122. doi: 10.1177/0886109908314327

Clance, P. R., & S. A. Imes (1978). The impostor phenomenon in high achieving women: Dynamics and therapeutic intervention. *Psychotherapy: Theory, Research, and Practice*, *15*, 241-247.

Collins, P. H. (1986). Learning from the outsider within: The sociological significance of Black feminist thought. *Social Problems*, *33*, 14-32.

Collins, P. H. (2000). *Black feminist thought: Knowledge, consciousness, and the politics of empowerment* (2nd ed.). New York, NY: Routledge.

Corey, F. C. (1998). The personal: Against the master narrative. In S. J. Dailey (Ed.), *The future of performance studies* (pp. 249-253). Annandale, VA: National Communication Association.

Cuádraz, G., & Pierce, J. (1994). From scholarship girls to scholarship women: Surviving the contradiction of race and class in academe. *Explorations in Ethnic Studies*, *17*, 21-44.

Delgado, R. (2000). Story-telling for oppositionalists and others: A plea for narrative. In R. Delgado & J. Stefancic (Eds.), *Critical race theory: The cutting edge* (2nd ed.) (pp. 60-70). Philadelphia, PA: Temple University Press.

Diamond, E. (Ed.). (1996). *Performance and cultural politics*. New York, NY: Routledge.

hooks, b. (1981). *Ain't I a Woman: Black women and feminism*. Boston, MA: South End Press.

hooks, b. (1989). *Talking back: Thinking feminist, thinking black.* Boston, MA: South End Press.

hooks, b. (1990). *Yearning: Race, gender and cultural politics.* Boston, MA: South End Press.

hooks, b. (2003). *Rock my soul: Black people and self-esteem*. New York, NY: Washington Square Press.

hooks, b. (2010). *Teaching critical thinking: Practical wisdom*. New York, NY: Routledge.

Hull, G. T., Scott, P. B., & Smith, B. (Eds.). (1982). *All the women are White, all the Blacks are men, but some of us are brave: Black women's studies.* Old Westbury, NY: The Feminist Press.

Johnsrod, L.K., & Sadao, K. C. (2002). The common experience of 'otherness': Ethnic and racial minority faculty. In C. S. Turner, A. L. Antonio, M. Garcia, B. V. Laden, A. Nora, & C. Presley (Eds.), *Racial and ethnic diversity in higher education* (2nd ed., pp. 185-201). Boston, MA: Pearson Custom Publishing. ASHE READER SERIES.

Jones, J. L. (2003). Sista docta. In L. C. Miller, J. Taylor, & M. H. Carver (Eds.), *Voices made flesh: Performing women's autobiography* (pp. 237-257). Madison, WI: University of Wisconsin Press.

Kennedy, R. (2008). *Sellout: The politics of racial betrayal.* New York, NY: Pantheon Books.

King, D. K. (1988). Multiple jeopardy, multiple consciousness: The context of a Black feminist ideology. *Signs: Journal of Women and Culture in Society, 14*(1), 42-72.

Kirk, G., & Okazawa-Rey, M. (2004). *Women's lives: Multicultural perspectives.* (3rd ed.). Boston, MA: McGraw-Hill.

Leverette, T. (2009). Speaking up: Mixed race identity in Black communities. *Journal of Black Studies, 39*(3), 434-445. doi: 10.1177/0021934706297875

Meyerson, D. E. (2003). *Tempered radicals: How everyday leaders inspire change at work.* Boston, MA: Harvard Business School Press.

Milem, J., Chang, M. J., & Antonio, A. L. (2005). *Making diversity work on campus: A research-based perspective.* Report by the Association of American Colleges and Universities.

Mutua, A. D. (2006). Theorizing progressive Black masculinities. In A. D. Mutua (Ed.). *Progressive Black masculinities* (pp. 3-42). New York, NY: Routledge.

Neubeck, K. J., & Cazenave, N. A. (2001). *Playing the race card against America's poor.* New York, NY: Routledge.

Ono, K. (1997). A letter/essay that I have been longing to write in my personal/academic voice. *Western Journal of Communication, 61*(1), 114-125.

Patton, T. O. (2004). Reflections of a Black woman professor: Racism and sexism in academia. *The Howard Journal of Communications, 15,* 185-200. doi: 10.1080/10646170490483629

Perkins, L. M. (2009). The history of Black women graduate students, 1921-1948. In L. C. Tillman (Ed.), *The Sage handbook of African American education* (pp. 53-65). Los Angeles, CA: Sage Publications.

Reynolds, T. (2002). Re-thinking a Black feminist standpoint. *Ethnic and Racial Studies, 25*(4), 592-606. doi: 10.1080/01419870220136709

Reynolds-Dobbs, W., Thomas, K., & Harrison, M. S. (2008). From mammy to superwoman: Images that hinder Black women's career development. *Journal of Career Development, 35*(2), 129-150.

Sikes, P., Measor, L., & Woods, P. (1985). *Teacher careers: Crises and continuities.* London, England: Falmer Press.

Solórzano, D. G., & Yosso, T. J. (2001). Critical race and LatCrit Theory and method: Counter-storytelling Chicana and Chicano graduate school experiences. *International Journal of Qualitative Studies in Education, 14*(4), 371-395. doi: 10.1080/09518390110063365

Steele, C. (1997). A threat in the air: How stereotypes shape intellectual identity and performance. *American Psychologist, 52,* 613-629.

Sue, D. W., Capodilapo, C. M., Torino, G. C., Bucceri, J. M., Holder, A. M. B., Nadal, K. M., & Esquilin, M. (2007). Racial microaggressions in everyday life: Implications for clinical practices. *American Psychologist, 62*(4), 271-286.

Trotman, F. K. (2009). The imposter phenomenon among African American women in U.S. institutions of higher education: Implications for counseling. In G. R. Waltz, J. C. Bleuer, & R. K. Yep (Eds.), *Compelling counseling interventions: VISTAS 2009* (pp. 77-87). Alexandria, VA: American Counseling Association.

Tuitt, F. (2008). Removing the threat in the air: Teacher transparency and the creation of identity-safe graduate classrooms. *Journal on Excellence in College Teaching, 19*(2), 167-198.

Turner, C. S. V. (2002). Women of color in academe: Living with multiple marginality. *The Journal of Higher Education*, *73*(1), 74-93.

Turner, C. S. V., & Myers, S. L. (2000). *Faculty of color in academe: Bittersweet success.* Boston, MA: Allyn and Bacon.

Walker, A. (1983). *In search of our mothers' gardens*. Orlando, FL: A Harvest Book Harcourt, Inc.

West, C. (1999). *The Cornel West reader*. New York, NY: Basic *Civitas* Books.

Wing, A. K. (Ed). (2003). *Critical race feminism: A reader* (2nd ed.). New York, NY: New York University Press.

EXPERIENCING DIFFERENCE IN THE CLASSROOM

TEACHING 'MAJORITY' STUDENTS

Chapter 12

Living Creativity
Teaching as Art

Marnel N. Niles

I wanted to be an artist when I grew up. I loved to paint, draw, write, and put things together. As a girl, I distinctly remember painting murals on my bedroom walls, doors, and dresser, and, much to the chagrin of my parents, carving pictures with a pen into the wooden banister. But I also remember writing until my hand hurt. I wrote stories, comic strips, and even lesson plans. It seems like even as a child, I understood that my creativity could add excitement to everything I touched. I still am passionate about doing many types of art, yet as an Assistant Professor of Communication who is a Black woman, I know that my choice of profession is not a sacrifice of my creativity; for *teaching is an art.* The classroom is a canvas waiting to be painted and repainted with vibrant colors of acrylic abstractions; this is a work that I know I must do.

Alice Walker (1983) supports this notion in her inspiring nonfiction book, *In Search of Our Mothers' Gardens*. In it, she writes about the anguish the Black woman slave must have felt when she was not allowed the freedom to create; that is, when her creative being was stifled. Because of this torment our foremothers suffered, she advocates the following mission for Black[1] women: "Therefore we must fearlessly pull out of ourselves and look at and identify with our lives the living creativity some of our great-grandmothers were not allowed to know" (Walker, 1983, p. 237).

The *living creativity* to which Ms. Walker refers is the creative spirit we each have that lives and breathes and bears fruit. It can manifest itself in many ways in the life of a Black woman, including in how she worships, moves, draws, narrates, and teaches. To suppress this living creativity is doing a disservice to who I am, to my spirit, and to those Black women who lived before me. This creative spirit must be nurtured and strengthened. It can never be hidden, for it adds excitement to everything it touches.

Alice Walker's (1983) text resonated with me on a personal and professional level, inspiring me to write this book chapter. Using a womanist approach, this chapter posits that the Black woman's creativity does not have to be suppressed in the classroom environment. Instead, the classroom environment must become a place of innovation and engagement, allowing the Black professor to continue on in her creativity, her community building, and her natural work, in spite of any struggle that may persist. I will begin the next section with a definition of womanism and a brief description of my experience working at my institution. Then I will discuss how womanism and positive marginality, a term used by Mayo (1982) and Hall and Fine (2005), can together provide suggestions for the minority female professor in the college and university classroom and how she can continue to be faithful in her work from the margins. I will provide personal examples as well as narratives from other Black female professors and conclude with a discussion on how womanism and positive marginality collectively explicate my effort to teach as an artist.

WOMANISM CONTEXTUALIZED: MY BLACK FEMALE PROFESSOR EXPERIENCE

Walker (1983) coined the term *womanist*, which "is to feminist as purple is to lavender" (p. xii), implying her intent not to focus on the differences between feminism and womanism, but to portray the closeness of their shades, or foundations. Walker provides other definitions of womanist, including "a feminist of color; [one who] loves music. Loves dance. Loves the moon. *Loves* the Spirit. Loves love and food and roundness. Loves struggle. *Loves* the Folk. Loves herself. *Regardless*" (p. xii, emphasis in original).

A womanist is a Black feminist who loves the struggle because she knows she will survive it; it is her living creativity that is her strength. This living creativity is a significant part of her identity and can be used in any environment—the college or university classroom is one of those environments that is ripe for this type of creativity.

It is important to note here that the Black woman's identity and creativity are complex and should not be essentialized; there is not one Black woman's voice nor is there one womanist voice. I am not the representative for Black women in the academy, though we probably share some similar experiences. Our identities are not the same, nor are our individual identities linear or stagnant. Instead, the womanist Black female professor's identity is dynamic. It is changing, fluid, and represents the intersections of race, class, ethnicity, culture, and sexuality. It is constructed through her environment and actions and constantly renegotiated (Georgakopoulou, 2002). Hylton and Miller (2004) write that, "identities are the rendering of stories that can be read from possible performances of persons" (p. 373), such as the performance of teaching. That is, teaching is one way the Black female professor can shape her identity. The Black female professor teaching at a majority institution will renegotiate her identity frequently, often because she may be one of few others like her at her institution. Yet, even as her identity is questioned and renegotiated, it is possible to, from the margins, become a stronger and more confident faculty member and teacher.

For example, I earned my Ph.D. at a historically Black university and immediately moved to the West Coast of the United States to work as an Assistant Professor at a Hispanic-serving institution. Recent statistics show that approximately 37% of the student population at my institution are White, 32% Hispanic, 14% Asian, and 5% Black. I was personally challenged moving into an environment that was different from my graduate school experience. This challenge happened to be even greater when it became obvious that African-Americans are not the largest minority group on campus but are outnumbered by the White and Hispanic populations. Thus, Black students and faculty are often overlooked in many aspects regarding resources, academics, and social support. I did not allow these obstacles to be deterrents to my esteem or my experience; I was strong and became stronger. I "loved myself, regardless." I loved "the struggle" (Walker, 1983, p. xii).

The struggle is not easy to love, but my experiences in the classroom give me the energy to do so. A note that I wrote on Facebook provides a vivid example of my enjoyment for the struggle. The following is an excerpt from the post written during my third year as an Assistant Professor:

> I'm teaching Gender Communication this semester, which is one of may favorite classes to teach. This semester, however, it seems as if I have the whole football team in the class. They make it interesting, but can also lead the class to laugh at some of our more serious class discussions. There is one football player, let's call him Dave, a Black guy, who makes a number of comments throughout the class, but to his fellow teammates (and not to the rest of the class), causing them to erupt in laughter. I can usually hear the comments, and they are often insightfully funny. At the beginning of class one day, I tell Dave I want to speak to him after class. For those of you who know me, my communication style is direct, sarcastic, and kind (think of it as an East Coast sort of

> thing). After class I fuss out Dave, telling him in a way that only a Black woman can, that he needs to get it together and start participating. He agrees.
>
> That was at the end of September [2009]. Though Dave is still a clown, he's been participating ("You see I'm participating now, right Dr. Niles?" he asked me when I saw him on campus the other day. "You aiight," I smiled in response, "Could be better." "Awww, C'mon, Dr. Niles!" I just laughed and kept walking. He knew I was proud of him). Earlier this week [a Monday in September of 2010], Dave did an oral presentation for one of the class assignments and he did an exceptional job: he provided examples and captured the audience's attention the entire time. It made my day.
>
> That was yesterday. Today, I'm home grading papers but still smiling to myself, not just because of Dave, but also because the Lord saw it fit that I have a career in which I can have mostly good, creative days at work.

This is the type of struggle that I love. The type in which "I forget all the titles, all the labels" and move forward because I know that "our people are waiting" (Walker, 1982, p. 133).

The results of the struggles that have come from my experiences teaching at a majority university have been mostly pleasant. This of course, cannot be credited solely to me; the faculty, staff, and student body at my institution tend to be liberal and open minded, resulting in what seems to be an acceptance or overlooking of who I am and what I represent. However, teaching at a university where one's race is represented by only 5% of the student body and an even smaller percentage in the entire university can be a lonely experience. This is compounded by the fact that I am the only African American faculty member in my Department and one of two African American female faculty members in the College of Arts and Humanities. In addition to working at a majority institution, the city to which I moved had a *significantly* smaller African American population than the previous one in which I had lived. My sense of isolation increased but did not affect my love for my decision to work at my university nor my need to bring my identity into the classroom.

The following is another example of why my choice to stay at my university has not decreased. In January of 2010, a White female student slipped a card under my office door. Part of the note read:

> Dear Dr. Niles,
> I wanted to thank you so much . . . for encouraging me to pursue a higher degree in communication. I'm so humbled that someone as passionate and inspiring as yourself, time and time again, helped me gain the confidence to set my sights higher. I've been so lucky to have been a student of yours.

Even amidst isolation, my students are instrumental in ensuring that my creativity never turns stagnant—and I know that both my students and I are able to reap the benefits of the struggle.

In essence, my struggle did not (nor should the struggle of the Black female professor) cripple my creativity or my desire to "order the universe [or classroom] in the image of [my] personal conception of Beauty" (Walker, 1983, p. 241). This beauty represents the creating and learning that occurs in the classroom, which adds excitement to everything it touches. It is similar to Walker's description of her mother's work in the garden: "She is [I am] involved in the work her [my] soul must have" (p. 241). The next section expounds on this notion by coupling womanism with positive marginality, a term that further gives voice to the Black female college professor's experience.

Positive Marginality, Womanism, and the Black Woman Professor's Classroom Experience

Psychologist Clara Mayo (1982) coined the term *positive marginality*, referring to the potentially advantageous viewpoint of those from the margins. The marginal role requires "the person to assess both the merits and faults of [the system]" (Smith, 1986, p. 105). In other words, a marginalized person can frame her or his marginalized status positively because she or he can be both "inside and outside of a group or system" (Smith, 1986, p. 105).

Hall and Fine (2005) use positive marginality as a framework from which to provide a detailed discussion about the friendship of two older Black lesbians, who were participants in their study. Using narrative analysis, they find that Black women "create spaces of energy and creativity" (p. 186) in both their personal and professional lives, akin to Mayo's (1982) idea of positive marginality. The authors write:

> The concept of marginality as positive has been echoed by a number of women of color—scholars, writers, and activists—who critiqued social arrangements but refused to view living at the margin of mainstream society as a site of low power, victimization, or even marginality. (p. 177)

Hall and Fine identify four important facets of positive marginality (pp. 177-178), all of which Black women professors at majority institutions can apply to their work (these will be discussed further in the next section):

1. *Critical watching and reframing*—This involves constantly perceiving how one is viewed through the eyes of non-Blacks and consciously assessing one's actions.
2. *The conversion of obstacles into opportunities*—One views obstacles "simply as challenges" (p. 178).
3. *The subversion of social institutions*—This requires engaging "social institutions with the aim of exploiting what is useful, resisting what is oppressive, and surviving within the institution" (p. 178).

4. *The evolution of lives of meaning*—This occurs when "people create lives in which they can grow and prosper, given the constraints with which they contend" (p. 178).

Each story that was told by the two women friends to each other and to the researchers showed that the women simultaneously defied and confronted what was expected of them by society. The authors also find that these two Black women created the four facets of positive marginality for themselves by using unharnessed anger and creating support systems (Hall & Fine, 2005, p. 186).

This study emphasizes how African-American female friendships are often grounded in support systems and positive marginality. Black women have the ability to find the "strength, vibrancy, and radical possibilities that lie and grow in the margins of social arrangements" (Hall & Fine, 2005, p. 177). In other words, those in the margins of society often display a strong ability to survive and cope; this includes Black faculty (Alexander & Moore, 2008).

Positive marginality can be also be used to understand the experiences of the Black woman in varying parts of her life, including her spiritual, professional, and emotional beings. It also provides further insight behind the meaning of Alice Walker's (1983) discussions about her mother's garden in which she writes,

> My mother adorned with flowers whatever shabby house we were forced to live in. And not just your typical straggly country stand of zinnias either. She planted ambitious gardens . . . with over fifty different varieties of plants that bloom profusely from early March until late November. . . . Whatever she planted grew as if by magic. . . . And I remember people coming to my mother's yard to be given cuttings from her flowers; I hear again the praise showered on her because whatever rocky soil she landed on, she turned into a garden. (p. 241)

Alice Walker describes her mother as an artist, whose art, or garden, allowed her to face any struggle caused by race, gender, or class. She was able to turn rocky soil into beautiful gardens. The rocky soil that seemed difficult to dig represents the obstacles faced by Black women that seem impossible to overcome. But the beautiful gardens represent the positive outcomes and opportunities that can result from the struggle. Oppression is not viewed as a blockade to living life positively; instead, it is seen as a challenge which "[forwards] momentum" (Hall & Fine, 2005, p. 186), a brushstroke that enhances the artwork and makes it more valuable. This means that teaching at an institution where I am a minority can be transformed into an opportunity to change or recreate the classroom environment into a place of community and engaged learning (hooks, 1994).

Positive marginality, coupled with womanism, is quite useful in understanding the art of teaching. Specifically, Hall and Fine's (2005) four facets of positive marginality have direct application for Black women and other women of color teaching at majority institutions. The use of positive marginality to understand Black women professors' classroom experiences allows for inclusion of the women's sense of self and culture by incorporating ideals such as resiliency and perseverance (Levine, 1977).

The following sub-sections further discuss and apply Hall and Fine's (2005) use of positive marginality and Alice Walker's (1983) womanism to the teaching experiences of Black female tenure-track faculty in academia. In addition to using my own experiences as the primary text for this chapter, I asked five other Black female assistant professors who teach at majority institutions to share their experiences as well. Specifically, I asked them to share the strategies they use in and out of the classroom to cope with any types of oppression or struggles they face and if/how they adapt their style of teaching to accommodate their majority students. I communicated with the women via email, Facebook messages, and telephone and also ensured them that their stories would remain anonymous and their identities confidential.

Critical Watching and Reframing

The first facet of positive marginality, as indicated by Hall and Fine (2005), is critical watching and reframing. At a majority institution, the Black female professor is a minority, especially in the classroom, because most of her students do not look like her. This means that she must constantly observe and assess student responses to her leadership of the classroom, her dialogue on particular topics, and her creativity in the course. If students are unresponsive to the professor, she will have to adjust (this may be a small or large adjustment) or reframe her interactions with her students.

For many Black female assistant professors, it is evident that majority students have difficulty responding to them as authority figures in the classroom. For example, three of the Black female professors I interviewed discussed their observations that some of their majority students initially did not view them as an authority in the classroom or in their field. One professor stated that she had even been challenged by some students, an experience echoed by another colleague in the following statement:

> I must admit that it is much more difficult to maintain authority with majority students than it is with minority students. They often question my ability, challenge my knowledge and skills, and are quite combative in dealing with me as it relates to grading, class assignments, and the like.

All three professors reframed and responded to these challenges by subtly establishing their credibility throughout the semester, but particularly at its beginning. One professor said, "I introduce myself to most of my classes as Dr. or Professor [last name omitted]. Generally, the title communicates that I am the authority figure in the class." Another wrote, "I refuse to let them call me by my first name, I do not care that colleagues in my Department allow it. I [also] start [the semester] hard, no exceptions for anything . . . grace comes later . . . after I know their work habits." Still another provided more details about her strategy:

> In general, the students are respectful and are clear that I am the authority figure, but some things that I remain diligent about to ensure that they are clear about my role is that I introduce myself at the beginning of the semester as Dr. [last name omitted], provide them with my academic and professional background, and [tell them] my research interests and what research I am currently working on. When I correspond with my students electronically, I sign my name Dr. [last name omitted] and provide my signature that lists my title (Assistant Professor). Should they call me "[first name omitted]" or "[first and last initials omitted]" as they sometimes do, I respond by signing my name Dr. [last name omitted] so that they are clear about how to address me. . . . I know how to be subtle in asserting my authority, and am not easily rattled by those who wish to challenge me.

More than their White counterparts, Black professors have to work harder to establish their credibility in the classroom because majority students are likely to assign credibility to older, White, and male professors (Hendrix, 2004). Even now, several students still refer to me as "Ms. Niles," something, I imagine, many of my White and male colleagues never encounter. It is important to me, and to the other women I interviewed, to be viewed as an authority figure in the classroom and the intentional or unintentional stripping away of our titles can be hurtful.

The new, tenure-track Assistant Professor must engage in critical watching and reframing; she cannot wait one day to begin observing her students' responses to her presence; this does a disservice to both the professor and the students. She must see how the students respond (both inside and outside of the classroom) to her womanhood, blackness, rhythm, and Spirit and ensure that she is viewed as an authority figure. There must be a valuation of her authority, credibility, and identity and, at the same time, there also must be a valuation of the students' identities. There must be a recognition of race and gender (of the professor and the students) and how these, in addition to class, sexuality, religion, and culture, develop into each person's identity. Once each role and identity is acknowledged and appreciated, the classroom can then become a transformative environment.

hooks (1994) suggests that, "one way to build community in the classroom is to recognize the value of each individual voice" (p. 40), including the voice of the minority professor. In instances where the voice, identity, or authority of the Black female assistant professor is opposed by her students, she can utilize womanist and positive marginality frameworks to resist internalizing these messages by finding the strength to reframe these negative messages into opportunities for change (this will be discussed in detail in the next section). Critical watching and reframing is necessary for the Black woman's survival in the academy. She must be particularly aware of the teaching environment she creates, establish her authority, and dare to make the classroom a place that is true to her culture and that values the voice of each person.

THE CONVERSION OF OBSTACLES INTO OPPORTUNITIES

A classroom where the professor is of a different race and/or ethnicity than the majority of her students can be an obstacle in itself. Students may focus on differences, particularly verbal and nonverbal differences, and because of them, may be distracted at various points throughout the class period. This challenge is one that can be turned into a learning opportunity in the classroom.

Houston (1997) writes that communication problems between Black women and White women occur because mutual understanding does not take place due to cultural differences and each group's history of suspicion of the other. In her study, Black women described their talk as: "speaking out; talking about what's on your mind; being very sure of oneself; speaking with a strong sense of self esteem; and reflecting black experiences as seen by a black woman in a white patriarchal society" (p. 189). White women described Black women's talk as: "using black dialect; using jive terms" (p. 189). I also suggest that Black women's talk is also viewed by their White counterparts as overly assertive or even aggressive.[2]

The classroom is one place where the non-Black student may perceive her or his Black female professor's directness (or "speaking out") as aggression. For example, a professor who was interviewed stated that one of her classroom strategies is to "speak to an issue." Similarly, if a student asks me a question, I answer it directly, even if she or he expected a different, more subtle answer. I usually refrain from speaking around an issue; I talk about it candidly, including more sensitive issues of race, gender, or sexuality. As a result, one female Asian student told me after completing the course, "When I first started this class, I was scared of you. That's why I dropped the other class." Likewise, another student, a White male, stated, "Black women scare me." Both of these comments support Jones and Shorter-Gooden's (2003) assertion that "since White women presumably provide the ideal model of femininity, and because Black women don't fit the same mold, they are mythologized as domineering, demanding, emasculating, and coarse" (p. 11). Initial and ignorant perceptions of Black female professors are often unfairly based on the supposition that Black women are "overbearing or too assertive" (Jones & Shorter-Gooden, 2003, p. 11; see also Collins, 2000).

These are opportunities for the Black female professor to turn this challenge into a teaching moment and create a liberating teaching environment. Though students may be unaccustomed to having a female professor be so direct, if the directness is coupled with respect and concern, the student will begin to appreciate this type of communication. In addition, the professor-student interaction can be used as a case study in any communication course.

For example, in an organizational communication course, I asked my students how they thought I would be perceived if I went to an interview at a prestigious law firm with my hair in an afro (how I usually wear it). The students responded that I would probably not get the position because my hair would be viewed as unprofessional. I then pose the question, "Why is it then, for my hair to be viewed as professional, do I have to either put a chemical in my hair or spend at least four hours getting my hair flat ironed or pressed?" Following this, we have an honest and straightforward discussion about how racial and gender differences can play a role in organizational communication. The result is of having these types of personal, applicable discussions about topics to which the students can relate is a type of learning that I believe will bear fruit.

Another professor discussed her method of turning the "obstacle" of her race and gender into an opportunity by purposely working toward making herself approachable:

> I also work to ensure that my students feel comfortable approaching me. I do this through my lectures and class presentations. Often, I use pop culture references, hip-hop lyrics, campus events, use slang terminology, make jokes, tell personal stories, or anything else that indicates to them that I am human and that I can relate, on some level, to what's going on in their world. [As a result,] my students have said in my evaluations that my classroom style is casual and relaxed but that the work is challenging and interesting. This is what I strive for.

In other words, what may seemingly begin as an obstacle (in the classroom) can be turned into an opportunity by transforming it into a teaching tool for students. Strategies that pave the way for a higher level of learning may be more effective if they initially come from a place of struggle.

THE SUBVERSION OF SOCIAL INSTITUTIONS

In her book, *Teaching to Transgress*, bell hooks (1994) writes, "as budgets are cut as jobs become even more scarce, many of the few progressive interventions that were made to change the academy . . . are in danger of being undermined or eliminated" (p. 33). This quote is extremely relevant to my institution where, as a state university, our budget was recently reduced by 26 million dollars, student fees increased, student enrollment decreased, classes and programs were cancelled, and faculty furloughs were mandated. Students come to class concerned about graduating on time and tired from working full-time to pay their tuition and fees. It is difficult to survive, let alone remain positive, in an institution where students have difficulty paying for their classes and faculty and administrators are being laid off. In spite of this, faculty of color must subvert certain messages from their social institutions while simultaneously staying engaged in them. In addition, they must "[exploit] what is useful and [resist] what is oppressive" (Hall & Fine, 2005, p. 178). For example, one Black female professor explains how she silences the social institutions:

> One thing I do to encourage students to engage in conversations with me is to provide my cellular number on the syllabus, and to encourage students to send me text messages and to call me when they have questions, want to talk, or need some assistance. I encourage students to call me Sunday [and] Saturday, and I also tell students that if they have a problem or concern about life in general to give me a call. I tell the students that if they are in trouble with the police or get arrested for something, to give me a call; I'll make an attempt to speak highly of them to the police officer.

Another professor speaks about how she reaches out to her students:

> Every child I pass I can say their [sic] name. I said the name of one former student on campus who walked past me and she said, "Dr. [last name omitted], you remember me?" And I said, "Of course I remember you, how's Mrs. [student's mother's last name omitted]?" And for me to be able to call her mother's name made me feel good. It's about creating relationships to get those kids rockin'.

These Black women extend their relationships with their students beyond the classroom in order to provide them with a source of support, particularly when the institution in which the students learn is also the one that is causing them difficulties.

Other forms of oppressive social institutions can also manifest themselves in the classroom. For example, Collins (2000) argues that the controlling images of Black women in media are reproduced in the classroom environment. In various mediums, Black women are portrayed as sexual deviants, freaks, or hoochies (Collins, 2000); these images are, often subconsciously, in the minds of students, even as they are physically sitting in the classroom. Similarly, other controlling images of specific gender, racial, ethnic, and religious groups are also brought into and reproduced in the classroom. Black men are stereotyped as dangerous, sexual, and unintelligent (Hall, 2001), Asian women and men are shown as quiet and highly intelligent (Lee, 1996), Islamic men and women are thought of as terrorists (Begawan, 2006), Hispanic men and women are perceived as family-oriented and poor (Jackson, 1995), White women are viewed as weak and pure (Edmondson Bell & Nkomo, 2001), and the list goes on. With these types of images in the back of their consciousness, students enter the classroom ready to learn with what they believe is an "open mind"; however, these controlling images often frame their perceptions of course topics.

Again, the Black female professor must intentionally make the classroom an environment that resists these types of messages. For example, recently a White male student gave a presentation in one of my courses about the Muslim Students Association (MSA) on campus. He began with, "I decided to present about MSA because I come from a conservative background and I tend to think that all Muslims are terrorists. So I wanted to learn about them so I wouldn't think that way." To admit, this introduction to his presentation was startling, yet I was impressed with the conscious effort made by the student to challenge his assumptions. I would like to think that the classroom environment that I helped to create played a role in the choice of organization for his project.

Both of these examples—budget cuts and preconceived ideas about minority groups—represent institutions that can negatively affect the Black female professor and the students in her classroom. However, it should also be the duty of this same professor to challenge these social forces. Here is an opportunity for the womanist professor to love the struggle while pulling herself, and her students, through it. The professor must intentionally subvert these oppressive social institutions that have damaging ramifications to real classroom learning. This may mean speaking privately to students if it seems they are having financial or emotional difficulties during the semester or it may mean having a classroom discussion about the impact and implications of budget cuts or institutional policy changes. It may also mean spending class time discussing or viewing images of oppressed groups that are contrary to the stereotypical ones mentioned above.

The Black female professor must find ways to keep the classroom, and her relationship with her students, transformative, and never oppressive. This will not always be an easy feat, yet even amidst grueling oppressions, she must promote a positive and thoughtful classroom environment. Any fear must be transformed and resisted so the students see a source of strength, especially when they become concerned about how they may be affected by a changing environment. hooks (1994) surmises:

> Learning from other movements for social change, from civil rights and feminist liberation struggles, we must accept the protracted nature of our struggle and be willing to remain both patient and vigilant. To commit ourselves to the work of transforming the academy so that it will be place where cultural diversity informs every aspect of our learning, we must embrace struggle and sacrifice. We cannot be easily discouraged. We cannot despair when there is conflict. (p. 33)

The professor initiates the formation of the classroom environment and culture; that is, she will often be the person students go to when they are suffering academically, financially, or emotionally. It is up to her to cultivate a setting where students understand that any struggle they individually or collectively face, especially those resulting from institutional and government mandates, can be overcome.

THE EVOLUTION OF LIVES OF MEANING

Attempting to use teaching strategies to foster a creative and open classroom environment that values each individual voice will not work if the Black professor is in an environment where she herself cannot learn, grow, or be true to herself. This growth is driven by a Spirit, which I believe is God. Akbar (2003) contends, "true spiritual growth is guided by the knowledge which cultivates the growth of the mind. . . . Being spiritual will release us for transcendental growth and self mastery (p. 104). Once there is the allowance for and the continuous accomplishing of growth, the Black female professor will then be able to give her full energy into constructing a transformative classroom experience.

One Black female faculty member wrote to me in a Facebook message stating, "I wouldn't say that I have yet to rise above any struggles in the classroom." I asked her if there is anything outside of the classroom to help her cope with these struggles and she responded:

> Unfortunately no. Right now I am so focused on my family's finances, being a mommy and a wife, being a professor and doing my research that there is nothing I do outside of work. I would like to start exercising again and maybe take some sewing lessons, but who knows when that will happen.

The Black female professor must have an outlet for any negative or stressful classroom experiences. Alexander and Moore (2008) write that African American faculty must consciously address and nurture their spiritual, physical, social, and emotional well-beings; this has to be done before the Black female professor becomes engaged in the classroom and must persist as she continues to teach. For example, I asked two other Black female professors working at predominantly White institutions if they had outlets for wearisome classroom experiences. One stated, "I am very active in my community and in my sorority. I host a lot of things. I travel. The University is not my life. It's just part of it." Another responded, "Girl, Bible study. I mentor middle school kids. I hit the art galleries. I do make-up classes. That's my balance. I need to be in my space without the responsibility of being somebody's momma."

Alexander and Moore (2008) state that as part of the growth process, Black professors should seek mentors, participate in community activities, and view themselves as strengths to their institution and community. Engaging in these types of activities and esteem promotion will result in an appreciation of self and a predilection toward one's work.

THE ART OF TEACHING

Teaching is a sometimes difficult art to create, yet as a womanist who "loves struggle," (Walker, 1983, p. xii) it becomes a necessary piece that needs to be created and recreated. “To be an artist and a black woman, even today, lowers our status in many respects, rather than raises it: and yet, artists we will be” (Walker, 1983, p. 237). In spite of being at an institution where I can easily fall into a lonely isolation and where my salary has decreased due to mandated budget cuts, I find that it is the struggle that makes me stronger; it is something I have to do and will. This love can transcend comfortably into a transformative classroom atmosphere.

hooks (1994) advocates that the classroom should be a place where all students are valued and recognized in order for “transformative pedagogy” (p. 41) to take place. I argue that creating this type of classroom environment is a natural fit for Black women and womanists, in particular, because we have a love for ourselves and a love for our community. Relatedly, Akbar (2003) posits that the person of African descent has a sense of connectedness with her universe and a fundamental belief that her inner being comes from God. This essentially means that community is more important than the individual and that “relationships are vital” (Akbar, 2003, p. 98). This perspective is also useful when applied to the college class that is taught by a Black female. She brings with her a sense of connectedness, even if her students are not predominantly of African descent. This viewpoint allows the classroom (or canvas) to be an engaged community (hooks, 1994) in which the Black female professor will “enter the classroom with the assumption that we must ‘build community’ in order to create a climate of openness and intellectual rigor” (hooks, 1994, p. 40).

For instance, the first day of each semester is when I see the most surprise/uncertainty on my students’ faces. They are not predominantly African American (in a class between 27 and 31 students, I usually have one or two African American students). Very few of my students have had an African American teacher in their lives; less than one-fourth of them have had a Black professor and virtually none have had a Black female professor. Though most of them have never had a Black female professor, their astonishment is peaked further when this revelation is coupled with their mental attempt at determining my age (outside of the classroom most assume I am a student). Furthermore, I wear my hair in an afro and introduce myself as *Doctor Niles*. At the culmination of these realizations, the students are either nervous, scared, or excited; perhaps all three.

Though these observations may seem disheartening, I find that overall, my students are attentive and respectful. In some ways, I feel as if they are this way *because of* my race, age, and gender. Because they have never had a professor like me—Black, young, and female (with natural hair)—the students seem to be increasingly attentive. I also believe I grab their interest and attention because in a sense, I know how to speak their language; I am not as far removed from their generation as some of the more seasoned faculty on campus. I attempt to use the mixed emotions and interest of the students to begin to create or, using artist’s terminology, paint, a classroom community of engaged learning.

One method of transforming the classroom into a community where each student's voice is valued is to ask uncomfortable questions of students about uncomfortable subjects. I find it especially important to bring discussions of race into the classroom, regardless of whether the course is Organizational Communication, Gender Communication, or Group Communication. Because most of my students have not had academic or social experiences with Blacks (and because the local city's African-American population is less than 15%), I believe it is important for my students to hear candid discussions about race throughout the entire semester because they may not hear or be able to discuss it elsewhere. Overall, I have received encouraging student responses to these discussions, though initially students are hesitant to respond in class. At first, my questions are often met with silence, fidgety hands, and eyes focused on blank (or invisible) sheets of paper. I am comfortable enough with myself, with silence, and with uncomfortable topics, to wait. I find that by the end of the semester, most, if not all, students have grown in their understanding of cultural communication issues and so have I. We are able to pose questions of each other and together, try to find the answers, resulting in a continuous recreation of an exciting classroom community.

CONCLUSION

The stories in this chapter told by Black female assistant professors show both our enjoyment and disdain for our professions. We enjoy teaching and communicating with our students and make significant efforts to reach out to them on a personal level. However, we also have difficulties with our students. Some students sometimes feel fearful of their professors, while others do not view us as credible. As a result, Black female assistant professors face unique struggles in the classroom because of our race and gender; however, many of these obstacles can be turned into opportunities for transformative learning, resulting in the creation of a masterpiece.

This masterpiece will never be easy to create, but the result of it can be a classroom that represents an engaged and innovative space, provided the Black female professor is unafraid to bring her identity into the classroom and fearless in allowing the creation of a new type of classroom environment. This new type of classroom environment is one where there is community, appreciation of varying voices, and respect—a type of environment in which the womanist Black female professor, though on the margins, has the ability to create by utilizing her strength to promote a transformative learning experience. These classes will benefit both the marginalized professor and her students because those courses that make the most impact on students are those that reach different areas of intellect; that is, the artwork that is more memorable and valuable is the piece that does not look like others. This type of classroom becomes powerful and exciting because of, and not in spite of, the Black female professor's struggles.

It is because of the struggles that Black women face that Alice Walker's (1983) mission, "to pull out of ourselves and look at and identify with our lives the living creativity some of our great-grandmothers were not allowed to know" (p. 237), is still instrumental today for all minority professors, and particularly for Black female assistant professors. It is up to us to use our living creativity to reframe and overcome these struggles and ultimately, pass on that "creative spark, the seed of the flower [our mothers and grandmothers] never hoped to see" (Walker, 1983, p. 240).

NOTES

1. The terms "Black" and African American" are used interchangeably to represent women of African descent who live in the United States of America.
2. Parker's (2001) study on African American women executives working in dominant culture organizations found that the women framed their direct communication styles in positive terms, in spite of research showing that this communication style is often viewed negatively by majority groups. Based on this and my personal experiences and observations, I find that Black women are often viewed as being more assertive or aggressive then they intend.

REFERENCES

Akbar, N. (2003). *Akbar papers in African psychology.* Mind Productions and Associates: Tallahassee, FL.

Alexander Jr., R., & Moore, S. E. (2008). The benefits, challenges, and strategies of African American faculty teaching at predominantly white institutions. *Journal of African American Studies, 12,* 4-18.

Begawan, B. S. (2006, December 10). The Muslim stereotype. *The New York Times.* Retrieved from http://www.nytimes.com

Collins, P. H. (2000). *Black feminist thought: Knowledge, consciousness, and the politics of empowerment* (2nd ed.). New York, NY: Routledge.

Edmondson Bell, E. L. J., & Nkomo, E. M. (2001). *Our separate ways: Black and White women and the struggle for professional identity.* Boston, MA: Harvard Business School Press.

Georgakopoulou, A. (2002). Narrative and identity management: Discourse and social identities in a tale of tomorrow. *Research on language and social interaction, 35,* 427-451.

Hall, R. E. (2001). The ball curve: Calculated racism and the stereotype of African American men. *Journal of Black Studies*, *32*, 104-119. doi: 10.1177/002193470103200106

Hall, R. L., & Fine, M. (2005). The stories we tell: The lives and friendship of two older Black lesbians. *Psychology of Women Quarterly*, *29*, 177-187.

Hendrix, K. G. (2004). Student perceptions of the influence of race on professor credibility. In R. L. Jackson, II (Ed.), *African American communication and identities: Essential readings* (pp. 237-248). Thousand Oaks, CA: Sage.

hooks, b. (1994). *Teaching to transgress: Education as the practice of freedom.* New York, NY: Routledge.

Houston, M. (1997). When black women talk with white women: Why dialogues are difficult. In A. Gonzalez, M. Houston, & V. Chen (Eds.), *Our voices: Essays in culture, ethnicity, and communication* (2nd ed., pp. 187-194). Los Angeles, CA: Roxbury.

Hylton, P. L., & Miller, H. (2004). Now that we've found love what are we gonna do with it? Narrative understanding of Black identity. *Theory & Psychology*, *14*, 373-408.

Jackson, L. A. (1995). *Stereotypes, emotions, behavior, and overall attitudes toward Hispanics by Anglos*. (Report No. 10). East Lansing, MI: Julian Samora Research Institute.

Jones, C., & Shorter-Gooden, K. (2003). *Shifting: The double lives of Black women in America.* New York, NY: Perennial.

Lee, S. J. (1996). *Unraveling the "model minority" stereotype: Listening to Asian American youth.* New York, NY: Teachers College Press.

Levine, L. W. (1977). *Black culture and black consciousness: Afro American thought from slavery to freedom.* London, England: Oxford University Press.

Mayo, C. (1982). Training for positive marginality. In C. L. Bickman (Ed.), *Applied social psychology annual*, *3* (pp. 57-73). Beverly Hills, CA: Sage.

Parker, P. S. (2001). African-American women executives' leadership communication within dominant-culture organizations: (Re)conceptualizing notions of collaboration and instrumentality. *Management Communication Quarterly*, *15*, 42-82. doi: 10.1177/0893318901151002

Smith, A. (1986). Positive marginality: The experience of Black women leaders. In E. Seidman & J. Rappaport (Eds.), *Redefining social problems* (pp. 101-113). New York, NY: Plenum Press.

Walker, A. (1983). *In search of our mothers' gardens*. Orlando, FL: Harvest.

Chapter 13

"One of These Things Is Not Like the Others"

Experiences of African-American Women Professors with Majority-Race Students

Eletra S. Gilchrist

As a little girl, my parents always stressed the importance of a quality education—one that would prepare me for a competitive world and position me to be a self-sufficient and independent woman. Because education was highly valued in my family, I often watched educational programs as a child. My favorite childhood program was *Sesame Street.* Around the age of four, one of the things I looked most forward to on a daily basis was tuning in to *Sesame Street* and learning about a new letter, word, number, concept, or song. One of my favorite *Sesame Street* songs was "One of These Things is Not Like the Others," written by Joe Raposo and Jon Stone in 1970. This song taught me how to recognize differences among various items. For example, the television program might display three balls and one toy sailboat. The song would proceed to ask, "Three of these things belong together. Three of these things are kind of the same. Can you guess which one of these doesn't belong here?" I always enjoyed picking out the "odd" item that did not belong with the group. Little did I know then that my *Sesame Street* experiences would metaphorically describe my future profession.

As a tenure-track African-American female professor employed at a majority-race institution in terms of both student body and faculty demographics, I sometimes feel that I live the "one of these things is not like the others" reality on a daily basis. As a professor who teaches and researches human interactions, I have a heightened concern about the communication and experiences I have with students, most of whom represent the majority White race. Students have commented to me in face-to-face interactions as well as written on my teacher evaluations that I am one of the few, if not the only, African-American female professors they have ever had. As such, I recognize that my experiences with majority-race students are often quite different than many of my White colleagues' experiences.

Previous research has suggested that race (e.g., Gilchrist, 2004; Hendrix, 1997) and biological sex (e.g., Basow & Silberg, 1987; Centra & Gaubatz, 2000; Hargett, 1999) are active forces in the college classroom and play major roles in the interactions between teachers and students. Thus, women faculty members of color at majority institutions often encounter many unique and dynamic interactions with majority-race students that are not experienced by White male or female professors or even African-American male professors who teach at the same university (Bradley, 2005; Hudson-Weems, 1989). Because African-American women professors' experiences with majority-race students at predominately White institutions are often "not like the others," this chapter aims to acquire a deeper understanding of the pedagogical and relational perceptions felt by this sisterhood of intellectuals. Through autoethnographic accounts, this study seeks to fulfill a three-fold objective. Specifically, through an examination of their (a) teaching evaluations, (b) face-to-face encounters, and (c) overall unique experiences, this study aims to garner a deeper understanding of the interactions African-American female professors have with majority-race students.

Literature Review

The literature review focuses on how professor demographic features impact students' perceptions of and interactions with college and university professors. Because race and biological sex are two demographic features that make the experiences of African-American women professors especially unique with majority-race students, the impact of these two variables in the predominantly White college classroom is examined.

IMPACT OF PROFESSOR RACE IN THE COLLEGE CLASSROOM

The impact of a professor's race in the college classroom dates back to the days of legal segregation when even erudite African-American educators, such as W.E.B. DuBois, Carter G. Woodson, Alain Locke, E. Franklin Frazier, and Rayford Logan, were not regarded as competent enough to educate White students (Cross, 1998). During this time, most African-American professors were limited to teaching only at Historically Black Colleges and Universities (HBCUs). The landmark Brown v. Board of Education decision in 1954 cleared the path for desegregation of United States' schools and universities. While this allowed more African-American students to enter White institutions, the number of minority professors employed at these universities remained sparse. Consequently, during the 1960s, African-American students led militant protests and demanded more minority professors at predominately White institutions. In addition, the National Association for the Advancement of Colored People (NAACP) filed suits contesting the failure of colleges to provide equal employment opportunities to African Americans. In order to silence the protests and keep peace on the newly desegregated campuses, university administrations began to hire more minority professors at majority-race institutions in the 1970s (Nelson & Pellett, 1997).

Since the days of desegregation, college classrooms have been perceived as facilities used to train and instruct students in a liberated and diversified environment. Yet, many majority-race United States colleges remain "permeated with much subtle, covert, and blatant racism" (Feagin, Vera, & Imani, 1996, p. x). The impact of race becomes present when observing the number of minority-race faculty members at these institutions. Turner and Myers (1999) found that for every professor of color hired at predominately White institutions in the United States, three White professors are also hired. Johnson (2002) added that more than 90% of classroom instructors are White at majority institutions. African Americans tend to comprise a small percentage of faculty members at these colleges and universities, and the majority of those employed as faculty members work in the non-tenurable ranks of instructors and lecturers (Reddy & TuSmith, 2002). Sutherland (1990) argued that predominately White institutions tend to ascribe "token status to Blacks" and "offer Blacks low salaries and non-tenurable positions," and further, that "the temporality implied by these appointments fosters a climate in which the Black scholar remains peripheral and inconsequential to the White institution" (p. 20). The only areas of campus employment in which minority group members are highly represented include the clerical and secretarial ranks and service and maintenance work. In these areas, minorities are disproportionally overrepresented (Reddy & TuSmith, 2002).

In addition to the disproportionate faculty numbers, distinctions are further seen between African American and White professors in the following areas:

workloads, tenure, faculty support, and salaries. Specifically, African-American faculty are regarded as the most overworked faculty members in that they are expected to serve on many university and student advising committees, as well as participate in institutional, community, and service activities to ensure that the minority perspective is represented (Anderson, Astin, Bell, & Cole, 1993; Murray, 1998). Some professors of color have become burned-out due to excessive demands and have left the professorate (Gititi, 2002; Turner & Myers, 1999). The professors who remain at the collegiate level often quickly discover that their excessive service and advising responsibilities generally carry little weight in performance reviews. Consequently, African-American professors at White institutions tend to have a more difficult time moving up the tenure and promotion ladder compared to their White cohorts (Gititi, 2002; Murray, 1998; Turner & Myers, 1999). Furthermore, many African-American faculty members receive a general lack of support for their scholarship. For example, African-American professors are often not made aware of funding opportunities for research projects or conference presentations, and they are not mentored by senior faculty members (Murray, 1998; Turner & Myers, 1999). As a whole, professors of color assert that majority-race universities do not support their research interests on race because the experiences of minorities are not regarded as universal. Yet, departments provide limited opportunities for majority-minority peer collaboration scholarship (Gititi, 2002; Murray, 1998; Reddy & TuSmith, 2002; Turner & Myers, 1999). To add insult to injury, Whites at colleges and universities in the United States generally have higher salaries than African Americans at all levels, including administrative, teaching, support, clerical, and service positions (Murray, 1998).

Workload, tenure and promotion practices, faculty support, and salary caps are just some of the many distinctions between African American and White professors at majority institutions. Perhaps one of the most salient points of difference between the two professor groups involves teacher-student interactions. African-American faculty members employed at predominantly White institutions can face some unique teacher-student interactions when communicating with majority-race students. For example, Gilchrist (2004) found that White students at majority universities persuade African-American college teachers with more polite and endearing compliance-seeking strategies than they use with college teachers of their same race. Additionally, African-American professors often must work harder to establish and maintain their classroom credibility than their White colleagues. Hendrix (1997), for instance, found that White students hold African-American professors to more stringent standards than White professors. Consequently, African-American professors frequently strive to establish their classroom credibility by emphasizing their credentials, experience, and knowledge early in the course (Hendrix, 1997). However, some African-American professors are not given the opportunity to prove themselves because some White students drop the professor's class simply because of the teacher's race, or they may enroll in another section of the class taught by a White instructor (Gititi, 2002). Even when the teaching credentials and credibility are established, students at majority-race institutions tend to rate African-American instructors lower on teacher evaluations than they rate White faculty members (Leong, 2002). Because professor race is frequently a salient force in majority-race classrooms, African-American professors commonly have significantly lower job satisfaction and quality of life than their White counterparts (Niemann & Dovidio, 1998).

IMPACT OF PROFESSOR BIOLOGICAL SEX IN THE COLLEGE CLASSROOM

In addition to race, there is compelling evidence that biological sex may also play a role in teacher-student interactions. Bradley (2005) generalized that "all women faculty often receive unequal treatment from students" (p. 520). Sandier (1986) posited that women faculty often have different teaching experiences than their men colleagues; many of the experiences involve negative sex bias by their own students, such as not being called professor or doctor or being challenged in front of the class by students. Sandier also argued that students have biological sex-related expectations of their instructors in that students expect women faculty to be more supportive, personal, and forgiving than men faculty. This suggests that students expect women instructors to be more communicative and receptive to questions from students (Brady & Eisler, 1999).

Basow and Silberg (1987) studied 16 pairs of instructors based on rank, discipline, and years of experience, and they found that male students rated women professors less favorably than men professors. Male students also have a tendency to evaluate women professors in terms of their attractiveness, as opposed to their intellectual capabilities and contributions (Canada & Pringle, 1995). In later research, Centra and Gaubatz (2000) found that male students perceive male teachers as more organized and systematic instructors compared to female instructors. These findings by Centra and Gaubatz are plausible since male students are perceived to "expect and exert male privilege" (Canada & Pringle, 1995, p. 180). However, Hargett's (1999) research indicated that both male and female students tend to rate male instructors as more credible than female instructors, implying that students automatically give more classroom credibility to men professors and give less classroom credibility to women professors.

Gilchrist (2008) used univariate analyses and found significant interactions between students' and professors' biological sex and how students seek compliance from their professors. Specifically, female students tended to persuade female professors to comply with their requests by emphasizing that they shared the same biological sex. In contrast, male students persuaded female professors to comply with their request by pointing out that their biological sex differed. These results suggest that students take into account professors' biological sex when seeking compliance in college classrooms. Previous research advises that a professor's biological sex does indeed impact teacher-student interactions and to claim otherwise is to ignore the *chilly climate* endured by women faculty. Sandier (1986) used the term *chilly climate* in reference to the confluence of problems women in the academy are confronted with, including gender bias and discriminatory practices.

AFRICAN-AMERICAN WOMEN PROFESSORS AND MAJORITY-RACE INSTITUTIONS

African-American women professors employed at majority-race institutions represent a unique group of professors because they are often marginalized in the academy based on both the racial and biological sex limitations previously described. Race and biological sex as dual lenses of marginality often confine these professors to an *otherness* position. *Otherness* is a metaphor that describes the idea that one group of people is not like the dominant group (Bartleet, 2008). In this sense, *otherness* often refers to women and people of color. For example, African-American women professors are not like the *other* professors (e.g., men and majority-race women) that students primarily encounter in classrooms at majority-race institutions. When people are confined to an *otherness* position they can face a different set of expectations and criteria for judgment that often results in discriminatory practices (Bartleet, 2008). From previous literature, Stanley (2006) found that besides the term *otherness*, a mix of words and phrases are used to metaphorically describe the overall unique experiences of African-American women professors teaching at predominantly white colleges and universities, such as 'multiple marginality,' 'living in two worlds,' 'the academy's new cast,' and 'silenced voices' (p. 3). These forms of marginality can impact the professors' quality of life in the academy and their teacher-student interactions. In addition to being underrepresented, African-American women faculty are perceived to be the most stressed and least satisfied of all faculty in the academe (Benjamin, 1997; Malveaux, 1998).

Because race and biological sex constitute salient and significant forces for African-American women professors, this study explored the following question: Per autoethnographic accounts, what unique experiences do African-American women professors employed at majority-race institutions report regarding their classroom interactions with majority-race students?

METHODOLOGY

PARTICIPANTS

This study included a purposive sample of tenure-track African-American women professors who currently teach at majority-race or predominately White institutions of higher education. Membership records from the African-American Communication and Culture Division of the National Communication Association were used to locate qualifying participants. I emailed each professor to inform her about the study and request participation. I also asked the professors to recommend additional potential participants who met the study's criteria.

Through purposeful and network/snowballing sampling procedures, 16 tenure-track African-American women professors employed at majority-race colleges and universities participated in the study. The participants ranged from first-year tenure-earning professors to those currently going through the tenure and promotion process. In terms of department sizes, the participants reported teaching in departments ranging from 4 to 29 full-time tenured or tenure-earning faculty members. Of the 16 participants, 13 of them represented departments in which they were the sole full-time African-American woman professor; 3 participants taught in departments with one additional professor of their same race and biological sex; no participants represented a department comprised of three or more tenured or tenure-earning African-American women professors.

PROCEDURE

Data were collected through a survey-interview format. Participants who agreed to participate in the study were emailed a consent form and an open-ended survey. Professors answered questions regarding their perception of how students view them based on credibility and overall teaching effectiveness. Professors further assessed their teacher evaluations and the face-to-face interactions they have with majority-race students (see Appendix). Completed surveys were emailed to me for analysis.

DATA ANALYSIS

This study's objective was to explore the overall unique experiences that African-American women professors employed at predominantly White institutions have with majority-race students through the professors' auto-ethnographic accounts. Thus, it was appropriate to analyze the meaning of the messages contained in the professors' written responses through qualitative content analysis. Qualitative content analysis explores the meaning of messages (Frey, Botan, & Kreps, 2000), and a qualitative approach focuses both on "explicit and implicit concepts and empowers the researcher to use his or her judgment in determining, on a case by case basis, whether a particular linguistic token references a particular concept in the given context" (Bazerman & Prior, 2004, p. 15). Qualitative content analysis further allows researchers to act as tools for analyzing the data (Hoepfl, 1997).

Frey, Botan, and Kreps (2000) recommend using two coders to enhance a study's validity. Thus, a trained research assistant and I performed the qualitative content analysis by following the process outlined by Auerbach and Silverstein (2003). Based on their suggestions, the research assistant and I examined the professors' written answers and looked for *repeating ideas*, which are defined as concepts "expressed in relevant texts by two or more research participants" (p. 54). We then categorized the repeating ideas into *thematic constructs*, which are viewed as abstract concepts that organize a group of themes by placing them into a theoretical framework (Auerbach & Silverstein, 2003).

RESULTS

To explore their interactions with majority-race students, the African-American women professors employed at predominantly White institutions assessed their teaching evaluations, face-to-face encounters, and overall unique experiences.

TEACHING EVALUATIONS

Initially, based on a review of their teaching evaluations, four dominant themes emerged from students' report about the professors' overall credibility and teaching effectiveness: (1) positive with no racial or gender implications, (2) sole African-American woman professor, (3) challenged and questioned credibility and authority, and (4) negative with racial and gender implications.

POSITIVE WITH NO RACIAL OR GENDER IMPLICATIONS. One theme indicated that students rate the professors very positively and that race and gender do not play a part in how students evaluate teaching effectiveness on written evaluations. One respondent said, "My teaching evals are high. The students write that I am crystal clear in terms of my expectations from them and that I am engaging and fun." Another professor commented, "My evaluations are solid; no student comment has ever given me reason to think they thought less of my effectiveness due to my race or gender or the combination of the two."

SOLE AFRICAN-AMERICAN WOMAN PROFESSOR. Another prevailing theme appearing in teaching evaluations suggested that the professors were many of the students' first and only African-American female professors. As stated by one participant, "Most students [including both minority and majority students at my university] have never had a professor of color in their three to five years of attendance based on my classroom polls." Another professor added:

> A student said that I was the first female African-American teacher he/she ever had. He/she commented that the class was enjoyed a great deal, although he/she did not expect to, primarily because having a Black female teacher was a new experience.

CHALLENGED AND QUESTIONED CREDIBILITY AND AUTHORITY. Some students also challenged and questioned the professors' credibility and authority via

via the written evaluations. Reflecting on her experiences at a former majority-race university, one professor said:

> My credibility was constantly in question by at least 20% of my students. The area in which my institution resided was known for being one of the most segregated cities in the country. Some students were not happy when they walked into a class and saw that the professor was a Black woman. For example, one student wrote on an evaluation, 'She is partial toward Black issues because she is always bringing up stuff about diversity in her lectures.'

According to another professor, "The students have indeed attacked my credibility and suggested that I was not knowledgeable about the subject. One student even wrote that my vocal quality was not appropriate enough to be a communication professor."

NEGATIVE WITH RACIAL AND GENDER IMPLICATIONS. Per their written evaluations, some students labeled the professors negatively and made explicit comments about the professors' race and gender. As stated by one respondent, "I have been called racist, sexist, power-hungry, and accused of having a poor attitude." According to another professor, "My students have indicated that they think I am too Black, too much of a woman, and too young to be called doctor." Another professor stated that one of her students gave her a compliment and an insult all in one statement by saying, "She's a pretty sharp teacher, for a Black woman."

FACE-TO-FACE INTERACTIONS

After assessing their teaching evaluations, the professors then recounted their face-to-face interactions. The African-American women professors indicated five overarching themes prevalent in their one-on-one encounters with majority-race students: (1) open and accepting, (2) credible and respectful, (3) avoidance, (4) intimidating and difficult to approach, and (5) challenge authority.

OPEN AND ACCEPTING. One theme intrinsic to the professors' accounts of their face-to-face teacher-student interactions suggests that some majority-race students are open and accepting to the professors and their teaching methods. One respondent articulated, "Based on face-to-face exchanges, I think students find my style very open and accepting." Another professor said, "I think my students find me somewhat of a mystery; so they are very open to communicating with me and trying to get to know me better on a more personal level."

CREDIBLE AND RESPECTFUL. Another prevailing theme found in the professors' accounts indicates that students collectively view them as credible and respectful forces in the classroom. One participant said, "For the most part, my students consider me to be a credible instructor." Another added:

> I believe the students see me as being very credible because I bring in real-life examples, including examples of race that many have never personally experienced. I also feel the students believe I'm credible because they come into my office asking for my advice in terms of life and academic issues.

AVOIDANCE. Per the professors' accounts, some majority-race students avoid nonessential face-to-face interactions with them and choose to communicate with them only on an as-needed basis. One professor recalled a time when her teaching and research agenda made her a suitable match to chair a White male student's thesis committee. However, the student chose a White male faculty member to chair the committee whose teaching and research interests were less than an ideal match. "It was as though he totally ignored my expertise," the professor recounted. Another participant stated, "They [majority-race students] will talk to me about relevant academic issues, but they seem to avoid getting to know me on a more personal level, even though I always make myself available to them."

INTIMIDATING AND DIFFICULT TO APPROACH. According to the professors, some of their students perceive them as intimidating and difficult to approach; thus they often hesitate to engage in face-to-face interactions. Reflecting on her teacher-student interactions, one professor said, "Initially students, particularly White males from rural areas, hesitate to approach and trust me as an instructor. I believe this to be a matter of race as well as gender and age." One professor recounted a time when she overheard a majority-race female student tell a group of peers, "I find her so difficult to approach. She really intimidates me."

CHALLENGE AUTHORITY. Some African-American women professors also indicated that their majority-race students challenge their classroom authority. As articulated by one professor:

> There have been times when I feel that students question my credibility when it comes to teaching the topic of race. They often have resistance to learning about race, which is coupled by the feelings of guilt they have for being part of the dominant group that has historically oppressed Blacks and other marginalized groups.

Another professor added:

> On a few occasions, I have had students (usually White males) challenge my authority. During my first year, after an exam, one student said, '*we* have to rethink the format,' and thought that he should come to my office and give advice on how to structure the class.

UNIQUE EXPERIENCES

After exploring their written teaching evaluations and face-to-face encounters, the professors then recalled any unique experiences they have had with majority-race students. Specifically, these experiences are perceived to be distinct to African-American women professors who teach at predominantly White institutions, and they are not commonly shared by professors representing different racial and gender demographics. Four themes emerged: (1) less formal, (2) less disclosive and trusting, (3) held to higher standards, and (4) treated according to stereotypical beliefs.

LESS FORMAL. The professors noted that often majority-race students refer to them in a more informal manner compared to how they interact with professors representing more traditional demographics. For example, students readily call them *Miss* or *Mrs.*, as opposed to *Doctor.* As stated by one respondent, "Students do tend to refer to me as 'Mrs.' instead of 'Dr.,' and I don't like this. I'm fairly certain they don't refer to most men professors as 'Mr." rather than 'Dr.'" Some majority-race students go so far as to call the African-American women professors by their first names. One professor described an instance when she was a new professor and a White female graduate student constantly called her by her first name. According to the professor:

> I had to have multiple conversations with her who insisted on calling me by first name, which I perceived as an attempt to equalize us. . . . I was offended by her assumption that we were colleagues or friends, neither of which we were.

LESS DISCLOSIVE AND TRUSTING. The respondents also indicated that majority-race students tend to be less disclosive and trusting of them compared to how they interact with White men or women professors or even Black men professors. One participant summed up her experiences with majority-race students as "often cold and distant . . . characterized by an atmosphere of mistrust." She added:

> They don't trust me, and to be perfectly honest, I'm not sure I trust them. I know they will smile in my face just to get what they want, then turn around and talk about me to the department chair and write ridiculous things on my teaching evaluations.

Another professor said, "I think they're less disclosive and less trusting in their communication with me, particularly White male students. Their body language and communicator style suggest to me that they're more comfortable in conversations with White male professors or White female professors."

HELD TO HIGHER STANDARDS. A repeating theme suggests that African-American women professors are collectively held to higher standards than their colleagues of different demographics. To give the professors in question proper credibility and respect, majority-race students tend to hold them to more stringent expectations in terms of dress, verbal and nonverbal delivery, knowledge level etc. One participant said:

> I have been critiqued by students on the following issues: style of dress, vocal tone (e.g., aggressive, harsh, loud), and demeanor (e.g., mean, negative). I have discovered that these critiques are exclusive to women of color on my campus; they don't ever seem to "pop-up" on evaluations of White faculty.

According to another respondent:

> Some of my White colleagues can get away with wearing jeans, T-shirts, and sneakers. I could never come to class dressed like that because my credibility is on the line. Students judge every move I make, every place I go, everything I wear, and everything I do and say. I feel like I must always *prove* to my students that I deserve to be here.

Treated According to Stereotypical Beliefs. Per the professors' comments, majority-race students are knowledgeable about common stereotypes associated with African-American women, which range from passive and submissive at one end of the spectrum to power-hungry and demanding at the other end. Because the students are aware of these stereotypical beliefs, they commonly expect the professors to reflect these characteristics in classroom settings. Based on her experiences with these stereotypical assumptions, one professor affirmed:

> Students expect me to offer more extra credit work, accept late work routinely, and treat them like a 'mammy' in terms of demonstrating a stereotypical subservience when assisting them with course work that they should have been able to manage on their own. Some students also have a hard time dealing with my authoritarian, assertive style. They expect me to be docile, passive, and overly accommodating.

Another professor reasoned that her students also expect her to display the stereotypical image of the submissive and easy-going African-American woman and are, therefore, put-off by her high standards for quality work. "Some students tell me that I'm a hard grader and my expectations for the quality of their work are unreasonable," the professor recounted.

Discussion

Bradley (2005) put it best when she asserted, "unique challenges confront African-American women professors," and these professors have "distinct career development paths and encounters" (p. 518). Interactions with majority-race students arguably comprise some of the most unique experiences for these professors. Therefore, the purpose of this study was to explore these teacher-student interactions based on the professors' autoethnographic accounts.

ASSESSMENT OF WRITTEN TEACHING EVALUATIONS

When the professors assessed their teaching evaluations, four dominant themes emerged concerning how students view the professors in terms of overall credibility and teaching effectiveness. The remarks were varied and diverse, with some students offering relatively standard evaluations that were generally positive and harbored no racial and gender implications. These comments are ideal for any faculty member and imply that not all students view African-American women professors negatively. However, the content analysis suggests that these positive comments constitute more of the minority rather than the majority of comments that the professors receive from students. Many written comments the African-American women professors received were unique to them and would not likely be shared by their colleagues. For example, some students commented that the professor was their sole African-American woman professor. This shows that African-American women professors are somewhat rare in the collegiate setting. In fact, only 2.5% of the full-time instructional faculty in degree-granting institutions are African-American women (Patitu & Hinton, 2003). Because there are so few African-American women professors, many students are not accustomed to seeing these women in positions of authority, which metaphorically can place them in a position of *otherness*. As stated in the literature review, African-American women professors are not like many *other* professors (e.g., men and majority-race women) that students commonly encounter in the classroom. Therefore, it is not surprising that the professors in this study also indicated that the students challenged and questioned their credibility and authority on written evaluations. These findings concur with Bradley (2005), who posited, "Some White American college students perceive African-American women professors to be incompetent and feel at liberty to challenge their authority" (p. 520).

The last recurring theme that appeared when the professors assessed their teaching evaluations is perhaps the most disturbing. Some students wrote negative comments laced with racial and gender implications. It is unlikely that professors representing more dominant demographic features would get some of the written comments that the participants in this study received. Per respondents' autoethnographic accounts, students have labeled them *racist*, *sexist*, and *power-hungry*. As previously stated, one student even audaciously wrote, "She's a pretty sharp teacher, for a Black woman." Why was it necessary for the student to include the latter part of this evaluation? These examples support the research of Pope and Joseph (1997), whose investigation revealed that African-American women faculty often receive derisive student evaluations with hurtful and offensive comments such as, "Bitch, go back to Africa," "Black bitch," and "You are here only because of Affirmative Action" (p. 252). In other words, an examination of African-American women professors' written teaching evaluations suggests that their experiences are unique and complicated in ways not shared by all faculty members. It is arguable that African-American women are among the few professors who receive evaluation comments riddled with both offensive racial and gender connotations. From this, it appears that some majority-race students use the anonymous course evaluation process as a dividing tool to distinguish the in-group from the out-group. In Nakayama and Krizek's (1995) discussion of whiteness as a strategic rhetoric, the scholars argue that the *center* is a discursive cultural space of privilege and power, whereas the *margins* reflect a discursive system of naming oppression. Inferring from Nakayama and Krizek's theoretical perspective, it is plausible that students view teaching evaluations as dividing forces that remove African-American women professors from the *center* and place them in the *margins* as a group that "doesn't belong" in predominantly White educational settings (Raposo & Stone, 1970).

Assessment of Face-to-Face Interactions

Similar to the themes that emerged when the professors reflected on their teaching evaluations, varied findings also resulted when the professors evaluated their face-to-face interactions with majority-race students. Two themes (openness/acceptance and respect) imply positive and constructive interactions. These themes further suggest that some majority-race students desire open communication and overall healthy interpersonal relationships with African-American women professors. These are ideal face-to-face encounters that virtually all professors desire from their students. At first glance, the themes of openness/acceptance and respect could indicate that majority-race students do not interact with the professors in this study any differently than they interact with majority-race or male professors. However, the three other themes that emerged (avoidance, intimidation, and challenges to the professors' authority) contradict the first two themes and connote negative and destructive interactions.

Some of the professors posited that their majority-race students communicated with them on a limited basis out of necessity, or they avoided them altogether. This theme echoes the sentiments by Gititi (2002), who theorized that some White students commonly avoid or drop a class because of the professor's race. The question becomes, why do the students avoid the professors? Perhaps the answer lies in another prevailing theme—majority-race students find their African-American women professors intimidating and difficult to approach. According to Bradley (2005), one way that society has typecast African-American women is based on the *Sapphire* stereotype. Sapphire was a character from the 1950's television show, *Amos and Andy*, who was the nagging, complaining, and sassy wife of her television husband, Kingfish. Kingfish often ignored her because of her loud and obnoxious behavior, while others regarded her as unintelligent and incompetent. African-American women who display a confident and assertive demeanor in their professional careers are commonly perceived as a *Sapphire* and are, therefore, avoided (Benjamin, 1997). In other words, because the majority-race students perceive African-American women professors as intimidating, they may choose to avoid unnecessary or social interactions with them. Men or majority-race women professors are rarely questioned for displaying intelligence, confidence, or assertiveness in the classroom. However, as previously noted, students at predominantly White institutions are not accustomed to regularly being taught by African-American women professors. Thus, when these professors epitomize the essence of confidence or "exhibit any level of assertiveness, they are frequently labeled as 'loose cannons' or trouble-makers" (Trotman, 2009, p. 80). These negative perceptions further illustrate that the experiences of African-American women professors are "not like the others" (Raposo & Stone, 1970).

The final emerging theme illustrated that majority-race students commonly challenge the professors' authority in face-to-face interactions. This theme is quite the contrary to the previous two (i.e., avoidance and intimidation/difficult to approach). The question now becomes, why do some majority-race students avoid African-American women professors due to intimidation, yet other students openly challenge and question the professors' authority? According to Bradley (2005), the answer again lies in how society has typecast African-American women. While the *Sapphire* image reflects a confident and assertive character, the *Mammy* stereotype is just the opposite. The *Mammy* typecast began during slavery when an actual mammy served as the primary caregiver to the master's household. Mediated images have portrayed her as happy, subservient, and always eager to attend to other's needs (Yarbrough & Bennett, 2000). So while some majority-race students view African-American women professors as a *Sapphire* who should be avoided, others view the professors more like a *Mammy* who works for them and does whatever is demanded by the dominant group. When students harbor these stereotypical images, they may challenge and question minority-group professors considerably more compared to majority-group professors. Thus, as reported by the participants in this study, some students openly tell the professors how they should teach the class and conduct classroom policies. With this rhetoric, the students are implying that they know more about classroom instruction than the professors. These face-to-face interactions further illustrate that some majority-race students place African-American women professors in an *otherness* position and, as summarized by Stanley (2006), desire to "silence" their voices in the professors' own classrooms (p. 3).

OVERALL ASSESSMENT OF TEACHER-STUDENT INTERACTIONS

The participants were asked to evaluate their overall interactions and identify unique experiences with majority-race students. The professors' autoethnographic accounts indicate that their experiences with majority-race students can be challenging and filled with obstacles that are not commonly shared by their colleagues who represent dominant demographics. Four themes emerged that suggest majority-race students interact with African-American women professors less formally, trust and self-disclose less to them, hold them to higher standards, and treat them according to stereotypical beliefs. The professors theorized that these four themes are likely not specific and significant to the interactions that other professors have with their students, especially White men professors. The question is, why were the participants' interactions with their students plagued by these defining characteristics? The answer potentially lies in the students' overall perception of the professors' classroom credibility.

According to Hendrix (1997), compared to White professors, African-American professors are held to higher standards by White students; thus, these professors frequently make concerted efforts to establish and maintain their classroom credibility by stressing their credentials, teaching experience, and knowledge level at the onset of a course. Additionally, Hargett's (1999) research implies that students automatically grant more classroom credibility to men professors in contrast to women professors because both male and female students tend to rate male instructors as more credible than female instructors. The findings from this study mirror Hendrix's (1997) assertions on professor race and Hargett's (1999) assumptions pertaining to professor biological sex. According to Trotman (2009), "The African-American woman is not only relatively new to the academy, but brings with her the added stigma of presumed intellectual inferiority and incompetence" (p. 79). Myers (2002) adds, "The perception that African-American women are incompetent pervades much of their career, forcing upon them the undeserved stress of providing a defense they should not need to give and fighting to prove merit when merit is unquestionably apparent" (pp. 21-22). Although Myers argues that merit should be apparent and without question, this may be easier said than done for many African-American women professors at majority institutions.

The participants were asked whether or not they believe they have to work harder to establish their classroom credibility and have favorable interactions with their students compared to their colleagues representing the majority race and sex. Of the 16 participants in this study, 14 answered yes, while only 1 participant said no, and 1 other answered that she was not sure. One participant said, "I feel like I have to be perfect. I cannot afford to make any mistakes/errors, or students may think I am incompetent. I do not believe my White or male counterparts have this pressure." Another commented, "Without a doubt I have to work harder, be more prepared, and prove that I am a credible member of the academic community. My students have much higher expectations of me." One professor added:

> I am convinced that I work twice as hard as my majority colleagues to gain the trust of students, and to be perceived as credible. I feel compelled to be conscious of my use of language, style of dress, and expressions of respect.

These statements affirm that African-American women professors are subjected to an *otherness* position and are not readily granted classroom credibility and respect. This lack of perceived credibility can infiltrate their teacher-student interactions with majority-race students and foster an atmosphere characterized by informality, distrust, uncertainty, and stereotypical behaviors. These conditions can create a *chilly* and uncomfortable working environment for the professors and affect their overall satisfaction in the professorate (Niemann & Dovidio, 1998; Sandier, 1986).

LIMITATIONS AND RECOMMENDATIONS

While this study provides a more in-depth understanding of the unique experiences African-American women professors have with majority-race students, it is not without limitations. Sample size is perhaps one limitation of this study because data were collected from only 16 professors from the target population. Future research should seek a larger sample size to increase the study's validity. However, as a disclaimer, it is relatively challenging to acquire a large sample of African-American women professors employed at predominantly White institutions because as previously mentioned, these individuals comprise only 2.5% of the full-time instructional faculty in degree-granting institutions (Patitu & Hinton, 2003).

Data were collected through the professors' autoethnographic accounts of their experiences with majority-race students. One of the greatest strengths of autoethnography is that it allows individual voices to be heard, especially those voices from marginalized groups. Aggregated data commonly reported in quantitative research does not provide opportunities for individual voices to be heard (Foss, 1988). Thus, autoethnography was the appropriate methodology to use for this study in order to understand teacher-student interactions from the professors' point of view. Nonetheless, the findings could be strengthened and further validated by comparing the professors' perceptions with those of their students. For example, forthcoming research could survey both professors and students regarding their classroom interactions and look for points of commonality among the two sets of comments. Another recommendation is to observe a classroom taught by an African-American woman professor that is comprised mostly of White students and document how the majority-race students interact with her both verbally and nonverbally. The observations could then be compared with the professor's accounts of her teacher-student interactions.

CONCLUSION

Overall, findings from this study suggest that African-American women professors experience many unique interactions with majority-race students. The professors initially assessed their teaching evaluations and reported that students use a range of measures to evaluate the professors' teaching effectiveness. Via written evaluations, students may rate the professors positively without mentioning racial and gender implications, single out each professor as the students' sole African-American woman educator, challenge and question the professors' credibility and authority, or rate the professors negatively based on racial and gender implications. When the professors evaluated their face-to-face interactions with majority-race students, a mix of themes also emerged connoting positive as well as negative perceptions. Specifically, when engaged in face-to-face interactions, majority-race students may communicate with the professors in a manner that suggests openness and acceptance, respect, avoidance, intimidation, or they may challenge the professors' authority. Finally, a collage of recurring themes surfaced when the professors recounted their collective unique experiences with majority-race students. The professors indicated that compared to professors representing dominant demographic features, students relate to them less formally, are less disclosive and trusting, hold them to higher standards, and treat them according to stereotypical beliefs.

The study's findings collectively inform African-American women professors that when they join the faculty at majority-race institutions, they are essentially signing up for the unknown. Their experiences may be jointly rewarding and fulfilling, but they may also be riddled with challenges and negative perceptions that are not faced by White faculty or even African-American male professors because these educators endure on a day-by-day basis multiple forms of oppression, including racism and sexism (Hudson-Weems, 1989). This oppression characterizes the position of African-American women professors at majority institutions as one that is unique and, "not like the others;" that is, sometimes they "just doesn't belong" (Raposo & Stone, 1970).

References

Anderson, M., Astin, A. W., Bell, D. A., Cole, J. B. (1993). Why the shortage of Black professors? *The Journal of Blacks in Higher Education*, *0*, 25-34.

Auerbach, C. F., & Silverstein, L. B. (2003). *Qualitative data: An introduction to coding and analysis.* New York, NY: New York University Press.

Bartleet, B. (2008). 'You're a woman and our orchestra just won't have you': The politics of *otherness* in the conducting profession. *Hecate*, *34*, 6-23.

Basow, S. A., & Silberg, N. T. (1987). Student evaluations of college professors: Are female and male professors rated differently? *Journal of Educational Psychology*, *79*, 308-314.

Bazerman, C., & Prior, P. (Eds.). (2004). *What writing does and how it does it: An introduction to analyzing texts and textual practices.* Mahwah, NJ: Lawrence Earlbaum.

Benjamin, L. (1997). *Black women in the academy: Promises and perils*. Gainesville, FL: University Press of Florida.

Bradley, C. (2005). The career experiences of African American women faculty: Implications for counselor education programs. *College Student Journal, 39*, 518-527.

Brady, K. L. & Eisler, R. M. (1999). Sex and gender in the college classroom: A quantitative analysis of faculty-student interactions and perceptions. *Journal of Educational Psychology, 91*, 127-145.

Canada, K., & Pringle, R. (1995). The role of gender in college classroom interactions: A social context approach. *Sociology of Education, 68*, 161-186.

Centra, J. A., & Gaubatz, N. B. (2000). Is there gender bias in student evaluation of teaching? *Journal of Higher Education, 71*, 17-33.

Cross, T. (1998). The Black faculty count at the nation's most prestigious universities. *The Journal of Blacks in Higher Education, 19*, 109-115.

Feagin, J. R., Vera, H., & Imani, N. (1996). *The agony of education: Black students at White colleges and universities*. New York, NY: Routledge.

Foss, S. K. (1988). What distinguishes feminist scholarship in communication studies? *Women's Studies in Communication, 11*, 9-11.

Frey, L., Botan, C., & Kreps, G. (2000). *Investigating communication: An introduction to research methods* (2nd ed.). Boston: Allyn & Bacon.

Gilchrist, E. S. (2004). *Students' use of compliance-seeking strategies with Black and White graduate teaching assistants.* Unpublished doctoral dissertation, University of Memphis, Tennessee.

Gilchrist, E. S. (2008). *Unconventional classroom persuasion: An investigation of students' seeking compliance from male and female professors.* Paper presented at the National Communication Association Convention, San Diego, CA.

Gititi, G. (2002). Menaced by resistance: The Black teacher in the mainly White school/classroom. In B. TuSmith & M. T. Reddy (Eds.), *Race in the college classroom: Pedagogy and politics* (pp. 189-199). Piscataway, NJ: Rutgers University Press.

Hargett, J. (1999). Student perceptions of male and female instructor level of immediacy and teacher credibility. *Women and Language, 22*, 46.

Hendrix, K. G. (1997). Student perceptions of verbal and nonverbal cues leading to images of Black and White professor credibility. *Howard Journal of Communications, 8*, 251-274.

Hoepfl, M. (1997). Choosing qualitative research: A primer for technology education researchers. *Journal of Technology Information, 9*, 47-63.

Hudson-Weems, C. (1989). The tripartite plight of African American women as reflected in the novels of Hurston and Walker. *Journal of Black Studies, 20*, 192-207.

Johnson, L. (2002). "My eyes have been opened": White teachers and racial awareness. *Journal of Teacher Education, 53*, 153-168.

Leong, K. J. (2002). Strategies for surviving race in the classroom. In B. TuSmith & M. T. Reddy (Eds.), *Race in the college classroom: Pedagogy and politics* (pp. 189-199). Piscataway, NJ: Rutgers University Press.

Malveaux, J. (1998). Retaining master jugglers. *Black Issues in Higher Education, 15*, 40.

Murray, B. (1998, June). Why are some minority faculty unhappy? *The APA Monitor Online, 29*. Retrieved June 25, 2009, from www.apa.org/monitor/ jun98/frus.html.

Myers, L. W. (2002). *A broken silence: Voices of African-American women in the academy.* Westport, CT: Bergin & Garvey.

Nakayama, T. K., & Krizek, R. L. (1995). Whiteness: A strategic rhetoric. *Quarterly Journal of Speech*, *81*, 291-309.

Nelson, S., & Pellett, G. (Producers/Writers/Directors). (1997). *Shattering the silences* [Television broadcast]. Washington, DC: Public Broadcasting Service.

Niemann, Y. F., & Dovidio, J. F. (1998). Relationship of solo status, academic rank, and perceived distinctiveness to job satisfaction of racial/ethnic minorities. *Journal of Applied Psychology*, *83*, 55-71.

Patitu, C. L., & Hinton, K. (2003). The experiences of African American women faculty and administration in higher education: Has anything changed? *New Directions for Student Services*, *4*, 79-93.

Pope, J. & Joseph, J. (1997). Student harassment of female faculty of African American descent in the academy. In L. Benjamin (Ed.), *Black women in the academy: Promises and perils* (pp. 252-260). Gainesville, FL: University Press of Florida.

Raposo, J., & Stone, J. (1970). One of these things (is not like the others). On *The Sesame Street Book & Record* [Record]. Columbia.

Reddy, M. T., & TuSmith, B. (Eds.). (2002). Introduction. *Race in the college classroom: Pedagogy and politics* (pp. 1-3). Piscataway, NJ: Rutgers University Press.

Sandier, B. (1986). *The classroom climate revisited: Chilly for women faculty, administrators, and graduate students.* Washington, DC: Project on the Status and Education of Women, Association of American Colleges.

Stanley, C. A. (2006). *Faculty of color: Teaching in predominantly white colleges and universities*. Bolton, MA: Anker Pub.

Sutherland, M. E. (1990). Black faculty in White academia: The fit is an uneasy one. *Western Journal of Black Studies*, *14*, 17-23.

Trotman, F. K. (2009). The imposter phenomenon among African American women in U.S. institutions of higher education: Implications for counseling. In G. R. Walz, J. C. Bleuer & R. K. Yep (Eds.), *Compelling counseling interventions: VISTAS 2009* (pp. 77-87). Alexandria, VA: American Counseling Association.

Turner, C. S. V., & Myers, S. L. (1999). *Bittersweet success: Faculty of color in academe*. Boston, MA: Allyn & Bacon.

Yarbrough, M., & Bennett, C. (2000). Cassandra and the "Sistahs": The peculiar treatment of African American women in the myth of women as liars. *Journal of Gender, Race and Justice*, *24*, 626-657.

APPENDIX

AFRICAN-AMERICAN WOMEN PROFESSORS' EXPERIENCES WITH MAJORITY-RACE STUDENTS

Instructions: This survey is designed to explore the experiences African-American women professors have with majority-race students at predominately White institutions. Please answer the following questions in as much detail as needed.

1. What is your professional title?

2. How long have you taught at a predominately White institution?

3. Considering the full-time tenured and tenure-track professors in your department, what is your departmental composition in terms of race and sex?

4. As a woman faculty member of color, why did you choose to teach at a majority-race institution?

5. Based on your *teacher evaluations*, how to you think your students perceive you in terms of overall credibility and teaching effectiveness? Feel free to cite specific examples or quote directly.

6. Based on *face-to-face interactions* and the *classroom experiences* you have with students, how to you think your students perceive you in terms of overall credibility and teaching effectiveness? Feel free to cite specific examples or quote directly.

7. As a woman faculty member of color, do you feel that you have to work harder to establish your classroom credibility and have favorable interactions with your students than your colleagues representing a majority race and sex?

8. Have your students ever commented that you are their first African-American woman professor? Please explain if applicable.

9. Do you feel that your students interact with you differently than how they interact with your colleagues representing a majority race and sex? Please explain your answer.

10. Please describe any unique experiences you have had with majority-race students.

WORKING WITH SCIENCE, TECHNOLOGY, ENGINEERING, AND MATHEMATICS (STEM)

14-15

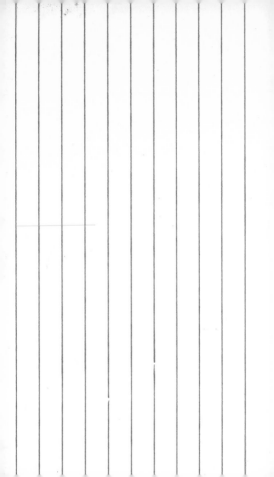

Chapter 14

Navigating New Terrains

Socialization Challenges of African-American Female Tenure-Track Faculty in the STEM Disciplines[1]

Cerise L. Glenn

Women of color have made significant strides in attaining advanced degrees and entering the job market. Despite these achievements, however, they continue to be underrepresented in academia, particularly in the sciences, technology, engineering, and mathematics (STEM) disciplines. Although these women have the educational background and qualifications to become successful faculty members, they often do not stay in tenure-track positions as long as their male or European-American female counterparts (Bonner, 2001; Green & Greene King, 2001; Gregory, 2001; Turner, 2002). Organizational socialization processes, the means through which people learn their roles in their professions, impact how these women learn the norms and values of their occupations. Since academia has been traditionally associated with members of majority culture and men, normative practices do not always include women and people of color. Efforts to incorporate underrepresented groups into organizational socialization discourses can be effective, yet they can also marginalize and alienate those who do not fit traditional organizational norms (Bullis & Stout, 2000; Buzzanell, 2000). Newer faculty of color and women often experience unique challenges adjusting to organizational culture and/or professional organizational roles. In addition to negotiating organizational discourse regarding their professional roles, they also simultaneously negotiate the impact of their occupational roles with the racial and gendered aspects of their cultural identities. At times, the multiple aspects of their social identities cohere; however, they can also contradict each other or result in additional tasks and demands (Allen, 2000).

Organizational socialization of diverse groups continues to be a growing issue in academia and in organizational communication scholarship (Ashcraft & Allen, 2003; Buzzanell, 2000; Frierson, 1990). In order to gain a deeper understanding of how organizational discourses influence newcomer occupational socialization for women of color, this chapter examines organizational socialization processes from the vantage point of African-American female assistant professors in the STEM disciplines. Organizational discourses include formal policies and documents, as well as communicative "micropractices," i.e. the everyday interpersonal interactions with others in the organizational environment. Examining how the participants understand and negotiate multiple organizational discourses illuminates barriers they encounter as they attempt to "learn the ropes" of their new professions (Allen, 2000; Mumby, 1993). Further, this chapter explores ways that the women's cultural identities, primarily race and gender, impact the development of their professional identities through socialization processes. So as to provide a context for the issues they confront and the strategies they utilize to mitigate the impact of these encumbrances to their potential career growth, in-depth interviews and participant observations were utilized to capture the voices of these women in the first three years of their careers as assistant professors. The chapter concludes with the theoretical and pragmatic implications that these encumbrances and proposed coping strategies have for women of color in academia in as well as for other university and college personnel.

Occupational Socialization and Cultural Identities in the Workplace

Organizational Socialization

The process of understanding professional expectations occurs through the internalization of organizational roles, norms, and values through organizational discourses. Organizational communication scholars assert that organizational socialization significantly impacts how new employees understand their job-related roles, develop professional identities, and integrate into organizational cultures (Bullis & Stout, 2000; Jablin 2001, 1987). Organizational socialization can also be described as the process by which newcomers, or "outsiders," learn and adapt to the organization's norms and rules, thereby becoming "insiders." Socialization occurs as organizational members adopt roles specific to the organization to which they belong (Bullis & Stout, 2000).

Socialization occurs in four stages: anticipatory socialization, encounter, assimilation, and exit (Jablin, 2001,1987). Anticipatory socialization occurs before members officially become part of a new organization. During this stage, prospective members and current members of the organization seek information about each other to determine if there is a good fit between the organization and the potential newcomer. Job interviews serve as an important mechanism of anticipatory socialization for new members. In the case of tenure-track professors, they often visit the university to learn about its norms, policies, and values. They meet current students, faculty, and administrators to ascertain more detailed information about the expectations and responsibilities of their positions. If the organizational members charged with the task of hiring new professors decide to make an offer and the candidate accepts it, he or she officially becomes part of the organization.

After accepting a formal job offer, organizational newcomers begin the encounter phase. That is, they gain an understanding of the "reality" of their new positions and begin to shape their organizational identities. They learn more about their job-related roles and develop expectations about what they will experience in their roles, as well as what others expect of them in terms of performance and outcomes (Jablin, 1982). For tenure-track faculty, these expectations center on teaching, research, and service—both to the university and to their respective fields. They often utilize socialization strategies, such as seeking a mentor, to obtain feedback from more experienced faculty. This feedback helps new organizational members increase their understanding of job-related responsibilities. Further, they use socialization strategies to find successful members of the organization to model in order to learn appropriate behavior and reduce uncertainty about ambiguous tasks and/or expectations (see DiSanza, 1993; Miller & Jablin, 1991).

Assimilation, the target of socialization, occurs when members have successfully internalized their job roles and have integrated into workplace culture (Jablin, 2001, 1987, 1982). When organizational members reach this stage of occupational socialization, they have "become an accepted, participating member of the organization" (Allen, 2000, p. 181), which means they have successfully adapted to and internalized the organization's norms and rules into their professional identities (Jablin, 1987). In the case of tenure-track faculty, they demonstrate assimilation through informal pre-tenure reviews and the formal tenure process. During the process of obtaining tenure, they present their work pertaining to teaching, research, and service to show they have performed their job-related duties and become an integral part of the university's culture. Obtaining tenure reflects successful assimilation. Unsuccessful attempts to assimilate into the organizational norms and expectations result in exit, the final (and often undesired) stage of socialization. At the exit stage, tenure-track professors prepare to leave the organization and usually begin seeking employment elsewhere.

Gender and Race in European-American and Male Dominated Fields

Although the stages of socialization apply to and describe how people develop professional identities and adapt to organizational cultures, a growing number of scholarship addresses how socialization processes are not the same for *all* people. People from diverse socio-cultural backgrounds may adapt to organizational practices in ways that may differ from the norm. Approaches to organizational socialization from the perspective of difference, particularly feminist approaches, discuss the ways in which other social identities, such as gender and race/ethnicity, impact "successful" organizational socialization (Allen, 2000; Bullis & Stout, 2000). Bullis and Stout (2000) assert that socialization literature that examines organizational newcomers often overlooks those who encounter barriers erected by discourses and institutional structures as they try to transition to the assimilation stage of socialization—that is, how race, gender, and class (socioeconomic status) often affect how people learn, adjust to, and perform their professional roles. Those who do not fit into the norms of more dominant social groups, such as racial and ethnic minorities, women, and those of a lower socioeconomic status, may be socialized in ways that do not cohere with other aspects of their social identities and/or may not be fully accepted by those with more social power (Allen, 2004, 2000; Collins, 2000; Glenn, 2008).

Existing research that primarily (and often exclusively) addresses gender in male dominated fields reveals that socialization differences between men and women can often disadvantage women in their careers. Professions in the STEM fields especially value masculine traits over those deemed more feminine; thus, women's gendered social traits that predispose them to be more submissive and caring do not cohere with more masculine social traits, which embrace logic and facts (Fels, 2004; Hewlett, Luce, & Servon, 2008). For instance, women may not be perceived as professional in male dominated workplace settings when they talk about work-family balance, which is generally considered feminine discourse (Buzzanell, 2000; Bullis & Stout, 2000; Fels, 2004; Frehill, 2004; Gallos, 1989). Conversely, women who do not adhere to traditional feminine roles, such as valuing relationships too much at work and competing for high profile positions, are accused of embodying more masculine characteristics (Fels, 2004). Women in STEM professions often opt to leave these fields because of hostile work environments, isolation from being the only female in the job, long work schedules, and uncertainty about career advancement (Hewlett, Luce, & Servon, 2008).

AFRICAN-AMERICAN FEMALE FACULTY IN THE STEM FIELDS

Women of color in the STEM disciplines in the United States have not received much attention in occupational socialization scholarship. To date, no published empirical communication research addresses women in these fields at majority White institutions. In general, this type of research is conducted from other disciplines, such as education and sociology, and/or consists of well-articulated position statements, calls to action, and anecdotal evidence. Research examining attrition of African-American female faculty (across all fields) reveals that they do not remain in tenure-track positions as long as men or European-American women (see Bonner, 2001; Turner, 2002). Similar to the previously discussed research on gender, scholars have posited various reasons for this disturbing trend. Bonner (2001), who examines women of color at Historically Black Colleges and Universities, and Bruns and Bruns (2005) suggest that women of color often face a hostile work environment, often referred to as "chilly climates," where they do not feel welcome in their new environments and/or encounter racism and sexism while fulfilling their job-related tasks. Research also suggests that African Americans face challenges from their majority culture students, which can impact their perceived credibility and course evaluations used for promotion and tenure reviews (Hendrix, Jackson, & Warren, 2003).

In addition to the occupational stress of working in "chilly climates," African-American women may also be more likely than their male or European-American female counterparts to spend more time engaged in service, particularly guiding and advising their African-American students in different departments (Gregory, 2001). Although this service is important, it often detracts from time that could be spent in roles that improve promotion and tenure, such as publishing. These additional time demands can contribute to difficulties African-American women experience related to obtaining tenure. These demands also contribute to the women's premature departure from academic posts prior to tenure reviews (Bonner, 2001; Burgess, 1997; Turner, 2002). Not only do African-American women experience tenure-related difficulties during the assimilation phase of organizational socialization, many of them also work in non-tenure track positions, for example, as adjuncts or term lecturers. As a result, they often experience role burnout and overload due to occupational stressors, or leave academia for other jobs altogether (Bonner, 2001; Brewer, Ehrenberg, & Goldhaber, 1995; Jordan-Zachery, 2004; National Center for Education Statistics, 2000; Turner, 2002). At various times during the organizational socialization process, these women may experience forms of discrimination which marginalize them. These types of discrimination can take the form of overt, openly hostile discourse, such as the following student comment to a Black female instructor: "Bitch, go back to Africa" (Allen, 2000, p. 192). They can also be covert and subtle, such as expressed formal and informal expectations to represent the "minority" voice on committees (Allen, 2000). Both overt and covert forms of marginalizing organizational discourses can make it more difficult for African American women in the STEM disciplines to advance and successfully adapt to the university environment.

RESEARCH METHODS AND DATA ANALYSIS

I used in-depth interviews and participant observation with five African-American female tenure-track assistant professors at Research Extensive and Intensive Institutions (formerly referred to as Research I institutions) to examine newcomer organizational socialization for African-American women in the STEM disciplines. Each of the participants is an organizational newcomer who has been in her tenure-track position for fewer than three years. Each woman engages in teaching, research, and service as part of her job-related tasks and shares the career goal of obtaining tenure. Since participants are at research institutions, they have smaller teaching loads and more emphasis on publications and obtaining external funding than at master's comprehensive and teaching universities. The data collection process entailed two semesters of multiple in-depth interviews and participant observation. Participant observation procedures included job shadowing (such as observing activities like teaching), obtaining grant information, and attending conferences. These data collection methods provided rich contexts and nuances to their experiences (Denzin & Lincoln, 2000; Lindlof & Taylor, 2002; Patton, 2002). I obtained informed consent, took extensive notes, and recorded the interviews as approved by the appropriate institutional review board. Information regarding name, age, university affiliation, and specific discipline of study were omitted to ensure anonymity and confidentiality. I assigned pseudonyms, Anastasia, Doreen, Laura, Katherine, and Malika, to the participants as I transcribed their interviews.

Consistent with the guidelines of Strauss and Corbin (1998), I used continuous data analysis that began with the first point of contact with the participants and continued throughout the data collection process. After the initial interview, I identified and connected ideas and themes from the interview transcriptions and the researcher's notes. After identifying preliminary themes regarding socialization, I gathered more data related to these themes through participant observation and additional interviews. For example, when a participant identified challenges regarding students' conduct in the classroom, I observed the participant while she taught courses (direct quotes from students were not included in the results since they arose from participant observation and the students did not sign informed consent forms). During a follow-up interview, the participant and I discussed the classroom interaction in relation to ideas generated during the previous interview. Ideas and thoughts were assigned into interconnected categories and then organized into common themes across the participants' experiences. After identifying preliminary thematic categories, I reviewed the data to recode and check for additional themes. The analysis resulted in overlapping themes, reflecting how multiple experiences influence their socialization processes in a holistic manner. After the final coding, I utilized member checks with three of the participants who reviewed the findings, which contributed to the validity of the data analysis (Lindlof & Taylor, 2002). The names of two of the themes were modified for clarity and the participants provided further details about their experiences.

CHALLENGES TO SUCCESSFUL ORGANIZATIONAL SOCIALIZATION

As noted earlier, the participants are assistant professors who aspire to become tenured associate professors. In order to achieve this goal, these women must successfully integrate into their work environments by learning their job-related roles regarding expectations for research, teaching, and service. These job-related functions apply to most assistant professors, regardless of cultural identity; however, the participants described ways in which their gender and racial identities can impede effective organizational socialization. They described how they experience and negotiate the following challenges: 1) exclusion from social networks and resources, 2) lack of understanding job-related tasks and expectations, 3) demands of additional roles, 4) finding appropriate mentors, and 5) questioning competence and "belonging."

EXCLUSION FROM SOCIAL NETWORKS AND RESOURCES

All of the participants felt that they were excluded, both intentionally and inadvertently, from many resources and social networks needed for successful occupational socialization. Interestingly, Anastasia and Malika found the STEM disciplines attractive because they thought they would avoid discrimination that their counterparts in the social sciences often face when trying to learn and fulfill the duties of an assistant professor. Anastasia explained the beginning of her career as an assistant professor:

> I thought that if I studied [field name omitted], there would be no race issues or problems because I'm a woman. Facts are facts. Period. Just numbers and data with no way for race to factor into it. . . . I want the bottom line to be about me. If I publish, I get tenure. If I don't, I won't. I didn't get any grants—my fault. It's all on me—no way discrimination can factor into that.

After completing her first year, she stated that she was wrong in those assumptions, as explained in the following narrative:

> I have to obtain grants to fund my research. I'm good at that, but sometimes I'm left out of the loop. People don't think about me when it comes time to collaborate or co-author projects. I feel like I'm alone. It's a little strange. There's

> no effort to connect me to funding sources. I have to make all those contacts myself. I feel the discrimination in an odd way. I don't think my colleagues are racist, they just exclude me from resources I need without thinking about it. In a way, that *is* discrimination. Treating me like I'm invisible, with no mentor or invitations for lunch or coffee. I mean they're friendly people. I just feel like I find out about too much stuff after the fact when I should've been included all along.

She particularly felt excluded when it comes to the assignment of students to work with faculty as research assistants. She said that when they meet formally, she discovered that her peers had already decided which students would be assigned to particular faculty members. Because the cohorts are so small, she noted that it is possible that she will only have one research assistant or not get one at all. Being left out on decisions like this creates barriers for her to succeed in her goal to get published because she does not have as much assistance as her peers.

Like Anastasia, Malika and Laura also felt excluded from resources, particularly those related to information regarding grants. These participants stated that being left out of important decisions and lack of access to information regarding their duties contributed to their feelings of isolation and exclusion from the resources needed to perform job-related tasks. They could not obtain the "inside" information and so they feel like organizational "outsiders" in their respective departments (Bullis & Stout, 2000; Collins, 1986, 2000; Turner, 2002). Laura expressed her desire to be an "insider," stating that, "it's isolating here," referring to her place of work. She continues to express her feelings of isolation in the following statement, "I'm on the team and I want the playbook that everyone else has, but no one will give it to me." Exclusion from social networks and resources, whether by oversight or intent, impede the participants' abilities to fully participate in important socialization practices. Additionally, when barriers exist to successful socialization, they may not understand all of their performance-related duties which they must account for during the tenure process, as discussed in more detail in the following section.

LACK OF UNDERSTANDING JOB-RELATED TASKS AND EXPECTATIONS

All of the participants discussed not fully understanding their position-related tasks and expectations, particularly as they relate to obtaining their own funding. For example, Doreen not only felt excluded from social networks and resources, but felt that she came into the assistant professor position at a disadvantage because she did not understand what her job entailed during the anticipatory socialization stage. This lack of awareness and encountering stereotypes further impedes her ability to perform well at her job (Allen, 2000; Bonner, 2001; Turner, 2002). Doreen explained that she did not fully understand what it meant to work at an "RI" (research intensive university) when she first accepted the assistant professor position. She explained:

> Sure I knew I would have to publish and teach, but raising my own money? I probably shouldn't admit this, but I didn't understand what I was getting into. Maybe I didn't ask the right questions at my interview or read my contract as carefully as I should have, but that should've come up sometime. Did they just assume I knew that? Should I have known that?

When prompted about ways she tries to find out about her responsibilities and learn ways she can fulfill them, Doreen responded:

> People treat me like I don't know anything. I know it's a shock to see a Black women in [field name omitted], but I shouldn't be treated like I'm here *just* because of my race and gender. I guess age plays a role in that, too. I'm the youngest one here. I can't ask questions because that just reinforces the stereotype. I mean I can just see them thinking, "She doesn't know this? How did she get this job? Clearly it couldn't be based on merit." I just sit back and try to gain as much information from watching them without them knowing I'm watching them.

Doreen's fear of being stereotyped prevents her from engaging in information seeking strategies that would help broaden her understanding of research funding (Allen, 2000). As previously noted, her lack of understanding this important aspect of her job may negatively influence her potential for promotion and tenure. Laura was also taken aback by the expectations to obtain her own funding. Although she knew she would have to raise money to support her research initiatives, she stated that, "developing grant writing skills have been challenging. . . . I found out that when it comes to writing grants, it's one out of every ten [applied for] that's funded." She continued, "If I could collaborate with other people . . . finding someone else to feed off of, it would be help." She described how she has tried to work with her colleagues, but they "treat me more like the hired help. I'm key personnel, but not co-PI [who has a controlling interest in how funds are dispersed]." The difficulty in obtaining external funding reflects aspects of a "chilly climate" where the participants do not feel welcome on important projects (Bonner, 2001; Bruns & Bruns, 2005). Laura's experience reflects the role of the "token," where she feels included in ways that merely show her representation without inclusion in key roles necessary to obtain the visibility and credit needed for tenure (Allen, 2000; Bonner, 2001).

Demands of Additional Roles

In addition to lack of understanding certain job tasks, the participants also discussed how their socialization processes are different from their colleagues', partially because they face different expectations. At times, these women gladly accepted additional roles; however, at other times they did so grudgingly in silence. Katherine, whose position is split between administration and an assistant professorship, states that, "Fifty percent of [her] time is administration" while two hundred percent of [her] time goes to organizing and preparing for class." She explained that she has to prepare large group lectures weekly, oversee numerous teaching assistants who lead the smaller classes, and oversee and visit all of the labs. Katherine admitted the time demands are high, but did not want to turn down the administration position because it was created out of initiative to diversify the institution. In addition, she was the only African-American *and* female in her area when she first accepted the position. Since this assignment is unique to her, she expressed doubt about her ability to successfully complete all of her responsibilities. She stated, "I don't know if I can take it. I may burn out in five years." Although she experiences work-related stressors such as role overload and perhaps burnout (Steers & Black, 1994), she quickly added that the positive strides she has been able to make regarding diversity in her department encourage her to continue.

Anastasia discussed how she was surprised when she was asked to teach this year because she should not have had any teaching obligations. She recounted her surprise and reaction to this request as she explained, "I'm all bought out [no teaching assignments because of research grants], but of course *I* get asked to teach anyway. . . . It's a class for this program on minorities in [field omitted] to support them. I'm the only one [African-American female], how can I say no?" She described how the request was not posed as an option, but more of an order. She was also told that the class would not take much time. Anastasia further elaborated that she finds this course challenging because she has to scramble for course material, particularly because she discovered it consisted of students in other STEM disciplines outside of her area of expertise. Additionally, the students need more support and affirmation than she can offer in a classroom setting. She wants her peers to understand the demands on her time, especially because she has not adapted to her job yet, but fears the negative reaction she would get not only from her peers in the department, but other faculty of color at her university (Allen, 2000; Turner, 2002). It is important for her to feel connected to the African-American faculty and she does not want to be excluded from them or perceived as uncaring or unsupportive of minority students' academic success.

Malika, Doreen, and Laura also expressed concern about the extra job-related demands from both peers and students. Malika and Laura discussed how they attend extra conferences to support minority students. They also feel pressured to recruit other women and minority students into their departments. Laura described a difficult situation regarding a request she has from a prospective African-American female graduate student *and* from one of her senior colleagues. Both the student and the colleague want to work together if the prospective student decides to attend the university. Her colleague will formally mentor and advise the student. The student, however, wants Anastasia to be her "extra mentor" since she is the only African-American female in her department. Anastasia explained:

> [The student] actually told me she preferred [colleague name omitted] as a formal mentor because she has a stronger research record and has more established networks. But she actually wants *me* to be her mentor and advisor. And [colleague name omitted] thinks that's a good idea because it frees up her time. . . . I understand those are good career moves for *them*, but come on. Now I'm supposed to be doing all the work, but I don't get the formal credit in my dossier. Of course I'm gonna help her [the student], but she needs to know that the graduate students I focus on are the ones here on *my* research money helping me with *my* projects. And I want to tell [colleague name], she can either mentor her or not. Now that's what I *wanna* do, but [pause] I have no idea what I *should* do. And the pressure's on because [the student] has also been admitted to another program and I really want her to come here.

Although the participants enjoy activities that help other students, this type of service often detracts from their ability to engage in other activities they need to obtain tenure (Bonner, 2001). All of the participants expressed frustration that these extra tasks are placed upon them in addition to, and not in place of, their obligations.

FINDING APPROPRIATE MENTORS

As Anastasia briefly referenced earlier, she believes that having a mentor would aid her as she tries to achieve her research-related goals. Malika, Doreen, Katherine, and Laura also do not have mentors in their departments and mentioned this as a barrier to positive socialization (Allen, 2000). Doreen stated:

> I just need someone I can safely ask questions. . . . I recently found out that I'm underpaid. Now that could be because I'm Black and female, but could it be because I didn't know how to negotiate a contract. How can I get a salary adjustment? How can I be mentored, now that I have the salary scale, to respond and get a raise?

Katherine feels that since she is the first African-American female in her position, having a mentor is not a viable option due to open animosity from her colleagues (she notes she was not a departmental hire, but obtained her position from a line created by someone high in administration).

Even though none of the participants have formal or informal mentors in their departments, they try to find ways to obtain mentors to assist them with concerns and issues regarding their professional obligations. Anastasia discussed the persistent manner in which she recently found a mentor at her university so she could learn appropriate ways to respond to the issues she encounters:

> I keep attending university functions. Tested the waters by talking about race and gender issues. I found a White male—he's great, but the exception—I could talk to. He helps me increase my boldness, not be so timid. Be really vocal about things. You have a voice so speak up about things—salary discrepancies, teaching loads that aren't equitable. Communicate about the culture of favoritism and exclusion of people. Communicate about faculty searches and how we decide to admit students.

Malika explained how she desires three different mentors at her university. She wants to form a mentoring relationship with someone outside of her technical area, a person within her discipline that has more influence than her departmental colleagues (such as a provost), and someone of color who has already obtained tenure. She is still trying to find all three of these people, and attends university events where she believes they will be present in order to foster these relationships. Currently, she relies upon her network of women of color in the STEM fields at other universities. Malika enjoys the solidarity of her professional networks, but finds she cannot obtain the information she needs because the women are primarily assistant professors seeking answers for similar issues and/or because they are not at universities that have as strong of an emphasis on research and grants. The principle of homophily suggests that women and people of color have difficulty finding mentors because they seek mentors of the same socio-demographic (see Allen, 2000; Burgess, 1997; Ibarra, 1993). The participants' experiences, however, suggest that they understand the importance of having male mentors and mentors of different racial backgrounds, but experience difficulty finding them.

QUESTIONING COMPETENCE AND "BELONGING"

The participants have also encountered troubling interactions with others at their respective institutions. They have endured direct and indirect challenges to their competence, as well as their sense of belonging to the university environment from students, colleagues, and staff members. Katherine explains:

> There were so many struggles when I first came here. . . . It takes a mature African-American female to get along with White . . . middle-aged men. They didn't want me here. People spread rumors. People wouldn't speak to me. For two years I asked myself, "Why am I doing this?" [She starts to cry.] For two years, I had tears every morning and every night. One said, "we don't have people of color in our community here. Why are you needed here?" I said that was completely out of line. In an off-the-record chat about all the adversity [a White male colleague] told me: "I don't know how you're going to make it here. It's not a welcoming environment. . . . " I had a lot of struggles because of the color of my skin. People weren't willing to give me a chance.

Even though some of her colleagues have begun to warm up to her, she still faces hostility, which makes it difficult to complete her numerous demanding tasks. As Bonner (2001) and Turner (2002) discuss, perceptions of a hostile work environment can negatively impact professors' abilities to perform their jobs well. Katherine counters this by attending conferences frequented by African-American professors and administrators. Two of these conferences are not directly related to her discipline, but she needs the motivation and solidarity from her peers to counter the stress at work.

Although Katherine experiences the most difficulties with her colleagues in her department, Doreen encounters the most overt challenges while teaching. She explained, "I'm at a disadvantage. The students [are] judging me more harshly. . . . They don't have questions about what's being covered. . . . They're testing me to see if I know what I'm talking about. Like the name Dr. [omitted] isn't enough to prove I'm competent." She elaborated "I just don't know. The stereotypes may still be pretty rampant. I have to rise above that. . . . It's a matter of getting respect from students [and] some faculty." Consistent with the findings of Hendrix, Jackson, and Warren (2003), Doreen believes that the students challenge her because of her race and gender and because they sense that some of her other peers do not respect her. She described earning the respect of her students and colleagues as part of her "extra" job-related tasks.

Laura experiences more subtle cues that make her feel like she does not belong in her position. She explained that no one has been rude to her, but she feels a tension that is difficult to articulate. When prodded for an example, she described how she keeps "shocking people that I (an African-American professor in the STEM disciplines) exist. I don't look like a professor. People think I'm a secretary and when I bust out the title, their jaws drop." Like Laura, Anastasia feels that people have "seemingly sly" ways of letting her know she does not "fit the mold" of a typical professor. She states, "There are stereotypes about women of color. I must prove myself even though I have a Ph.D. People think [I'm] not as qualified. When [I] do know something, it's surprising or intimidating." She recalls walking across the campus with a male staff member. When a faculty member approached them, he assumed that the staff member was the professor. She did not want to directly challenge the faculty member or embarrass her male colleague by asking why the faculty member assumed that her colleague was a professor. She expressed difficulty balancing the tensions of being vocal and standing up for herself with remaining silent about these issues so her colleagues will think she is more collegial, and not intimidating. She has, however, recently, begun discussing issues like these with her new mentor. She finds it helpful to express her concerns to him before she vocalizes them to her department.

Malika stated that she has a difficult time making sense of the challenges she faces. She is not sure whether to attribute them to "newcomer hazing," racism, and sexism, or not yet having time to adjust to her position. While she searches for mentors at her university (as discussed earlier), she relies on external networks to reinforce her sense of belonging to her profession. She explained, "I maintain and created networks so I could have people to talk to. Some of us were graduate students together. We're still very close—it's an all female ethnically diverse network. I'm the only African-American in that one. But I have another that's an all-African-American female support group." She further explained that while she "is trying to figure it all out, it's helpful to know I'm not alone. I'll always be the only one in the department. It's refreshing to know that that's not crazy."

Theoretical and Pragmatic Implications for Organizational Socialization

The experiences of new tenure-track African-American women in the STEM fields contribute to scholarship regarding organizational socialization. Jablin's (2001, 1987) model presents four additive, linear stages of socialization: anticipatory socialization, encounter, assimilation, and exit. It posits that entry to the next phase is predicated upon successful completion of the preceding one. The experiences of the participants, however, demonstrate that this does not always happen. Doreen, for example, did not fully understand her job duties and tenure expectations during the anticipatory socialization phase. Although she is currently advancing through the encounter stage and looking for ways to reach assimilation, she is still resolving uncertain expectations from the anticipatory socialization phase. She expresses frustration as she tries to obtain information to clarify her position since she did not completely understand them before accepting a tenure-track position. Doreen's experiences especially suggest that socialization is not a linear process, but one that can be cyclical regarding certain job expectations. According to Jablin's (2001, 1987) stages of socialization, the manner in which organizational members complete earlier stages of socialization fosters successful entry to the next stage of socialization (or exit). Doreen demonstrates how organizational members can experience aspects of these stages simultaneously. She is trying to obtain socialization information related to the anticipatory and encounter phases of socialization while trying to successfully assimilate to the university environment. Negotiating three phases at the same time intensifies the role stress she feels.

Organizational members can simultaneously negotiate the stages of socialization in ways that may remain hidden to those inside the organization. For instance, Malika looks for clarity from her personal circle of friends and colleagues in the STEM disciplines. While she is looking for a mentor at her university, she relies upon a network she helped form, even though they do not have experiences related to her particular position. Although this provides a "safe space" to ask questions and vent about her experiences, it also allows her to obtain information about her position without appearing to be unqualified to her peers.

Jablin (2001, 1987) asserts that modeling successful colleagues helps assimilation into the organizational culture. The participants attempt to utilize mentoring to achieve this task; however, as Bullis and Stout (2000) assert, barriers to successful assimilation exist for people of diverse populations. The experiences of the participants add empirical support for this assertion. Fear of being stereotyped and appearing unqualified often encumbers efforts to find mentors in the participants' respective departments. As noted earlier, prior research attributes the difficulty people of diverse groups have with obtaining mentors to the principle of homophily (see Allen, 2000; Burgess, 1997; Ibarra, 1993). The participants seek support from other women and people of color; however, they also express interest in obtaining mentors who are wise in areas where they need development regardless of race and gender. Even though they feel excluded from mentoring experiences in their departments, some have begun seeking mentors from other areas of the university. For example, Anastasia went to several events to find a mentor who was supportive. Malika has also started to seek mentorship from people outside of her area of expertise. Although these mentors are helping them with their socialization efforts, the lack of mentors in their fields, in addition to the lengths the participants must go to in order to find mentors, suggests that this is a great area of concern for women of color in the STEM fields.

The participants' stories also reflect how African-American women in research extensive and intensive universities can experience double binds, or paradoxical messages that result in confusing and contradictory ideas regarding job roles and expectations (Jorgenson, 2002; Putnam, 1986; Tracy, 2004). They each have additional service expectations and demands of their time related to supporting other women and minority ethnic groups at the university; however, working in this capacity detracts from job expectations that will look favorable for tenure and promotion. Anastasia's situation with the prospective graduate student reflects this contradiction. The student and her colleague want her to mentor the student because she is an African-American female. Anastasia also believes it is important for her to support African-American students in her field; however, the student and colleague want Anastasia to be her mentor in an *unofficial* capacity, which would result in no formal record of advising and mentoring Anastasia could put in her tenure file. Further, she would not receive the assistance students provide in completing research projects, which is also very important for tenure purposes. In addition, the expectation to teach a course for minority students even though she should have no teaching responsibilities for the semester reflects contradictory notions of her job-related responsibilities. If Anastasia elected not to teach the class, she could be perceived as uncaring and uncooperative even though she has also been informed to use the time to complete research related to her grant.

Pragmatic implications regarding socialization practices also exist for university personnel. Helping new tenure-track women of color find mentors would greatly assist them in becoming strong candidates for tenure. University personnel could also help women of color in these positions by protecting their time during the early stages of their careers. Training courses on obtaining grants, in addition to implementing a policy of not serving as a mentor the first year or semester in a new position, would allow these women to use their time in ways that will be rewarded in tenure evaluations without them feeling obligated to engage in additional roles placed upon them. Strategies such as these ultimately benefit both the professors and the institutions as they can help reduce role stressors that can lead to burnout.

CONCLUSION

This research bridges scholarship on women in the STEM disciplines with the limited amount of scholarship examining African-American women in academia, which primarily centers on the social sciences and humanities. The stories these women share may seem to paint a somewhat bleak picture; however, these women are resilient and find ways to successfully integrate into their professional environments. They engage in socialization strategies to increase their likelihood of success in obtaining their tenure goals, mitigate negative experiences, understand questionable occurrences, and maintain positive energy. Because they often feel excluded from socialization practices within their departments, they seek external mentors and networks to compensate for the information they do not get from these environments. This shows the creative ways that people who are socialized to be organizational "outsiders" search for "insider" information. Future research could build upon how these women create and maintain these connections, as well as explore how information gained from people of different university cultures "translates" to the culture of other university environments. For example, Malika's networks of women and women of color primarily consist of assistant professors at teaching universities. They most likely do not have much experiential knowledge about obtaining tenure that will enhance her understanding of her expectations at work, particularly in an environment where research funding plays a vital role in fulfilling job-related duties. Future research could also explore the double binds women of color experience when they are expected to be involved in job-related roles that will detract from their ability to complete projects necessary for promotion and tenure.

Women of color often face challenges to successfully learning and fulfilling their job responsibilities. Although they face overt and covert discrimination as extant research has noted, a focus on organizational socialization in the male and

European-American dominated STEM disciplines elucidates ways that women of color are often inadvertently relegated to positions of organizational "outsiders." Hopefully this research helps foster awareness of socialization issues for professors in similar positions, other faculty of color in different positions, and university personnel who work to effectively socialize new professors. Elucidating the challenges these women face can help achieve the common goal of helping professors successfully integrate into their university environments.

NOTE

1. This research was supported in part by a grant from the National Science Foundation and Purdue University through the Alliance for Graduate Education and the Professoriate (AGEP).

REFERENCES

Allen, B. J. (2000). "Learning the ropes": A Black feminist standpoint analysis. In P. M. Buzzanell (Ed.), *Rethinking organizational and managerial communication from feminist perspectives* (pp. 177-208). Thousand Oaks, CA: Sage.

Allen, B. J. (2004). *Difference matters: Communicating social identity.* Long Grove, IL: Waveland Press, Inc.

Ashcraft, K. L., & Allen, B. J. (2003). The racial foundation of organizational communication. *Communication Theory, 13*(1), 5-38. doi: 10.1111/j.1468 2885.2003.tb00280.x

Bonner, F. B. (2001). Addressing gender issues in the Historically Black College and University community: A challenge and call to action. *Journal of Negro Education, 70*, 176-191.

Brewer, D. J., Ehrenberg, R. G., & Goldhaber, D. D. (1995). Do teacher's race, gender and ethnicity matter? Evidence from the national educational longitudinal study of 1988. *Industrial and Labor Relations Review, 48*(3), 547-561.

Bruns, D. L., & Bruns, J. W. (2005). Sexual harassment in higher education. *Academic Exchange Quarterly.* Retrieved from http://www.highbeam.com/ doc/1G1-136071106.html

Bullis, C., & Stout, K. R. (2000). Organizational socialization: A feminist standpoint approach. In P. M. Buzzanell (Ed.), *Rethinking organizational and managerial communication from feminist perspectives* (pp. 47-75). Thousand Oaks, CA: Sage Publications, Inc.

Burgess, N. J. (1997). Tenure and promotion among African-American women in the academy: Issues and strategies. In L. Benjamin (Ed.), *Black women in the academy: Promises and perils* (pp. 227-234). Gainesville: University Press of Florida.

Buzzanell, P. M. (Ed). (2000). *Rethinking organizational and managerial communication from feminist perspectives*. Thousand Oaks, CA: Sage Publications, Inc.

Collins, P. H. (1986). Learning from the outsider within: The sociological significance of Black feminist thought. *Social Problems*, *33*, 14-23.

Collins, P. H. (2000). *Black feminist thought: Knowledge, consciousness, and the politics of empowerment.* New York: Routledge.

Denzin, N. K., & Lincoln, Y. S. (Eds). (2000). *Handbook of qualitative research.* (2nd ed.). Thousand Oaks, CA: Sage Publications, Inc.

DiSanza, J. R. (1993). Shared meaning as a sales inducement strategy: Bank teller responses to frames, reinforcements, and quotas. *Journal of Business Communication*, *30*, 133-160.

Fels, A. (2004). Do women lack ambition? *Harvard Business Review*, *82*(4), 50-60.

Frehill, L. (2004). The gendered construction of the engineering profession in the United States, 1893-1920. *Men and Masculinities*, *6*(4), 383-403. doi: 10.1177/1097184X03260963

Frierson, H. (1990). The situation of Black educational researchers: Continuation of a crisis. *Educational Research*, *19*, 12-17.

Gallos, J. V. (1989). Exploring women's development: Implications for career theory, practice, and research. In M. B. Arthur, D. T. Hall, & B. S. Lawrence (Eds.), *Handbook of career theory* (pp. 110-132). Cambridge, England: Cambridge University Press.

Glenn, C. L. (2008). Negotiating cultural identities and organizational terrains: African-American females at Predominantly White Institutions and Historically Black Colleges and Universities (Unpublished doctoral dissertation). Howard University, Washington, D.C.

Green, C. E., & Greene King, V. (2001). Black women in the academy: Challenges and opportunities. *The Journal of Negro Education*, *70*, 156-165.

Gregory, S. T. (2001). Black faculty women in the academy, status and future. *Journal of Negro Education*, *70*, 124-138.

Hendrix, K. G., Jackson II, R. L., & Warren, J. R. (2003). Shifting academic landscapes: Exploring co-identities, identity negotiation, and critical progressive pedagogy. *Communication Education*, *52*(3/4), 177-190.

Hewlett, S. A., Luce, C. B., & Servon, L. J. (2008). Stopping the exodus of women in science. *Harvard Business Review*, *86*(12), 113-114.

Ibarra, H. (1993). Personal networks of women and minorities in management: A conceptual framework. *Academy of Management Review*, 18, 56-87.

Jablin, F. M. (1982). Organizational communication: An assimilation approach. In M. E. Roloff & C. R. Berger (Eds.), *Social cognition and communication* (pp. 255-286). Newbury Park, CA: Sage Publications, Inc.

Jablin, F. M. (1987). Organizational entry, assimilation, and exit. In F. M. Jablin, L. L. Putnam, K. H. Roberts, & L. W. Porter (Eds.), *Handbook of organizational communication* (pp. 680-740). Beverly Hills, CA: Sage Publications, Inc.

Jablin, F. M. (2001). Organizational entry, assimilation, and disengagement/exit. In F. Jablin & L. L. Putnam (Eds.), *The new handbook of organizational communication: Advances in theory, research, and methods* (pp. 732-819). Thousand Oaks, CA: Sage Publications, Inc.

Jordan-Zachery, J. S. (2004). Reflections on mentoring: Black women and the academy. *PS Online*, October, 875-877. Retrieved from www.aspanet.org

Jorgenson, J. (2002). Engineering selves: Negotiating gender and identity in technical work. *Management Communication Quarterly, 15*, 350-380. doi: 10.1177/0893318902153002

Lindlof, T. R., & Taylor, B. C. (2002) *Qualitative communication research methods.* (2nd ed.). Thousand Oaks: Sage Publications, Inc.

Miller, V. D., & Jablin, F. M. (1991). An experimental study of newcomers' information seeking behaviors during organizational entry. *Academy of Management Review, 16*, 92-120.

Mumby, D. K. (1993). Feminism and the critique of organizational communication studies. In S. Deetz (Ed.), *Communication yearbook 16* (pp. 155-166). Newbury Park, CA: Sage Publications, Inc.

National Center for Education Statistics (2000). Salary, promotion and tenure status of minority faculty and women faculty in LLS. Colleges and Universities: US. Retrieved from http://nces.ed.gov

Patton, M. Q. (2002). *Qualitative research methods and evaluation methods.* (3rd ed.). Thousand Oaks: Sage Publications, Inc.

Putnam, L. L. (1986). Contradictions and paradoxes in organizations. In L. Thayer (Ed.), *Organization-communication: Emerging perspectives 1* (pp. 151–167). Norwood, NJ: Ablex.

Steers, R. M. & Black, J. S. (1994). *Organizational behavior* (5th ed.). New York, NY: Harper Collins.

Strauss, A., & Corbin, J. (1998). *Basics of qualitative research: Techniques and procedures for developing grounded theory* (2nd ed.). Thousand Oaks, CA: Sage Publications, Inc.

Tracy, S. J. (2004). Dialectic, contradiction, or double bind? Analyzing and theorizing employee reactions to organizational tension. *Journal of Applied Communication Research, 32*(2), 119-146. doi: 10.1080/ 009098804200021 0025

Turner, C. S. (2002). Women of color in academe: Living with multiple marginality. *The Journal of Higher Education, 73*, 74-93. doi: 10.1353/jhe. 2002. 0013

Chapter 15

MULTIPLYING THE OTHERS FROM THE MARGINS

EXPERIENCES OF A BLACK, FEMALE, JUNIOR FACULTY MEMBER IN A NON-STEM DISCIPLINE AT A STEM INSTITUTION

Kami J. Anderson

> *It is not, for a moment, to be assumed that enfranchising women will not cost something. . . . Above all, it will interfere with the present prerogatives of men and probably for some time come to annoy them considerably. (DuBois, 1999, p. 85)*

Drawing on the perspectives of Ellison's (1952) *Invisible Man,* Hendrix, Jackson, and Warren (2003) acknowledge the persistent proleptic tension that is present among African-American faculty. This tension is directly related to the multiple identities of African American faculty manifested through university activities such as tenure review, mentoring opportunities, and interactions between colleagues and students. The tension is often magnified at predominantly White institutions[1] (PWIs) because African American faculty are few in number but highly visible because the color of their skin makes them stand out in a "sea" of Whiteness. These multiple identities begin with ethnic identity and then branch out to include how we identify as scholars, researchers, professors, and advisors. As these identities are magnified, ironically, so are the invisibility and marginalization of African American faculty. To be both invisible and illuminated simultaneously highlights the tension to which Hendrix, Jackson, and Warren (2003) allude. Yet, from my experience, a greater tension exists within African American faculty members when multiple types of invisibility and marginality merge. Such a combination further complicates their position of otherness ascribed to them by their institutions. In my specific case, these different forms of invisibility and marginalization that combine to complicate my position of otherness include the invisibility felt from being one of few African American faculty at a predominantly White institution; the invisibility felt being a junior faculty member who is dismissed because I am perceived as too "new" to offer a valid opinion; the invisibility from being a female faculty member on a campus where the male to female faculty ratio is approximately four to one; and the invisibility of being part of a discipline, i.e. Communication, that has historically not received the same degree of merit and recognition on a campus traditionally geared toward offering technical degrees.

Thus, the purpose of this chapter is to explore the particular challenges I face as a tenure-track, African American, female junior faculty member teaching in a non-STEM discipline at a traditionally STEM (Science, Technology, Engineering, and Mathematics) institution. This chapter will also suggest strategies for increasing the possibility of success in academe for similarly challenged faculty. This exploration takes place at the personal level, grounded in my experience and examined through a reflective Afrocentric framework. I will also use my personal reflections as the lens through which to apply Alexander and Moore's (2008) recommendations for African American faculty who find themselves in a similar position.

Otherness, Marginalization, and Identity

Otherness

Let me first begin by expanding on the notion of "other" so that it is possible to discuss the multiple layers of otherness I face at my institution. The concept of "other" has been used to describe the ways in which one group is chosen as the representative of the "norm" regarding behavior and communicative practices. Any person or group that does not belong to this select category is seen as outside of or "other than" the norm (Hecht, Jackson, & Ribeau, 2003; Nakayama & Krizek, 1995; Orbe, 1998). Nakayama and Krizek (1995) argue that placing one set of experiences as "normal" or assuming a position of "uninterrogated space" (p. 293) is the basis on which othering begins. At my institution, the uninterrogated space is where quantitative scholarship and the pragmatics of all things related solely to science, technology, engineering, and mathematics guide pedagogy and the collegial discourse of those faculty who have achieved tenure on the campus.

The concept of the other is extremely relevant to my experiences as an Assistant Professor, as I am affected by the previously mentioned multiple layers of otherness. The first layer comes in the form of being a junior faculty member. Junior faculty are othered to the point of being muted on my university campus because it is often assumed by senior faculty that junior faculty have no knowledge of campus politics and procedures. In university meetings when junior faculty offer suggestions, senior faculty will often talk over them so junior faculty cannot be heard. Senior faculty may also begin to murmur and have side conversations, not listening to what junior faculty have to say. This can lead to junior faculty not having a desire to speak up in meetings and choosing instead to fall silent. Senior faculty usually do not behave in this manner when other senior faculty are speaking, thus positioning junior faculty as unequal colleagues, undeserving of the same caliber of respect.

The second layer of otherness comes from the department and discipline of which I am part. My university has, within just the past three years or so, begun the arduous process of moving from a strictly technical university to being newly comprehensive and more inclusive of majors outside of the STEM fields. Therefore, both the field of Communication and a department that offers a Communication degree are new to the university. My department is a combination of English, Technical Communication (traditionally the only Communication degree offered), and Media Arts. Before the department offerings expanded to include courses such as Organizational Communication, Small Group Communication, Media, Culture and Society, and others, the senior faculty within my department were only responsible for teaching the core courses of Composition and Public Speaking. Because of this, senior faculty in other departments perceive our department as nothing more than the department that helps the students in the STEM majors to be better writers.

When our department creates proposals for new course offerings or degree changes, we are often met with meticulous scrutiny by the university curriculum committee. There are always many questions asked of our department about how our courses support the technical degrees the university offers. The department also has to include more than the required information for degree proposals, making sure that our communication courses fit the existing technical format for the application of course content as well as the learning outcomes. The expectation is that students should primarily receive hands-on learning with only minimal theory being introduced to the pragmatics of the course.

Because my institution is dominated by Whites and males, the third and fourth layers of otherness come from the cultural groups with which I identify, namely, African American and female. Numerous scholars have examined the specific challenges faced by African American and female scholars in academia (Alexander & Moore, 2008; Ashcraft & Pacanowsky, 1996; Kogler Hill, Bahniuk, & Dobos, 1989; Sandler, 1991; Spitzack & Carter, 1987; Thompson & Dey, 1998). These challenges include lack of voice within the university community, lack of respect from students, mothering students in the mentoring and advising processes, and difficulty in the promotion and tenure process for African American female faculty. These challenges are detrimental to my professional growth since they further complicate my position of otherness within the university.

MARGINALIZATION AND IDENTITY

The aforementioned layers of otherness strongly influence my experience in the academy, particularly because they are a significant part of my identity and because they individually and collectively lead to my marginalization on campus. It is important to pause briefly to conceptualize two terms that will be used frequently in this reflection: marginalization and identity. First, the concept of *marginalization* is borrowed from a definition set forth by Orbe (1998) when discussing muted groups. Marginalized groups, according to Orbe, are those groups that are not seen as being a part of the dominant voice within a group or organization. Thompson and Dey (1998) further refer to "multi-marginality" (p. 325) when discussing the stress put on African American faculty. This concept describes the multiple ways in which African American faculty are marginalized at majority institutions such as in "their scholarly agenda; . . . their teaching agenda; and in the larger college community based on an institution-preferred agenda" which is not very inclusive (Thompson & Dey, 1998, p. 325). This marginalization comes from the dominant voice within institutions that deemphasize and devalue the voices of African American faculty. At my STEM university, the most dominant voices are those of whites, males, and senior faculty members. These voices together operate to create a dominant discourse of neutrality and objectivity, which results my multi-marginality.

Second, *identity* is defined as how one constructs a personal, lived biography, replete with agency and uniqueness. Identity has become the catalyst for critical examination of how individuals are able to utilize personal agency to define themselves through a dominant lens. In the field of academia, the dominant paradigm of White patriarchal hegemony (Jhally, 1998) has influenced the dialogue of the identity of the professoriate and left scholars and faculty who do not conform to this notion of collective identity muted.

AFROCENTRICITY: A REFLECTIVE LENS

For this discussion, it is important to be able to utilize theoretical frameworks which allow for a strong voice and position within the context of discussing the other, allowing me to assert power in this reflection. The notion of Afrocentricity moves Blacks from the periphery to the center. Afrocentricity is a metatheory that creates a world for the marginalized. In the academic world, it provides a space for my voice to challenge the perception held by the dominant voices of the university regarding the identity of African American, female junior faculty members in the Communication department. The Afrocentric lens allows me, a multi-marginalized African American female, junior faculty member to have a place to reflect on my marginality and develop strategies to ensure the possibility of success regardless of my otherness. It also offers a rhetorical space to dissect the identity that emerges from the multiple layers of otherness I encounter. The Afrocentric lens further allows me a platform for engaging in fair rhetorical exchange with dominant university voices in an environment that appears unequal. This is because Afrocentricity values the other as an equal source of information in rhetorical exchanges (McPhail, 1996) and emphasizes the importance of listening to multiple perspectives on an issue. According to Asante (1998), Afrocentricity allows people of African descent to have a rhetorical structure that reflects their historical and cultural experiences. An Afrocentric study would effectively depict this reflection and keep issues that are of primary concern to the Diaspora in the forefront, such as how marginalized groups can still assert identity and voice within the dominant group, often resulting in positive change, thereby using their marginality as an advantage.

Although its basis is in the richness of the African Ancestral history, Afrocentricity is also founded on the experiential situations of Blacks who choose to embrace it. Asante (2007) states that "the Afrocentric method seeks to uncover the masks behind the rhetoric of power, privilege, and position in order to establish how principal myths create *place*" (p. 27, italics added). The myths to which Asante refers are those that have been put in place to create control for a dominant group over a marginalized group. Using this perspective allows for the assertion of my place and position within my institution, which may seem resistant to the environment of the university.

The definition of space and place are poignant factors in describing identity in the majority university setting because African American female junior faculty who understand their space and place at a majority university can gauge and manipulate interactions in order to clearly shape the personal biography of their identities as professors and scholars. For example, Stewart (2008) recounts the story of a Black female respondent whose "interaction within the institution made evident the salience of her racial and gender identities" (p. 196). This respondent was able to use interactions with members of the dominant group to understand how Blackness was viewed and perceived, how the sentiments that were experienced were communicated to all parties involved because of this view, and how critical it was for the respondent to recognize the salience of her identities as African American and female in order to affirm her own presence at the institution. It can be inferred from this example that it is possible to examine how the salience of identity is developed within the environment of the STEM institution and more specifically, how an African American, female, non-STEM, and junior faculty member is able to define her identity within a STEM institutional environment.

At the STEM institution, genuine dialogue between students and non-STEM faculty is difficult because of the search for neutrality within STEM disciplines and the foregrounding of technical skills within disciplines. Further, in the traditional STEM university, professors and instructors lecture while students work diligently on mathematical formulas used to design and create complex plans. The basis of interpersonal interaction is limited to what will allow the student to complete a task. This limits critical reflection and constructive dialogue between instructor and student. STEM students, because of the technical skills they need to solve problems in their fields, utilize a method of problem solving designed to promote universality and culturally neutral language (Abell, Bryan, & Anderson, 1998; National Academy of Engineering, 2004; Smith & Waller, 1997). This causes the engineering or construction student in a Communication course, for example, to assert the dominant norms of the institution for the sake of comfort in understanding. For instance, in my public speaking course, the engineering and construction majors rarely participate in class discussions and tend to opt out of the one-on-one meetings to discuss speech topics, preferring instead to just complete the task and risk poor performance over interpersonal interaction. In this environment, Afrocentricity places the African American, female, non-STEM junior faculty member in a location apart from the dominant voice of that particular environment. This standpoint allows her to affirm her presence and contributions to the university as well as her scholarship endeavors; however, there is still need for professional cooperation to exist between the two.

THE CHALLENGES: AN ATTEMPT TO PUSH TO THE MARGINS

Earlier in this chapter, I argued that I face multiple layers of invisibility as an African-American, female, junior faculty member on campus. This invisibility comes from my inability as a female faculty member of color to feel as if I am a full member of the campus faculty due to the disconcerting silencing of my voice. I refer here to a process that "renders marginalized groups as largely muted because their lived experiences are not represented in [the] dominant culture" (Orbe, 1998, p. 4).

The marginalized groups at my STEM institution are African-American faculty, junior faculty, female faculty, and faculty in the field of Communication. The field of Communication demands its scholars to consistently and persistently engage in public dialogue and critique of the discipline in order to promote advancements in the field. As Communication scholars, we understand this to mean, publish, publish, and publish again. Additionally, scholarship is an important qualifier for the tenure process. At the STEM institution where I teach, there are few humanities professors who sit on the tenure review committee. Therefore, it is typically more acceptable to the tenure review committee to see evidence of quantitative research on the list of scholarship in the tenure review packet. This expectation places my research at the margins since I mostly engage in qualitative scholarship given that it is most appropriate for my research interests. My scholarship is further marginalized based on the primary subjects of my research, i.e. people of color. Research with African Americans as the primary subjects falls under close scrutiny at the university unless such studies examine that group in relation to the STEM discipline. This is illustrated best by two anecdotes.

The first anecdote recalls a grant writing process with the grant office at my university. I prepared an extensive proposal for a longitudinal examination of the identity construction of African Americans in the United States. The advice I was given by a non-White female faculty member, after a one-week review of my proposal, was to consider revising my research so that it was no longer solely African American, but inclusive of other ethnic and cultural groups as well. For the purposes of this particular study, that would have changed the scope of the research questions. When I asked why this would be necessary, I was told that it was because there was not usually university support for my area of research and with the accreditation assessment taking place that year, it would be difficult to justify why this was noteworthy research for the university. As a scholar, my research interests were deemed unworthy of university support by a colleague based solely on the subject of my research.

The second anecdote refers to an incident at the annual recognition reception for faculty who have published or presented throughout the year. For this reception, I was being recognized for the publication of my dissertation as well as for presenting several papers throughout the academic calendar year. The president of our university gave remarks where she proceeded to announce the long list of research that had been conducted during the year in order to toot the horn of diverse scholarship. She listed a very diverse group of research around technology, science, business, and mathematics. However, she failed to mention my ten publications and five presentations as well as the scholarship of other humanities faculty, which focused on qualitative humanities research. At the close of the reception, a colleague expressed regrets at the oversight and confided (in a lowered voice) the need for me to keep writing and publishing so she can push them to the forefront with the other publications. As stated earlier, quantitative research is typically viewed as scholarly research at my institution. The omission of non-quantitative scholarship from the "brag list" of faculty scholarship is further indication of that trend.

It has become the silent expectation among African Americans in general, and African American faculty in particular, that in order to be successful, one must put forth an effort that is 150 percent better than the performance of their White counterparts. This effort is also expected of women and other traditionally underrepresented groups. As a member of four marginalized groups, my effort has exponentially increased to a performance level seemingly impossible to maintain. The question remains, how can one continue to perform 600 percent better than her counterparts and still have a semblance of sanity for tenure review?

POWER FROM THE PERIPHERY: SHOWCASING MY OTHERNESS

Although this multi-marginality and otherness could seemingly pose serious concerns at a majority institution, I argue that there is power from the periphery using the Afrocentric paradigm. Afrocentricity includes and highlights "self-defining characteristics and self-determining actions" (Asante, 1998, p. 21). These actions should encourage empowerment and agency among people who may not have power and agency within a particular environment. For me, these actions assist in defining my identity within the STEM institution.

There are two key ways in which I am able to circumvent these challenges and create my own place. Alexander and Moore (2008) point out several strategies for "thriving at predominantly White institutions" (p. 11) and assert that these recommendations help to "lessen the negative emotional, psychological, physical, social, legal, and spiritual effects" (p. 11) that marginalized faculty at majority institutions experience. As a member of the "isolated faculty" (Alexander & Moore, 2008), I have the tendency to unknowingly reinvent the wheel in solitude because the challenges are similar for all minority faculty. After reviewing this article, it is apparent that what I believed to be "tricks" for getting through my own institution are no different than the suggestions recommended here for all faculty who find themselves in minority positions at their universities. The solutions I have found allow me to assert my identity as an African American, female, junior faculty member whose research on African American identity is substantial and noteworthy and whose service to the university and community secures my place as a scholar and mentor. Alexander and Moore posit several recommendations regarding how African American faculty can thrive at majority institutions and successfully attaining promotion and tenure, thereby having a satisfying career at a majority institution. Below are a few of their key recommendations that will be addressed further in this chapter, some of which are personally easier to adopt than others (Alexander & Moore, 2008, pp. 11-14):

1. Consider yourself from an asset and strengths perspective.
2. Develop other interests and employable skills.
3. Attend and present your research at professional conferences that are attended by a critical mass of African Americans.
4. Network.
5. Seek mentors.

Consider Yourself From an Asset and Strengths Perspective

Part of the advantage of being a member of the department that houses the Communication courses at my institution is that it is a new department that is gaining popularity not only among the students as majors, but also among the faculty. New hires are able to carve out their own scholastic niche and produce scholarly work despite the invisible constraints put forth by the administration. As enthusiastic "newbies," we are eager to write, publish, and quickly negotiate the balance between teaching and scholarship so that we can feverishly make our presence known within our discipline. Examining my ability to continue to write despite the minimal requirements put forth by my institution falls into the first recommendation from Alexander and Moore (2008): "consider yourself from an asset and strengths perspective" (p. 11). Attaining my own academic, writing, and publishing goals with rigor within my field has allowed me to be one of few professors within my department to boost the scholarship of our unit. This is seen as a strength within my department as well as by the Dean of the School of Arts of Sciences as we move toward becoming a comprehensive university. The appeal of faculty who are successful in research garners attention from students as well as grantors.

As stated previously, my department is new in both its development and course offerings. Presently, we do not have a formal Communication department, and we have limited faculty expertise in some areas of the discipline, although we offer a wide array of Communication courses. We offer seven Communication courses each academic year, including 14 sections of public speaking each semester. At present, I am the only tenure-track faculty in Communication Studies in my department available to teach the Communication courses we offer. The only other available faculty member is a full-time lecturer. This position makes it difficult for administrators to de-value my work performance (Alexander & Moore, 2008). However, projecting myself as seemingly "indispensable" within my department is not void of drawbacks. As the only faculty member with the credentials required to teach many of the Communication courses we offer, I find that I also have the heaviest course load of all other faculty within the department, teaching five courses each semester while being asked to sit on committees to push the Communication Studies agenda for the department. Nonetheless, being in this position allows for my voice to be stronger among the dominant dialogue. As a result, to date, our department has had few proposals for new degrees and concentrations rejected by the State Board.

Develop Other Interests and Employable Skills

Another suggestion offered by Alexander and Moore (2008) is to "develop other interests and employable skills" (p. 12). With my university situated in one of the larger southern metropolitan areas in the United States, consulting opportunities are copious. These opportunities are reflective of my skills within and outside of the discipline. It has saved me from being an African American faculty member who has "allowed [herself] to be defined by one area" (Alexander & Moore, 2008, p. 12). I have had numerous contracts for consulting work in the area of Communication and have been able to capitalize on my foreign language interpreting skills in a variety of outlets within the metropolitan area. This has allowed me to not be heavily dependent on my institutional salary, especially this past year when mandatory furlough days resulted in a reduction in pay during the school year.

My other interests have also allowed me to be able to have a network outside of the university that supports my professional development. The individuals with whom I have worked while consulting have become sounding boards for research ideas as well as unbiased eyes for reviewing my works for publication. This has proven invaluable for even this chapter: when I was unable to turn to colleagues at my university for support, I was able to rely on colleagues across the country to assist with feedback.

Attend and Present Your Research at Professional Conferences That are Attended by a Critical Mass of African Americans

Alexander and Moore (2008) state that attending conferences presents "opportunities to receive feedback on your research and have your work affirmed by others who share a similar worldview" (p. 14). Participating in and attending conferences has helped to challenge my scholarship and network with other African American scholars who share similar research interests as well as experiences at their predominantly White or majority institutions. One example of this is the opportunity to contribute a chapter to this text, which was birthed in a panel at a national conference in which I participated in 2008.

Through their reflective study, Alexander and Moore (2008) are able to alleviate a great deal of my preoccupations of feeling less than adequate within my department. Their suggestions also helped to mitigate feeling offended by colleagues who seemed to "withhold important university or departmental information" (p. 6). The suggestions they give for looking at strengths, having other employable skills, and attending conferences are steps that I have taken in order to keep a relatively comfortable (yet always precarious) position within my department. However, there are recommendations (i.e. network and seek mentors) from Alexander and Moore that are difficult for me to follow given the climate and culture of my institution: a STEM institution that is resistant to questions about policies and procedures from anyone who is not part of the Faculty Senate. The Senate is usually comprised of senior faculty with junior faculty present only when a department is too small to send senior faculty to represent them.

NETWORK

It is difficult to "network" with faculty on my campus. Networking is described by Alexander and Moore (2008) as "crucial for academic survival" (p. 12); however, the African American faculty members on campus have a "survival of the fittest" mindset and fear that any support or connection to other minority faculty will appear clandestine and so further isolate them from advancement within the university. Non-minority counterparts do not see any advantage in networking with minority faculty, so relationships remain superficial and quickly end if the benefits of such relationships do not seem weighted in their favor. Additionally, White female faculty are less inclined to be collegial to African American female faculty. Interaction is kept superficial and academic partnerships through authoring or projects are rarely initiated and often only happen on the suggestion of a White male colleague.

This environment makes this multi-othered and multi-marginalized faculty member feel as though I conduct my research in a bubble without any feedback from colleagues within my university. It also means that a great deal more time is taken to complete my projects as I have to send my work to colleagues in other states and wait for them to have the time to review and send feedback, a process which sometimes can take as long as a month to complete from start to finish. Being able to have colleagues on my campus that could offer feedback would prove more efficient and would more than likely free up time for me to add more writing projects.

SEEK MENTORS

A second recommendation that is difficult to achieve is seeking mentors. Not having enough African American senior faculty makes it difficult for African American junior faculty to be able to be properly guided through the tenure process. There is no established program for junior faculty to receive mentors at my institution. Overzealous senior faculty who volunteer their services do so to capitalize on a junior faculty members' lack of knowledge of university dynamics. These same senior faculty also become dismissive of junior faculty and do not offer any true mentorship for professional growth. They often become annoyed with questions junior faculty may ask. In this regard, mentoring serves primarily as a notch to add to senior faculty's tenure packets as university service and not necessarily to project junior faculty into a position of comfort and maneuverability within the institution.

For example, the White female, senior faculty member who volunteered to mentor me during my first semester at the university has provided nothing more than superficial interaction since her offer. She may stop by my office to say "hello" and ask how I may be doing that day, but when I begin to ask a question that needs her expertise, she quickly reminds herself of a student appointment and dashes off to her own office. Our relationship does not delve any deeper than being mere colleagues. This same colleague was able to put on her university résumé that she mentored a junior faculty member, which counts as service to the department for the post-tenure review. My solution to this is to continue to seek mentors from my graduate career, including advisors and former professors within my discipline, who have proven their genuine interest in my success in this career and have helped with the feelings of solitude in the ivory tower. These mentors cannot provide insight directly related to my institution with regard to promotion and tenure, but can provide feedback and open opportunistic doors for scholarship and research outside of my institution.

CONCLUSION

The plight of African American faculty often appears dismal at best. Added to the other challenges created as a result of being a female and junior faculty member, it seems as if hopes for advancement and achievement are an improbable dream. STEM institutions have not historically allowed for non-STEM disciplines to soar, which is yet another load to bear. As a result, the faculty member who is multi-marginalized and othered must continue to travel an unclear, but worn path.

Using Asante's (2007) concept of Afrocentricity and Alexander and Moore's (2008) recommendations, I have argued that a seemingly powerless position can be transformed into a position of strength for the multi-marginalized scholar. Asante argues that the Afrocentric paradigm provides an intellectual activity for the scholar that can be healing from the margins. Writing about the multiple layers of my otherness in this reflection can be seen as cathartic as it permits an outlet to discuss the ways in which I see my own agency and the agency of other people of African descent. My ability to utilize my Afrocentric perspective as "the therapeutic nature of . . . intellectual activity" (Asante 2007, p. 4) has created a place for junior faculty scholarship as well as attempted to relocate the place of my scholarship at the university. However, writing is not the only way I position myself as an asset.

The ways in which I have begun to assert power—in my position from the margins—have become a model among groups who follow this path at my institution. Junior faculty are now more than ever writing and publishing more often than our senior faculty counterparts. African-American faculty are seeking networks outside of the university in order to ensure they have a foundation for professional growth and development and then returning to the university with innovative ideas for pedagogy and university cohesion that set a standard that majority faculty are racing to reach. Since the first reflection on this topic, there has been a significant increase in the number of female faculty who voice concerns around dominant policies in public forums, such as faculty discussion boards and faculty correspondence to administration demanding compromise and change. These changes bring hope to the multi-marginalized and othered faculty member. I am hopeful that empowerment through our multiple identities will elicit a stratus of change as exponentially salient to the dominant voice as my otherness has been for me.

Note

1. Although literature often refers to "predominantly White institutions" (PWIs), the term "majority institutions" is used to denote both the ethnic majority and the discipline majority present at my university.

References

Abell, S. K., Bryan, L, A., & Anderson, M. A. (1998). Investigating preservice elementary science teacher reflective thinking using integrated media case-based instruction in elementary science preparation. *Science Teacher Education*, *82*, 491-509.

Alexander, R., & Moore, S. E. (2008). The benefits, challenges, and strategies of African American faculty teaching at predominantly White institutions. *Journal of African American Studies*, *12*, 4-18.

Asante, M. K. (2007). *The Afrocentric manifesto.* Malden, MA: Polity Press.

Asante, M. K. (1998). *The Afrocentric idea.* Philadelphia, PA: Temple University Press.

Ashcraft, K. L., & Pacanowsky, M. E. (1996). "A woman's worst enemy": Reflections of narrative of organizational and female identity. *Journal of Applied Communication Research, 24,* 217-239.

DuBois, W. E. B. (1999). *Darkwater: Voices from within the veil.* Mineola, NY: Dover Publications.

Ellison, R. (1952). *Invisible man.* New York, NY: Random House.

Hecht, M. L., Jackson II, R. L., & Ribeau, S. A. (2003). *African-American communication: Exploring identity and culture.* Mahwah, NJ: Lawrence Erlbaum Associates.

Hendrix, K. G., Jackson, R. L., & Warren, J. R. (2003). Shifting academic landscapes: Exploring co-identities, identity negotiation and critical progressive pedagogy. *Communication Education, 52,* 177-190.

Jhally, S. (producer) (1998). Cultural Criticism and Transformation [motion picture].

Kogler Hill, S. E., Bahniuk, M. H., & Dobos, J. (1989). The impact of mentoring and collegial support on faculty success: An analysis of support behavior, information adequacy, and communication apprehension. *Communication Education, 38,* 15-33.

McPhail, M. L. (1996). *The rhetoric of racism.* Lanham, MD: University Press of America.

Nakayama, T., & Krizek, R. L. (1995). "Whiteness: A strategic rhetoric." *Quarterly Journal of Speech, 81,* 291-300.

National Academy of Engineering (2005). *Educating the engineer of 2020: Adapting Engineering education to the new century.* Washington, DC: The National Academies Press.

Orbe, M. P. (1998). From the standpoint(s) of traditionally muted groups: Explicating a co-cultural communication theoretical model. *Communication Theory, 8,* 1-26.

Sandler, B. R. (1991). Women faculty at work in the classroom, or, why it still hurts to be a woman in labor. *Communication Education, 40, 6-15.*

Smith, K., & Waller, A. (1997). New paradigms for engineering education. Conference presentation. *Frontiers in Education,* November 1997.

Spitzack, C., & Carter, K. (1987). Women in communication studies. *Quarterly Journal of Speech, 73,* 401-423.

Stewart, D. L. (2008). Being all of me: Black students negotiating multiple identities. *The Journal of Higher Education, 79,* 183-207.

Thompson, C. T., & Dey, E. L. (1998). Pushed to the margins: Sources of stress for African American college and university faculty. *The Journal of Higher Education,* 69, 324-345.

Concluding Thoughts

Since the 1970s, the number of women faculty of color in majority institutions has increased in the United States and Canada. Recent statistics have shown that in 2007, the number of women junior faculty of color in the United States was 20,908 (Chronicle of Higher Education, 2009). This development can be attributed to the increase in the number of doctoral degrees awarded to women of color in addition to the rise of the availability of tenure-track faculty positions at higher education institutions that encourage women of color to apply. Undoubtedly, this growth has positively influenced colleagues, students, administrators, and institutional policies at American and Canadian universities. Through their research and other activities on college campuses, women junior faculty of color have simultaneously transformed academia and prepared the pathway for those who follow. We have carved unique' niches for ourselves as our research, service, and teaching tend to reflect our cultures and our academic interests, all of which benefit our most important constituents, our students, given that faculty of color are more likely to teach students to be culturally conscious citizens (Turner, 2000), which helps to create a more rounded academic environment.

However, despite these gains, it must be noted that our presence in academic spaces has only increased marginally when compared to the growth in numbers among our White male and female cohorts over the past 30 years. In fact, as Leggon (2004) noted in her address to audience members at the American Association for the Advancement of Science (AAAS) annual meeting in Seattle in 2004, "There have been only miniscule increases in faculty—especially women—of color in the science, technology, engineering and mathematics (STEM) fields." The rate of increase in Ph.D.s awarded to women faculty of color and faculty positions becoming available to us is not in keeping with our actual presence on university campuses. For instance, as of 2005, Black female faculty only represented 6.7% of the 274,117 female faculty and 2.7% of the 675,624 total faculty employed at degree-granting institutions (Henry & Glenn, 2009). In 2003, "only 62 African American women and fewer Latina and Asian women were presidents or chancellors of the 3,191 U.S. colleges and universities" (Santovec, 2010, p. 22).

This picture is decidedly imbalanced as is evident from the chapters in this edited volume. Women junior faculty of color are still searching for our mothers' gardens, looking for safe spaces where we can be intellectual, creative, and woman. This yearning is a result of the constant acknowledgement and awareness of our differences from others in the academy. As previously mentioned, we are still disproportionately represented at majority colleges and universities. We are still questioned about the significance of our scholarship and service as we work toward tenure. We are still judged harshly by our majority students on teaching evaluations. We still experience discriminatory retention, tenure, and promotion processes and are forced to interact with unprofessional colleagues. We are still viewed as the "Other" while our voices are silenced. And we still question ourselves, wondering if we truly belong.

Yet even amidst these negative experiences, there are supportive faculty, students, and administrators and enough positive moments to make us understand the necessity of our teaching, scholarship, and service, and the necessity of continuing in the struggle. Most importantly, what makes these negative experiences absolutely bearable, what makes us able to strive, give and create, is that we managed to escape the dreaded disease of an absolute lack of models. Dr. Alice Walker (1983) named this disease in her book from which this volume is titled and spoke of its monstrous mark on one's psyche, identity, and ultimately, one's life. She referred to it as an "occupational hazard" (p. 4) for artists but generally for anyone who has no professional or creative antecedent. Thankfully, the women who contributed to this volume have the shoulders of models such as Walker on which to rise and chronicle our own stories so that they are neither lost nor distorted. On this foundation we continue to search, seeking solutions, seeking to save our own lives.

The individual experiences of the women included in this volume are unique, yet they provide tremendous insight about the collective experiences of those marginalized in the academy. Our shared experiences both expand and are expanded on by a number of theories and frameworks that are relevant to the Communication discipline. For example, positive marginality, critical race theory, standpoint theory, relational dialectics, autoethnography, Afrocentricity, expectancy violation theory, subaltern silencing, organizational socialization, womanism, postcolonial feminism, postmodernism, and Black feminist thought all provide spaces that are (or attempt to be) accepting of the voices of women faculty of color. These perspectives add breadth and depth to the examination of women faculty of color working in the field of Communication, in addition to other disciplines such as science, technology, engineering, and math (STEM) as well as education, psychology, sociology, law, and the like. Through the lens provided by these theories and frameworks, we see that women junior faculty of color are strong, even in the face of overt and subtle discrimination.

These theories and frameworks also provide insight into the numerous methods women of color junior faculty use to survive our challenging experiences in the academy. These methods can be positive, such as openly discussing one's racial, ethnic, and gender background with students and faculty, working diligently to ensure course syllabi and assignments are clear, serving on committees that enhance institutional and community diversity initiatives, mentoring students of color, mentoring majority students, confiding in a trusted colleague or mentor, and creating new undergraduate and graduate courses. However, the strategies of survival women faculty of color use can also be potentially harmful. Examples of this include silencing or muting oneself, attempting to do too much service while sacrificing scholarship, not taking time out for rest, and denying that racial, ethnic, age, or gender discrimination even exists. These are occupational hazards that women of color junior faculty face because we are seeking to survive in a place that does not accept us. We cannot deny that these strategies, fatal as they are, sometimes prove to be the most utilitarian in a context where one's livelihood is at risk. But, as many of us have come to realize, it is not enough to just survive. We need to live and in so doing, save not only our own lives but those of others. To appropriately survive in the academy, it is important that we continue to use positive survival strategies that will result in retention, tenure, and promotion as well as increased job satisfaction.

Communicatively, the aforementioned theories and frameworks provide an understanding of how we, as women of color junior faculty, make sense of our experiences. This is best exemplified in the recommendations made by the authors of the various chapters to women of color who are thinking about or have already entered into the academy and to faculty and administrators at majority institutions. These recommendations can be divided into five primary categories which may be useful to the field of Communication, the overall organization of academia, and to faculty members in general.

First, *the institutional messages that are sent to tenure-track women of color are often contradictory but we have learned to make sense of this tension.* We are told that we are wanted at our institutions, but understand that various nonverbal and even verbal messages tell us otherwise. As such, the following recommendations from the chapter contributors are evidence of women of color learning to work with contradictory messages:

- Know that your experiences may be jointly rewarding and fulfilling, but that they may also be riddled with challenges and negative perceptions that are not faced by White faculty or even men professors of color. Don't be afraid to both appreciate and regret aspects of your tenure-track journey.

- Dare to be a "different kind of professor" who is decisive, responsible, and able to maintain her standpoint in an uncertain and anxiety-ridden environment, while also demonstrating caring for, interest in, and love for others.

- Understand that you will be marked as the "Other" and be aware that this marking may result in student and faculty resistance.

Second, and related, *women junior faculty of color often have to construct meaning based on low-context communication and subtle behaviors, resulting in ambiguity of job functions.* Colleagues and administrators may intentionally or unintentionally withhold job-related information from women junior faculty of color, such as information about grants, the retention, tenure, and promotion process, and even about informal gatherings with other colleagues. As a result, we have to make our own paths and find creative ways to obtain information. These same women may also have ambiguity of job-related functions because they silence themselves, thereby preventing them from asking questions for fear of being perceived as unqualified or as merely fulfilling affirmative action quotas. The following recommendations are what women faculty of color can follow to gain clarity about work-related tasks:

- Share your insights and experiences, ask questions, articulate contentions, and risk transforming or reinforcing your viewpoints through such dialogue.

- Select students who are women and people of color to work alongside you at graduate and undergraduate levels.

- Seek mentorship, network, and get connected.

- Be a team player and build and develop relationships with individuals inside and outside of your department and university.

Third, *women of color in junior faculty positions have to strategically monitor and actively perform communicative behaviors that do not reinforce negative stereotypes, but instead cause us to "blend in" and ultimately receive retention, promotion, and tenure.* Women of color have to learn to "play the game" if they want to achieve tenure, which often means superseding and/or contradicting preestablished expectations about our abilities. Behaviors that reinforce stereotypes, such as appearing too "aggressive" or too "passive" are avoided as they unfortunately have formal and informal consequences such as biased tenure reviews and unfair student and faculty evaluations. This is a seemingly lose-lose situation since, in trying to avoid being labeled as typically aggressive, we silence ourselves, which in turn plays into the stereotype that we are passive and have nothing worthwhile to contribute. However, there are several useful recommendations made below that can help us navigate this minefield successfully:

- Select an institution that best fits your aspirations but do so with an understanding of the institutional culture. Know what it takes to obtain tenure and focus your time on that which moves you closer to it.

- Educate yourself about your rights in your institution and fight for these rights.

- Give careful consideration when selecting the types of service activities you will participate in to maximizing visibility, time, talent, and energy.

- Balance research and teaching with reasonable service required of junior faculty members. You might be excited about getting to know your institution by serving it and its student populations, but this might affect your ability to focus on research.

- Build personal relationships with students, other faculty, and administrators to demonstrate the inaccuracy of stereotypes they may have about you.

Fourth, *despite discovering that the global village is really an academic ghetto where university campuses are concerned, women junior faculty of color with international backgrounds resist exploitation.* Although such women are marked as the subaltern and therefore invisible on university campuses by virtue of our third world origins, we have devised ways to counter ethnocentrism and promote social justice, as may be deduced from the following recommendations:

- Rather than succumb to assimilationist discourses, women junior faculty of color with international backgrounds should embrace your difference, knowing that your very presence in academic institutions may be used to challenge and question mainstream Western ideologies.

- Create a new reality that encourages *doing* difference instead of talking about it. This can be done through the dialogic properties of everyday communication, which can be transformative.

- Seek mentorship and locate allies who care enough about you individually and who respect and understand your cultural differences. A mentor can help one get that proverbial foot in the door when your independent/individual efforts will not.

And finally, *in spite of the attempted silencing of women junior faculty of color by our institutions, we have found creative ways to manifest our power and reclaim our voices.* Even with frequent disregard from majority colleagues of our intellectual contributions as well as our own self-questioning and self-muting, women faculty of color on the tenure track do not give up easily. We are learning to recognize that we are valuable in the academy, as substantiated in the following recommendations by chapter contributors:

- Write reflective qualitative essays on the experiences of women faculty of color; this will help you in coping with your own frustrations, and also allow other faculty members to understand what women faculty of color go through in academia.

- Recognize the progressive possibilities of your "outsider within" positions.

- Work it from the outside; the view from the fringes can be spectacular.

- Have confidence in yourself and your ability to be as competent as any other colleague.

Collectively, these insights and recommendations show that women junior faculty of color have the ability to make it in academia though the process will be difficult, lonely, and tiresome. For new, tenure-track women faculty of color, this book serves as a poignant view into the past and present and provides a glimpse of what the future of the academy may become. It is the editors' hope that the future will be one of positive changes.

> *Where we have pleaded for understanding, our character has been distorted; when we have asked for simple caring, we have been handed empty inspiration appellations. When we have asked for love, we have been given children. In short, even our plainer gifts, our labors of fidelity and love, have been knocked down or throats (Walker, 1983, p. 237).*

But we will keep searching.

Dr. Marnel N. Niles

Dr. Nickesia S. Gordon

REFERENCES

Chronicle of Higher Education (2009). Number of full-time faculty members by sex, rank, and racial and ethnic group, fall 2007. Retrieved from http://chronicle.com/article/ Number-of-Full-Time-Faculty/47992/

Henry, W. J., & Glenn, N. M. (2009). Black women employed in the ivory tower: Connecting for success. *Advancing Women in Leadership Journal*, Volume 27. Retrieved from http://advancingwomen.com/awl/awl_wordpress/black-women-employed-in-the-ivory-tower-connecting-for-success-2/

Leggon, C. (2004, February). Women of color: Numbers are low and not increasing, but hope rests in new strategies for improvement. *Georgia Tech Research News*. Retrieved from http://gtresearchnews.gatech.edu/newsrelease/smnumbers.htm

Santovec, M. L. (2010, March). Recruiting more women of color to student affairs. *Women in Higher Education, 19*(3), 22-23.

Turner, C. S. V. (2000, September/October). New faces, new knowledge. *Academe Online*. Retrieved from http://aaup.org/AAUP/CMS_Templates/AcademeTemplates/ AcademeArticle.aspx?NRMODE=Published&NRNODEGUID={CB90DAAC2F91480E-9B18C9E6AD67AA61}&NRORIGINALURL=%2FAAUP%2Fpubsres% 2Facademe%2F2000%2FSO%2FFeat%2Fturn.htm&NRCACHEHINT=NoModifyGuest

Walker, A. (1983). *In search of our mothers' gardens: Womanist prose*. Orlando, FL: Harvest.

INDEX

L

M

N

O

P

R

S

T

U

V

W

ABOUT THE EDITORS

MARNEL N. NILES (Ph.D., Howard University) is Assistant Professor of Communication at California State University, Fresno where she teaches courses in Organizational Communication, Group Communication, Gender Communication, and Special Event Planning. Her research interests include organizational and small group communication, particularly as they are linked to the intersections of gender and race. She has written about decision-making processes in the National Aeronautics and Space Administration and Black female friendship groups, and presented at numerous regional and national conferences. Dr. Niles has also examined Black females, hair, health, and identity. Her publications include an article in the *Journal of Alliance of Black School Educators* and a co-authored book chapter in the *Routledge Handbook of Applied Communication Research*. This is Dr. Niles' first book.

NICKESIA S. GORDON (Ph.D., Howard University) is Assistant Professor of Communication at Barry University where she teaches Media Programming, Media Management, Communication Research, and Television Production courses as well as introductory communication courses such as Introduction to Communication and Introduction to Mass Media. Her current research interests examine the intersections among gender, mass media, and popular culture. She also has an active research agenda in media globalization, media consolidation and convergence, and the implications that these have for programming and regulation in the Caribbean media environment. Dr. Gordon has published several research articles based on her research focus including the *International Journal of Communication* and *Wadabagei: A Journal of the Caribbean and Its Diasporas*, and a book, *Media and the Politics of Culture: The Case of Television Privatization and Media Globalization in Jamaica (1990-2007)*. This is Dr. Gordon's second book.

About the Contributors

RUKHSANA AHMED (Ph.D., Ohio University) is Assistant Professor in the Department of Communication at the University of Ottawa. Her primary area of research is health communication with an emphasis on interpersonal communication across cultures and within organizations; she is also interested in issues of gender and communication and communication and development. Dr. Ahmed has authored and co-authored articles in peer-reviewed journals such as *Communication Studies* and *Journal of Cancer Education* and presented numerous papers at regional, national, and international conferences.

KAMI J. ANDERSON (Ph.D., Howard University) is Assistant Professor in the Department of English, Technical Communication and Media Arts at Southern Polytechnic State University in Marietta, Georgia. Dr. Anderson has published extensively in both English and Spanish in scholarly and trade journals as well as in national U.S. news publications. Her primary research focuses on the construction of identity and the current state of social identity for African Americans and African Americans who are fluent in foreign languages.

MARCIA ALESAN DAWKINS (Ph.D., University of Southern California) is Visiting Professor at Brown University and Assistant Professor of Human Communication at California State University, Fullerton. She is interested in political communication, diversity, rhetoric, and new media. Her forthcoming book, "Things Said in Passing," is a critical analysis of instances of racial passing as a new model of rhetoric. Dr. Dawkins writes on these and other issues related to contemporary communication for *The Huffington Post*, *Race-Talk*, *MixedandHappy.Com*, and *Truthdig's* Webby-award winning political blog.

MICHELE S. FOSS-SNOWDEN (Ph.D., University of Florida) is Assistant Professor of Communication Studies at California State University, Sacramento. She teaches classes in presentational speaking, rhetorical criticism, media criticism, and communication theory. Dr. Foss-Snowden's current research interests include the representation of race and gender in entertainment media and the effects of diversity and multiculturalism in the organization.

KAMILLE GENTLES-PEART (Ph.D., University of Michigan, Ann Arbor) is Assistant Professor of Communication at a private university in New England where she teaches in the area of international communication. Her scholarship addresses how the cultural identities of media audiences inform how they interpret media messages, and how media in turn shape the identities of their audiences.

ELETRA S. GILCHRIST (Ph.D., The University of Memphis) is Assistant Professor in the Communication Arts Department at The University of Alabama in Huntsville. Her research focuses on communication pedagogy, interpersonal communication, and cultural studies from both quantitative and qualitative perspectives.

CERISE L. GLENN (Ph.D., Howard University) is Assistant Professor in the Department of Communication Studies at the University of North Carolina at Greensboro. Her research interests include cultural identity and identity negotiation, African-American communication and culture, occupational socialization and identification of diverse groups, organizational culture, and third wave/intersectional feminism.

RACHEL ALICIA GRIFFIN (Ph.D., University of Denver) is Assistant Professor in the Department of Speech Communication at Southern Illinois University at Carbondale. Her research interests span critical race theory, Black feminist thought, Black masculinity, popular culture, and gender violence. All of Dr. Griffin's current research projects speak strongly to notions of power, privilege, and voice. She has presented at national conferences, keynote addresses, social justice events, and diversity training sessions.

PERUVEMBA S. JAYA (Ph.D., University of Rhode Island) is Associate Professor in the Department of Communication at the University of Ottawa. Her research interests are gender diversity and multiculturalism in the workplace, immigration and gender, South Asian immigrant women's experiences, immigrant issues, interpersonal communication, and intercultural communication. Dr. Jaya has published in journals such as *Journal of Behavioural and Applied Management*, *Journal of International Business and Entrepreneurship*, and *Canadian Ethnic Studies*. She has presented several papers at national and international conferences.

ANNETTE MADLOCK GATISON (Ph.D., Howard University) is Assistant Professor and Basic Course Director at Southern Connecticut State University. Her primary areas of specialization are intercultural communication and rhetoric. While attending Howard University she served as an Assistant Coach for both the Policy Debate and Individual Events speech teams. Before teaching at the college level, Dr. Madlock Gatison spent several years working in the corporate sector as a computer programmer analyst and project manager.

YUPING MAO (Ph.D., Ohio University) is the Academic Developer of the Master of Arts in Communications and Technology program at University of Alberta in Canada. Her research focuses on organizational, health, and intercultural communication. Dr. Mao has presented her research in national and international conferences in both Canada and the U.S. and has published her work in *Review of Communication*, *Teaching Ideas for the Basic Communication Course*, *Howard Journal of Communications*, and *Feminist Media Studies*.

AHLAM MUHTASEB (Ph.D., University of Memphis) is Assistant Professor of Communication Studies at California State University, San Bernardino. Dr. Muhtaseb considers herself an activist scholar and her research interests include online communication, narrative theory and identity, and Muslim communities in the United States. She has conducted field research in the Palestinian refugee camps of Beirut and is currently working on a film about 1948 and its significance in the Israeli-Palestinian conflict.

ANGELA PRATER (Ph.D., Bowling Green State University) is Assistant Professor of Communication at Northampton Community College in Pennsylvania. While her primary research interests are media and body image, she has collaborated with authors in the areas of ethnicity and education. Dr. Prater has presented her research in national and international conferences in both the U.K. and the U.S.

YUXIA QIAN (Ph.D., Ohio University) is Assistant Professor in the Department of Communication Studies at Albion College. Dr. Qian specializes in organizational communication with related interests in intercultural and health communication.

JEANETTA D. SIMS (Ph.D., University of Oklahoma) is Assistant Professor in the Department of Marketing at the University of Central Oklahoma where she teaches business communication and marketing communications courses. She is accredited in public relations and her program of research includes strategic communication in organizations, social influence and persuasion, and organizational diversity. Her co-authored research has been published in *Communication Monographs*, *Communication Research*, *Corporate Reputation Review*, and *Mass Media & Society*.

ELVINET S. WILSON (Ph.D., Arizona State University) is Assistant Professor of Communication Studies at Indiana University, East where she teaches courses in gender and communication, interpersonal conflict and communication theory. She is skilled in conflict mediation and conducts research on Caribbean migration and diversity in higher education. Her research centrally examines the processes by which cultural identities are constructed and negotiated in a variety of contexts.